MUSIC FOR THE MULTITUDE

★

'Astonishingly successful . . . conveys a vast deal of information clearly and agreeably and without condescension.' THE TIMES LITERARY SUPPLEMENT

'The meaning of modes, notation, counterpoint, rhythm, harmony, fugue, and form—in fact, the whole fearsome list which scares the ordinary man away from serious music—is made as clear as any non-musician will demand.' SUNDAY TIMES

'Lively, well informed, and eminently readable. There is hardly an aspect of music that is not covered.' RALPH HILL
(Radio Times)

DURING the last few years a new delight in brightness and colour has emerged—a delight which deserves to grow and prosper. To catch this spirit for book production is one of the aims of *Mermaid Books*. The literary quality of the books themselves is naturally always the decisive factor: but the conviction behind the production of *Mermaid Books* is that books at a low price can look more attractive, more colourful, without sacrifice of dignity or durability. This conviction has been amply confirmed by the warm welcome given to the titles published so far.

Titles now available

MONICA DICKENS
*One Pair of Hands
*One Pair of Feet

JOYCE CARY
†Mister Johnson

AGNES KEITH
*Land Below the Wind

VICKI BAUM
†Danger From Deer

C. S. FORESTER
†The African Queen
†The Ship
†Mr Midshipman
Hornblower
†The General

BERGEN EVANS
*The Natural History
of Nonsense

V. SACKVILLE-WEST
*The Eagle and the Dove

REGINALD ARKELL
†Old Herbaceous

PAUL GALLICO
†The Lonely

DANE CHANDOS
*Abbie

H. E. BATES
†Colonel Julian
and other stories

NORAH LOFTS
†The Brittle Glass

ERIC HODGINS
†Mr Blandings Builds
his Dream House

SIDNEY HARRISON
*Music for the Multitude

BRIGADIER JAMES
HARGEST
*Farewell Campo 12

RACHEL KNAPPETT
*A Pullet on the
Midden

*Non-fiction

†Fiction

SIDNEY HARRISON

Music for the Multitude

London
MICHAEL JOSEPH

First published by
MICHAEL JOSEPH LTD.
26 Bloomsbury Street
*London, W.C.*1
NOVEMBER 1939
NEW AND REVISED EDITION 1947
FIRST PUBLISHED IN MERMAID BOOKS (REVISED AND RESET) 1954

Made and printed in Great Britain by Purnell &
Sons, Ltd. Paulton (Somerset) and London, and
set in Times New Roman type, 9 point, leaded

CONTENTS

CHAPTER I

Music and Magic

ONCE upon a time, as soon as a story-teller said 'once upon a time,' people felt themselves being taken to a land where anything might happen. Now, however, we know too much of the past. For a good many years we have been exploring, digging, deciphering—stocking our museums and cataloguing our documents and finding out what actually did happen—until anybody who wants to tell a story of magic and wonderment is compelled to pretend that it will take place in the future.

Any artist who attempts to bring to life an ancient scene must be sure that his 'local colour' is correct, for quite an industry has grown up to supply accurate representations of historical backgrounds.

Theatrical costumiers will dress you in clothes of any period. Fake antiques are available to furnish your stage sets. Weapons and armour, wigs, ornaments, 'props,' and scenery recall Imperial Rome, Arabian Nights, Baghdad, Saxon England, or Aztec America in convincing detail. It is almost possible to buy samples of period dialogue ready-made.

But only in recent history is there any period-music. For music there is still a 'once-upon-a-time.'

Let us imagine that a number of film chiefs have asked us to organise a vast museum of 'properties' and sound-tracks so that whenever they make an historical film they may be sure of avoiding mistakes.

We begin at the beginning. The dim, nightmarish world of pre-historic monsters and vanished races of men yields us a few fragments of skeleton from which we may guess what our remote ancestors looked like. We reconstruct some primitive implements from long-buried flints. We note a few impressions of character and occupation from the drawings which they left on the walls of their caves.

But there is nothing for the microphones to record. We cannot guess at the speech, if any, of the cave man. We do not know what cries came from creatures now extinct. There are drawings and paintings to show that men and women danced. We do not know to what music. The prehistoric world is a spectacle performed in silence.

The earliest civilizations give us the illusion that at last we have some sounds to record when, in fact, we can only look at instruments, or pictures of them, and wonder what was played on them. There is mention of them in stories. The Bible, for example, tells us of many instruments, but their names, as translated by the bishops, recall the dulcimers and sackbuts of Stuart England rather than the actual instruments of ancient Palestine, just as the apple that Eve gave to Adam recalls our orchard fruit rather than anything native to the Garden of Eden.

With artistic Greece we begin at last to have clear speech. The writing is so vivid that a tradition of speaking classical Greek has never died; and even if we cannot reproduce the exact accents of, say, half a dozen centuries before the Christian era, we can, by translation, sufficiently deceive an audience into thinking that they are eavesdropping on the gods and heroes, philosophers and statesmen that throng Greek legend and history.

Greek art is full of the mention of music; and although hardly anything of the music itself has remained, we are half-beglamoured into thinking that it must have been as lovely as the dancing figures on a Grecian urn.

> Heard melodies are sweet, but those unheard
> Are sweeter; therefore, ye soft pipes, play on;
> Not to the sensual ear, but, more endear'd,
> Pipe to the spirit ditties of no tone. . . .

But we must not make the mistake of thinking that music began with the Greeks, though the science of music did. They investigated the acoustical nature of sound—the wavelengths, vibrations, echoing surfaces, etc., that still occupy the attention of sound-engineers. There is no question of their inventing 'scales,' thereby providing a starting-point for musicians. Rather they took musical patterns which had already been arrived at intuitively generations earlier, and demonstrated that these were not only artistically satisfactory, but in close correspondence with Nature's laws. The artist jumps to conclusions. The scientist, centuries later, verifies the artist's bold assertions.

Though we know almost nothing of ancient music we need not doubt its power and influence.

Thus Samuel prophesied to Saul: 'Thou shalt meet a company of prophets coming down from the high place with a psaltery, and a tabret, and a pipe, and a harp, before them: and they shall prophesy.'

Again: 'Elisha said, bring me a minstrel. And it came to pass when the minstrel played, that the hand of the Lord came upon him, and he said, Thus saith the Lord. . . .'

Music was supposed to have magic curative effects, as when David played the harp to drive away Saul's melancholy. And here we may observe the difference between magic music and religious music. The one, by the use of enchantment, seeks to compel the hidden spirits. The other, by supplication, tries to persuade. A modern example of music-magic comes from the Baganda tribe of Central Africa who used to behead a man and allow the blood spouting from the neck to gush into a royal drum before a new skin was stretched over it. Their belief was that when the drum was beaten, it would convey the vitality of the dead man to their king.

The mention of drums reminds us that, whether we observe the contemporary savage, or study the habits of early mankind, we find people devoting great energy and skill to the practice of dancing. At first, this seems rather odd. One might think that primitive people have more urgent problems than to invent, practise, and remember elaborate dances. But perhaps this is the reason:

We moderns, with all our knowledge, live in the midst of a mystery. Some people hold religious beliefs which attempt to explain it. In the absence of direct evidence of the legal-scientific sort, they have faith —that the universe began in such and such a way, exists for a good purpose, and will proceed according to the will of its Creator. Other people, abandoning the puzzle as insoluble, call themselves atheists or agnostics.

Primitive man had very little knowledge. He was not only puzzled: he was afraid. Not only was the great plan of existence mysterious: the simplest, everyday objects were mysterious and perhaps hostile too. He did not distinguish very clearly between living and inanimate objects. So long as a thing moved, it seemed reasonable to suppose that a 'spirit' dwelt in it. The wind was a spirit's breath; a stormy sea was a spirit's anger; the growing crops were fed by 'mother' Nature. Primitive men saw the world in terms of themselves. Like themselves, the spirits were moody, sometimes generous, sometimes treacherous, and, being powerful, would have to be put into a good mood by the gift of sacrifices. (Like men, the spirits were vain and could be flattered.)

But how could one communicate with them? Primitive man, like many a civilized man after him, wondered how he might get in touch with the mysterious powers and ask them for practical favours such as health, abundant harvests, the conquest of enemies, and children for his womenfolk, for he had not yet learned to ask for such more subtle gifts as peace of mind, the power to resist temptation, and spiritual rather than bodily health. Throughout history, men have sought for a system of communication—a universal something that all settled processes have in common—something that seems to link all natural movements together and connect them with the fundamental forces of the world.

Again and again, after delving into profound questions of metaphysics and philosophy, enquirers have found that the search has led them to a quality that pervades the ceaseless process of change going on around us and in ourselves—rhythm.

It is almost impossible to define rhythm. It is the to and fro alternation between activity and rest, between departing and returning, between light and darkness, between growth and decay. The stars move rhythmically, the seasons recur rhythmically, we breathe and walk, sleep and wake, are born and die—making endless time-patterns. Modern science even tells us that matter itself perhaps consists of infinitely tiny, infinitely numerous movements—rhythmical wave-movements of the kind associated with electrical phenomena.

Without indulging in mystical rhapsodies, we may quite soberly assert that there is no quality more widely apparent in the universe than rhythm.

And when primitive men found that they themselves could set rhythms in motion—that there was an art of rhythm—they may well have felt that they possessed some of the creative magic that belonged to the spirits. This, maybe, is why, whenever they approached the gods with sacrifices, slaughtering their choicest animals or even their most beautiful young men and women on the altars of their idols, they came with dancing and beating of drums and loud cries.

If the origins of dancing are mysterious, so are the beginnings of song. Again, there is a good deal of guesswork in explaining how patterns in pitch came into existence as something akin to dancing and poetry. But the researches of the Greeks into what was among them a long-established art, revealed that even melody, regarded scientifically, has a rhythmical aspect (as we shall see later). Melody springs from the same roots as dancing; and just as dancing depends on the shape of our bodies and the condition of our muscles, so singing depends a good deal on the mathematical nature of sound-waves and the structure of our voice mechanisms and the way we arrange our lives—not just on artistic taste. Among peoples of the early civilizations, melody takes its place beside rhythm and dancing as essential to worship, recreation, and dramatic entertainment. Art of all kinds seems rarely to have been merely a means of individual self-expression.

CHAPTER II

Music Begins to be Scientific

WHY, then, if music is so old and so necessary, have we so few relics or documents that would allow us to perform some of the music of the ancients?

The chief reason is that musicians were quite unable to devise a really satisfactory way of writing sounds sung at definite levels of pitch. It is, indeed, a very difficult problem. It seemed much more difficult than writing spoken sound, and, anyway, there was no such urgent necessity as drove people to invent alphabets.

In writing messages and ideas, people began by drawing pictures of the objects the words referred to. But in most countries they found in the long run that an easier way was to arrange a code that referred to the movements of their mouths. In England we are agreed that 'H' means 'breathe out,' 'M' means 'hum,' 'S' means 'hiss,' and so forth. It does not matter what signs we use provided we are agreed on their interpretation. Most European languages manage with about a couple of dozen such signs. The rhythm and accents of words are fixed by usage and habit, and, in European languages at any rate, pitch is vague and has only an emotional significance. Whether you scream 'ham sandwich' at the top of your voice, or mutter it in an undertone, ham sandwich means ham sandwich. The pitch of your voice cannot make it mean swiss roll. (In the Chinese language such diverting possibilities *are* exploited.)

But in order to draw a plan of a melody—the height and depth of notes—you must have an agreed 'floor.' Ordinary heights are measured from the ground or, if we must be scientific, from sea-level. But if we are to imagine a scale as a sort of ladder of notes mounting upwards (the very word 'scale' means ladder) we need to know what it rests on. Or are we to think of it as something suspended in mid-air like the rope in the Indian rope-trick?

To many people to-day, accustomed to instruments of fixed pitch, particularly the piano, scales seem to present no problem. But anyone who has endured ear-training, even with the aid of instruments, knows how far from obvious a scale is. (Ask singers and fiddlers and other musicians who estimate their pitch as they go along.) It took mankind literally thousands of years to grope its way towards a satisfactory scale system. Even now it is important to remember that the prevailing system is valid (roughly speaking) for only Europe and America, and that modernistic musicians are now experimenting with new scale-divisions. We have no space in which to discuss Indian and Chinese and other systems. But we can explain how the European scale-system, after long development and adjustment, at last provided a basis for the swift evolution of music during the last few centuries.

Many very ancient melodies select only five notes out of an octave. Even so comparatively modern a tune as 'Auld Lang Syne' can be played on the black notes of the piano and is thus based on a five-note, 'pentatonic' scale.[1] Such a scale was arrived at by usage and experiment, and it was sufficiently confirmed by the earliest instruments. The natural proportions of simple instruments, and the operations of acoustical law, have guided men towards settled scales. The Greeks investigated the subject pretty fully, though they never succeeded in circumventing a difficulty that continued to bother musicians until only two centuries ago.

The problem and its solution will become clearer as we proceed, but here it is in simple outline. Men early recognized two simple 'concords'—notes that could be pleasantly sounded together. One such interval is the 'octave.' Another is the 'fifth.'

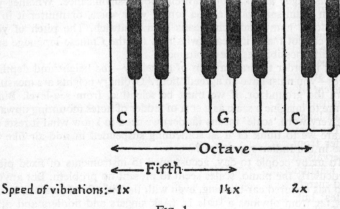

Speed of vibrations:- 1x   1½x   2x

FIG. 1

[1] This tune is not genuinely pentatonic. The other notes of the scale are implied. But it shows that pentatonic melodies are possible.

Now if we tune a series of octaves, then a series of fifths, we get a set of vibration-speeds proportioned as follows:

	C		C		C		C					C
Octaves:—	1		2		4		8	arriving in due course at 128				
	C	G		D	A		E	B				c?
Fifths:—	1	$\frac{3}{2}$		$\frac{9}{4}$	$\frac{27}{8}$		$\frac{81}{16}$	$\frac{243}{32}$	”	”	”	”	$\frac{531441}{4096}$

The fearsome end-fraction is equal to between 129 and 130. Thus the two series *almost* converge on one note—with a discrepancy of less than two vibrations in 130. (The lower series arrives at a note that is a little too sharp for the upper series.) Tuning by 'natural' method always produces some such 'error' somewhere, but the error did not become a problem until musicians began to be interested in chords or in 'modulating' from scale to scale. It was as late as Bach's day when they agreed, like fraudulent accountants, to 'wangle' the multiplication, dividing an octave into twelve exactly equal divisions and, as will be explained later, making all scales equally out of tune. (Few people nowadays can hear that they *are* out of tune.)

The Greeks arrived at a special system of scales that have been the subject of much argument ever since the early Church tried to re-establish them. But though the scholars are now sure that the Church system is very different from the Greek, they are quite unable to give us a convincing performance of Greek music. It is tantalizing to possess ancient treatises about Greek music without the music itself.

The eighteenth-century historian, Burney, made an attempt to print a Greek melody in European notation. Certain gramophone histories have attempted performances. Curt Sachs in his *Rise of Music in the Ancient World* gives his interpretation but speaks of the 'hopeless confusion in Greek theory.' For most musicians Greek music is a dead language.

The Greek 'modes' are sometimes referred to as scales, but they differ from ours in many ways. For example, they used very small intervals. If we could hear a Greek singer proceeding from a note to its neighbouring 'supplementary,' we should probably think that he had merely gone out of tune. An octave might be divided into seven notes; but, since some notes were very close together, others had to be further apart than the steps in our scales. So that whether we were to hear the 'enharmonic' or the 'chromatic' or the 'diatonic' versions of, say, the Hyperphrygian mode we should not recognize anything that *we* should call a scale or understand the words chromatic and diatonic as applied to them. The modes could not be transposed from lower to higher positions. Some were suitable for low voices only: others for high. They were not built according to the laws of harmony as we understand them or related to a beginning-note. This is odd, since Greek researches into the science of sound form the basis of our science of harmony. But the Greeks were not interested in chords and used instruments only in a subordinate capacity.

It is difficult for us, who can not persuade our singers to keep in tune, to imagine how Greek singers managed quarter-tones (though, of course, they may have had a truer sense of pitch than we have), or how their simple wind instruments were better able than our improved models to produce accurate pitch.

The names of the Greek modes were afterwards taken over by the medieval musicians, but they did not know that what we call a high note the Greeks called low, and vice versa.[1]

The effectiveness of Greek music is a matter for speculation. The Greeks themselves ascribed extraordinary powers to it. Burney, after admitting that his versions present 'but a rude and inelegant appearance, and seem wholly unworthy of so ingenious, refined, and sentimental a people,' quotes a story from Thucydides. 'When the Lacedæmonians went to battle, a Tibicen played soft and soothing music . . . lest by an ardent temerity they should have rushed on with too great impetuosity. . . . However in an engagement with the Messenians, they were very near being discomfited, when the celebrated Tyrtæus . . . immediately quitted the Lydian mode, and played in the Phrygian, which so animated their courage . . . that they obtained a complete victory.'

Burney slyly refers to Orpheus and 'such wonder-working bards'; and we may well wonder whether perhaps the Greeks—or at any rate the earlier Greeks—were really rather unsophisticated musicians, since simple people are always the most *violently* disturbed by music. Nobody knows with certainty. Nobody knows exactly what part music played in the Greek drama—though it was certainly important.

But we do know that Pythagoras investigated musical sound scientifically; and it is interesting to see how his investigations link up with our music (subject to the already mentioned tuning discrepancy—the 'comma of Pythagoras').

The Greeks were given to this kind of investigation. They catalogued all the tricks of speech-making, and made oratory a science and a danger. . . .

---

[1] Some authorities believe that the Greeks described as high those notes that came from high or long pipes and strings—our low notes.

Six centuries B.C., Pythagoras stretched a string tightly between two fixed points and observed its conduct. He found that if he plucked it, it emitted a note. Whether he plucked it vigorously or gently, the pitch of the note did not alter. To make the note go higher he had either to tighten the string; or to shorten it; or use a thinner string; or combine these methods. In a vigorous vibration, the middle of the string oscillated across a wider space and only in that sense travelled faster (making a louder sound). But the *number* of to and fro movements *in a second* remained constant. Which is what we mean when we say that the speed of the vibration of a given note does *not* alter.

(You obtain similar conduct from the swing at the bottom of the garden. Give it a vigorous push, and its occupant will feel herself rushing through the air with unaccustomed haste. But whether she swings gently or violently, the number of to and fro journeys per minute remains constant. The speed of the *vibration* does not alter.)

The stretched string disturbs the air round about, and 'waves' of sound travel very quickly in all directions. The waves travel, but the air itself, of course, does not suddenly start blowing a gale. Similarly the wash from a steamer travels in waves across a lake. Small boats nearby bob up and down, but they are not carried along. There is no *current* of water except in the quite special case of waves breaking on a shore. Individual globules of water are disturbed and communicate their excitement to their neighbours, as a man may jostle his neighbours in a crowd. The excitement travels. The crowd, as a body of people, remains where it was.

Sound waves from the stretched string, entering your ears, communicate their excitement to your ear-drum and give you the sensation of hearing.

It is possible to get a string to vibrate in two equal halves thus:

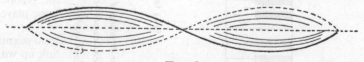

FIG. 2

Violinists often do it by placing a finger-tip very lightly half-way along a string and bowing with special care. Each half-string vibrates twice as quickly as the undivided string did, and the new note is an octave higher than the original one. If the string began by vibrating 256 times a second (giving a note roughly in tune with the 'middle C' on your piano) it now vibrates at 512, giving the octave higher.

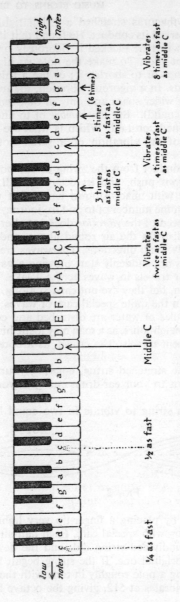

Vibrates 8 times as fast as middle C

(6 times)

5 times as fast as middle C

Vibrates 4 times as fast as middle C

3 times as fast as middle C

Vibrates twice as fast as middle C

Middle C

½ as fast

¼ as fast

high notes

low notes

The piano keyboard bases itself on a C — C scale (instead of, logically, A — A) because of historical evolution away from the "modes." C is always found to the left of a group of two black notes

Fig. 3

Straightway we have the two chief notes of a scale—the end ones—and we find that they sound so alike, for all their distance apart, that generations of musicians have insisted on calling them by the same name. Whether you divide the string into 2 loops (getting vibrations twice as fast) or 4 (getting vibrations four times as fast) or 8 . . . you will always get a note called C until you get too high for practical usefulness. (See Fig. 3.)

Other notes can be found, however, which, like the C's, conveniently arise from the fundamental note by simple division of the string. For example, G and E. G is obtained if the original string be persuaded to divide itself into 3 loops. E if it be divided into 5. (Four loops merely gives us another C.) Both of these new notes—these 'harmonics' or 'overtones'—occur in upper registers, but may easily be transposed down to within our octave by anyone with a musical ear. We now have this much of our scale:

Relative speeds of vibration:—

$$1 \qquad \frac{5}{4} \qquad \frac{3}{2} \qquad 2$$

low notes ←———————— C (d) E (f) G (a) (b) C ————→ high notes

giving us the simplest of all chords, the so-called 'common chord.'

To put it another way, the common chord (C E G) vibrates thus:

The lower C vibrates 4 times to E's 5 times	Simple mathematical
It vibrates twice to G's 3 times	relationships welcome to the nervous
It vibrates once to upper C's twice	system of our ears, making a 'concord.'

But, obviously, any of these notes can be regarded as a starting point. We could tune a new string to G-pitch and start dividing *it* into loops. We should get similar proportional vibrations and ultimately arrive at a new common chord—G B D.

Alternatively we could regard our original note (C) as being itself a harmonic derived from some lower note. It could be at the top of a chord F A C.

We need do no more than this to get all the notes of our ordinary modern scale 'C' major.

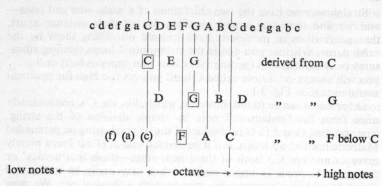

Does this process go on endlessly into a dim perspective of innumerable pitches? Fortunately not. Later on we shall observe how, if we pursue this idea on and on, we find that we soon arrive at the black notes of the piano. Then, to our relief, we find that common chords erected on black notes lead us back to the white ones. The whole arrangement turns out to be a sort of circular diagram. And by the time we have twelve white and black notes in every octave we can erect common chords wherever we like and never need a pitch that isn't already on the keyboard. The pitches that *aren't* on the keyboard are ignored in European music. And if your domestic keyboard should be a little above or below international radio pitch-level, the only practical difference it makes is to cause a slight adjustment to instruments and voices consorting with it—provided it is in tune with itself.

All this will appear in clearer detail when history brings us to the problems of notation and key-relationships. Happily, as we have already observed, the laws of simple arithmetic co-operate *almost* perfectly in this plan, and we shall see later how Bach persuaded his contemporaries to adopt a subtle compromise in tuning-methods.

For the moment it is enough to observe that a simple relationship between speeds of vibration gives us the scale-series of sound from which endless permutations and combinations make music. And it is important to remember that, at all times, humble, unscholarly people, inventing tunes out of their heads, knowing little of modes and scales, but guided by natural intuition, have used note-sequences which, if set out in scale-order, differ only very slightly from the balanced, 'corrected' scale of the modern piano.

While on the subject of overtones and harmonics, we may note one more point. Just as the bigger waves of the sea can be wrinkled with tiny wavelets, so big musical waves can have smaller, swifter vibrations superimposed on them. Almost inaudibly, but enriching the *quality* of the main tone, the harmonics of a note accompany it.

Modern scientists have investigated vibrating bodies with modern subtlety. They have found how it is that a string produces its main tone and some of its harmonics all at once. Most listeners are not aware of this, for, of course, we usually hear consciously only the main tone, which swamps the very faint upper harmonics. Nevertheless *a single string does produce a chord*. The string performs this conjuring trick by wriggling in a shape more complex than an ordinary loop. Mathematicians who analyse these things talk learnedly of 'sine curves' and propound obscure theorems; but the effect is almost as though, by some magic, the string were looped along its whole length, *and* in halves, *and* in thirds, etc., all at the same moment.

Other vibrating bodies—the air in organ pipes and wind instruments, the membranes on drums—behave in comparable ways, but they differ in the extent to which they select some overtones more emphatically than others. They vary in their willingness to divide into 'loops'; and, when they do divide, some divisions come about more readily than others. 'Pure' tones arise in the absence of overtones: 'rich' tones in their abundance: 'shrill' tones if the upper partials are more apparent than the lower ones (the lower ones being the concordant common-chord harmonics).

Which is why the 256 vibrations per second that produce approximately middle-C on the piano do not affect the ear in exactly the same way as 256 vibrations coming from a french-horn or a clarinet. In all these cases there are accompanying waves of other notes, too faint to be listened to, but effective enough to 'colour' the tone.

CHAPTER III

Sacred Instead of Magic Music

To say that the Romans were an unmusical people is to make a large generalization. It seems dangerous to assert that a world-empire, enduring for centuries, produced practically no music. But the encyclopædias, the dictionaries, the historical gramophone records are silent about the Romans. Even Burney, the father of musical histories, as Doctor Johnson is the father of dictionaries, writes only a very short chapter about Rome, and fills it with more stories than facts.

Burney's explanation of the Roman's lack of music is (*a*) that 'they were long more renowned as a military than an elegant and learned people,' and (b) 'that they wholly abandoned to their slaves the practice of the liberal arts.'

But there is another possible explanation. The Romans contributed practically nothing original to religion. They only adapted or organized the religions of other people. They imitated the Greeks; they borrowed from the Egyptians (making gods of emperors); and later they organized Christianity, by origin Jewish, into a state religion. Until their day, music and dancing had been essentially religious exercises. In the absence of genuine religious feeling these arts declined, for the formal observances of the patricians and the superstitions of the plebs were not such as would keep them alive.

And the early Christians were too ascetic, too convinced of the approach of Judgment Day, too hostile to sensual pleasures, to permit dancing.

Burney reminds us that the Christians in their earlier days of persecution were compelled to celebrate their rites 'in caves and deserts, without pomp and splendour. . . . On this account, and from the horror with which the followers of the new religion beheld the dissolute manners of the Pagans, the fathers of the Church declaimed bitterly against the public spectacles in which the ancient music was still practised; and to adopt into the Church theatrical melodies would have been a scandal and a mortal sin. . . . Besides, the new Christians, being chiefly illiterate, and of mean rank, would hardly have been capable of executing the refined and difficult music of the theatre, which was usually performed by skilful and eminent professors. Thus vanished entirely the idea of Greek and Roman secular music, with the knowledge of the Greek characters . . . as nothing remained to be expressed by them but simple sounds such as were common to Christians and Barbarians.' (St. Augustine said: 'It is better to dig or to plough on the Lord's Day, than to dance.')

Constantine the Great was the first Roman Emperor to be baptized. But, curiously, in giving imperial sanction to the once despised Christian religion he made it not Roman but Greek. For Constantine deserted Rome as a capital city and established himself at Byzantium. Here Greek culture asserted itself. Christianity had converted many Greeks, who were attracted to it on philosophic grounds. The scriptures were in Greek. Prayers were in Greek. Music also was in Greek. With the *Götterdammerung* of the pagan gods there appears the murmurings of a *Musik der Zukunft*.[1] But this music of the Christian future was

[1] *Götterdämmerung*—Twilight of the Gods, the title of a Wagnerian opera. The Wagnerian style was the *Musik der Zukunft* (Music of the Future).

not *completely* Greek. On grounds of sheer probability we may surmise that there was a Jewish element in it, and that the structure of Jewish verse, even in translation, would influence it. The surmise is supported by many scholars who judge that early Church 'plainsong' resembled synagogue chanting. In a religion based upon a book, the free rhythms of oratory and poetry replace the stricter rhythms of the dance, and the parallelism of Hebrew poetry helps to determine the style of declamation.

This early Christian music, then, was (with admixtures of other influences) Greek-Jewish. But it began to spread at a time when the barbarian invaders were breaking through the frontiers of the empire. It developed while the inhabitants of Rome, no longer masters of the world, not even masters of the western half of the divided empire, were giving themselves over to the strange cults and superstitions that help tyrants to explain their defeats. No one can tell how many influences music succumbed to or how many it resisted. Becoming the servant of a new purpose at a time when the civilized world was falling into disorder, it developed slowly, and its history remains obscure.[1]

At first it seemed that Byzantium would continue to take precedence over Rome both as a governmental and a religious centre. But when the empire split into two definite halves, with an emperor in each, Rome reasserted itself. And then, as the western empire gradually collapsed under the hammer-blows of the barbarian invaders, it came to survive as the centre of the Western Church instead of as an imperial metropolis.

The empire split in two. The Church split in two. And the music of the west, which had never been Imperial Roman, began to be Holy Roman. Unfortunately, the Dark Ages of barbarian chaos obscure the process of musical evolution as they obscure so many activities that are more easily recorded than music, and we do not know where Greek-Jewish music ends and European music begins, or indeed if there is any genuine connection between antique and medieval music.

Christianity was already three hundred years old when Constantine accepted it and nearly four hundred when Saint Ambrose of Milan made a pioneer attempt to codify plainsong. It was six hundred before Pope Gregory established the medieval 'modal' scales. It was eight hundred by the time Charlemagne ordained that Roman ritual and music should be observed throughout his Frankish (he and the Pope

[1] Any attempt to summarize the evolution of early church music must inevitably fail to be quite satisfactory. Research continues in this subject as it does in the field of medieval music. At the Benedictine 'Scriptorium' of Solesmes, the Roman Catholic Church has assembled for the purposes of study the photographs of hundreds of manuscripts, but these are not old enough to reveal the music of the first Christians.

called it Roman) empire. It was a thousand before plainsong and modes became the foundation of a recognized science of music. For a thousand years of the Christian era, the evolution of music is painfully slow and obscure.

The Church preserved what it could of culture and learning in the presence of the Visigoths and Vandals and Huns. Music was a powerful weapon of propaganda, enhancing the solemnity of ritual, making doctrine memorable, helping to drive out the Celtic and Teutonic languages, and, in the course of centuries, replacing them by forms of Latin that gave rise to Italian and French.

But even with the aid of Charlemagne it could not quite drive away the practice of pagan music and dancing. Charlemagne himself, though crowned Roman Emperor by the Pope, made a collection of the old Frankish songs. Dr. Eileen Power, writing of the peasants of his time, says 'they used to spend their holidays in dancing and singing and buffoonery . . . and the place they always chose for their dances was the churchyard; and unluckily the songs they sang as they danced in a ring were old pagan songs . . . left over from old May-day festivities . . . or ribald love-songs which the Church disliked. Over and over again we find the church councils complaining that the peasants (and sometimes the priests too) were . . . holding "ballads and dancings and evil and wanton songs and such-like lures of the devil." ' Sometimes the peasants listened to wandering bards singing the old songs that Charlemagne loved. And when Charlemagne's son, Louis the Pious, persecuted the minstrels, the minstrels remembered Charlemagne in their songs, until, in the later Middle Ages, he became a legend, a figure of romance like King Arthur.

(There is romance in the thought that Charlemagne, exchanging gifts with Haroun al Raschid, Caliph of Baghdad, introduced an Arabian organ—one is tempted to call it an Arabian Nights organ—to the musicians of the West.)

CHAPTER IV

Plainsong and the Modes

MUSIC was the first art to make an appearance in a definitely Christian form in the Dark Ages. Long before Christianity fostered its own styles of architecture or painting or drama, it produced music of a kind that was quite distinct from that known in pagan times.

About nine centuries A.D. the Schola Cantorum in Rome produced the earliest musical documents, which we may still examine. Already there was a tradition of plainsong—a subtly beautiful chanting in which an 'intoning note' occupies much of the time and many of the syllables. This prose-music is the remote forerunner of the recitative we know in oratorio and opera, and is distantly related to the cadenzas of instrumental music. It can be, and is, chanted by trained choirs, but in its essence it is solo music, since concerted music is difficult to hold together in the absence of regular rhythm.

The chief anthology of chants is that of the Gregorian collection, and in it our interest is chiefly centred on the music of the Mass, part of which varies according to the season of the year, part of which is repeated without variation daily. The variable part (the Proprium) 'consists roughly of about 300 Introits and Communions, 100 Graduals, 100 Alleluias, 20 Tracts, and 100 Offertories.' Some of these categories are 'responsorial,' in which the choir responds to a solo voice. The others, later in evolution, are 'antiphonal,' in which two sections of the choir sing alternately.

It is extremely difficult to convey the quality of this music to anyone who has never heard a Roman Catholic service. Its other-worldly serenity, its almost invariable rise to a central point with a fall thereafter, the absence of modern key-feeling or harmony or accompaniment, make it inaccessible at first hearings to the average English listener, though to millions of people it represents the purest expression of the holy spirit.

From the historian's point of view it is of enormous interest. A few, exceptional, metrical hymns have a rhythmic quality that suggests that in them we have perhaps a remnant of Greek-Roman music. These turn our gaze back into the past. But there are other elements that point forward—the 'sequences,' for example. Alleluia chants after the ninth century were often extended by lengthy passages, to which, later, words were added. And these (though Mother Church often condemned them as licentious) developed a modern quality of shape and movement. Nor is this all. These sequences were rhythmic, and therefore the words attached to them had to be rhythmic too. It is in these sequences, then, that we find what is probably the beginnings of our poetry, appealing to the ear by way of accent rather than (as in Latin verse) to the eye by way of vowel-quantity.

Once developments of this kind had begun, nobody could hold plainsong strictly within the old bounds. There arose 'tropes'— additional narrative passages that were destined to evolve into the earliest religious music-dramas. A stage began to be seen in church on which church-men and women and choir-singers played dramatic parts. Later, the 'mystery play' was transported to the market-place.

A whole treatise could be written on the connection between the evolution of plainsong and the organization of religious services—the use of choirs, the effect of monastic environment, the opportunities for experiment provided by life in the cloisters, the teaching of music in the orphanages (*conservatori*) that are the prototypes of our music schools. As time went on, singers found themselves paying more and more attention to whatever note a melody ended on. But the idea that a tune should finally come to rest on a note *towards which the whole melody seemed to be proceeding*, did not develop fully for some centuries; and it developed more swiftly outside the Church than in it.[1] To some extent it accounted for the transformation of the Ecclesiastical Modes (scales) of the Middle Ages into the modern scale.

What were these ecclesiastical modes? A few simple experiments make their essential character clear.

Between a note and its octave you may observe twelve steps. They are plainly visible on the piano keyboard. But in an ordinary scale, as used as the basis of a simple tune, there are only seven steps. (See Fig. 4.)

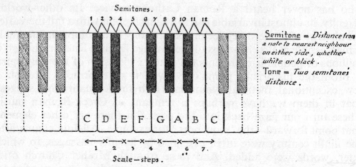

FIG. 4

How is it possible to proceed up a 12-step staircase in 7 steps? Obviously one cannot go upstairs two at a time, for that would give us only six steps. The answer is, that one can proceed two at a time *most* of the time. But twice during the journey one will have to proceed by a small step.

The piano keyboard somewhat disguises this because it puts the C-scale before all others as a normal, standard progression. At first sight, then, C-scale looks as though it proceeds by standard-size steps

[1] See references to Troubadours in the chapter 'The Medieval Musician.'

along evenly spaced white notes. Indeed, as we shall see later, the whole system of notation is based on the same plan of regarding C-scale as normal and as proceeding by equal steps. But in actual fact, it *doesn't* proceed by equal steps. Twice during the octave it proceeds by only half-steps.

Whereas most of its steps are of the two-at-a-time variety, which musicians call 'tones,' there are two examples of 'semitones.' The ear does not readily recognize this fact at first. But if you play the 12-note black-and-white scale (the 'chromatic scale'), you will come to hear that E-to-F and B-to-C are really part of *this* succession, and that a white-note scale does not consist entirely of tones.

In the majority of cases, if one wants to give an example of a semitone on the piano, one must use a black note as one of the two notes concerned, but E F and B C are white-note semitones.

Observe, by the way, that *any* two semitones, side by side, make a tone, and therefore a tone need not necessarily extend between two white notes separated by a black one. Here are examples:

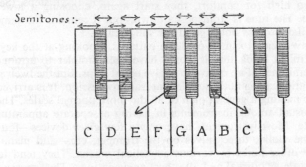

←—→ = 1 tone = 2 semitones (embracing 3 notes inclusively.)

FIG. 5

This is important, because it means that once we have decided on a certain order of tones and semitones as constituting a scale, we may begin on *any* note (white *or* black) and, provided we pick our way carefully enough, maintaining tones and semitones according to plan, may make a standard scale. Here is just one example of the scale transposed to a new position. (See Fig. 6.)

This 'transposing' of a line of notes to a new pitch seems, and is, complicated as we trace our way along the keyboard. But fortunately a musical person when singing can do it almost unconsciously 'by

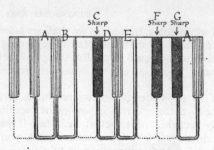

FIG. 6

ear.' Ordinary untrained people, humming a tune as they go about the day's work, usually pick their first note at random. If the tune then lies too high for comfort, they start again, choosing a lower starting-note. The tune is 'transposed down,' but it remains the same tune. A similar process holds good for sung scales.

Natural law seems to insist on scale patterns. Looking at the keyboard, you might think that it would have been simpler to arrange the twelve semitones of an octave in twelve equal steps. But the twelve-note, chromatic scale is not a simple, natural progression. It is arrived at only after making a general plan of all the more normal scales. The piano is unusual among instruments in having a separate apparatus for each note. Most instruments have only a few *given* devices—four strings on the violin, three valves on the trumpet, etc.—and manufacture their other notes by various acoustical means. They tend to regard one scale as normal and all others as deviations. They most of them have their own C-scale. The piano falls into line, making visible in black and white (literally in black and white) how the whole of musical notation runs its rather illogical course.

So far we have examined scales of the C-scale type, which has its tones and semitones arranged thus: C D EF G A BC. Medieval musicians, however, tried all sorts of other rearrangements, though they always used semitones twice in an octave. Here is a plan of their scales expressed in terms of white notes. (See Fig. 7.)

This white note plan is useful for reference; but, just as C-scale can be transposed to other positions, provided one preserves the given order of tones and semitones, so can these modal scales. They do not exist, as the original Greek modes seem to have done, always associated with a specific pitch, or a specific kind of voice or occasion.

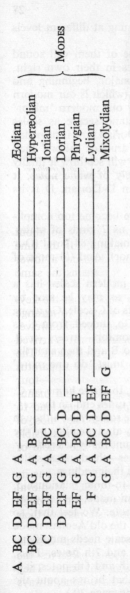

A	BC		D	EF	G	A
	BC		D	EF	G	A
	C		D	EF	G	A
	BC		D	EF	G	A
	BC		D	EF	G	A
	BC			EF	G	A
	BC			F	G	A
	BC		D	EF	G	

Æolian
Hypereolian
Ionian
Dorian
Phrygian
Lydian
Mixolydian

MODES

These names were borrowed from those of the Greek modes, but the medieval musicians were deluding themselves in thinking that they had brought Greek music to life.

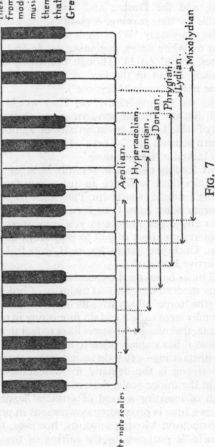

Aeolian.
Hypereolian.
Ionian.
Dorian.
Phrygian.
Lydian.
Mixolydian

White note scales

FIG. 7

The Hypereolian, also known as Locrian, was very little used in practice.

They are like any ordinary tune which can be sung at different levels according to the 'lie' of your voice.

If you play these modes on the piano, some of them will sound peculiar. Instead of making the effect of scales in their own right, they will seem merely to be fragments of C-major, beginning and ending on unaccustomed notes. But the Ionian (which is our modern major scale), the Aeolian (which is very nearly our modern 'minor' scale), and the Dorian and Phrygian scales stand secure as scales suitable for tune making. A good example of a Dorian tune is provided by the sea-shanty 'What shall we do with the drunken sailor?' Pick it out on white notes, beginning on A, and you will see how it finally 'comes home' on D. Though consisting entirely of white notes, it definitely is not in the key of C-major. It is in D-Dorian. D is its 'home note' ('tonic,' 'keynote').

Why did the modes die? (a) They would have become too complicated. Set out on the modern piano they give us 7 kinds of scales, each of which could begin on any of 12 notes, making 84 keys! (Our modern scheme has 24 keys—12 major, 12 minor). And (b) most of them lacked a 'leading-note.'

This leading-note—the seventh note of our modern scale—has a very important influence in tune-manufacture, as may be seen by making a simple experiment. Play some fragments of C-scale. Go along the white notes from C to F or from C to A. Go, indeed, from C as far as any other note, and you may stop in comfort—*except on B*. It requires an effort of will to play from C up to B and then shut the piano. Once you get as far as B, you feel you must 'do one more' and arrive home on C.

All tunes based on the C-scale tend, in the end, to arrive home on C. In any modern key, the vast majority of ordinary tunes end on the keynote (the 'tonic' which gives its name to the whole scale). And although there may seem to be a certain monotony in nearly always ending on the keynote, the man-in-the-street likes to feel that a tune really has ended—not that it has vaguely come to a stop. Modal tunes—the drunken sailor notwithstanding—often do sound rather vague in their endings.

So strong is the demand for a leading-note-to-tonic relationship, that in the minor scale, derived from the Aeolian mode, we go to the length of inserting a kind of artificial leading-note. We feel that, so long as a tune is proceeding downwards in pitch, the old Aeolian mode is satisfactory. Moving upwards, however, the scale needs modifying for melodic purposes by the raising of the 6th and 7th notes. Thus, instead of there being a semitone between the 5th and 6th notes, it is transferred to the 7th and 8th—the position that brings about the characteristic leading-note effect. (See diagram on page 30.)

For harmonic purposes, in those later centuries when chords were being developed, musicians manufactured an even more artificial minor scale in which, as compared with the Aeolian mode, only the seventh note is raised. In this we get semitones *three* times in the octave, leaving a consequent wide gap of a tone and a half between the 6th and 7th degrees.

Largely owing to this demand that a leading note should be only a semitone lower than the tonic, our minor scale structure is full of compromise. For example, A-minor scale may be regarded in two ways. If we remember its Aeolian origin we mentally link it with C major as being, for all its modifications, a white-note scale. If, however, we observe its strong association with its keynote, on which its tunes nearly always end, we link it with A major, which gravitates towards the same keynote. Examining it in this second way, we find that, whatever may happen round about the leading-note, there is always *a semitone between the 2nd and 3rd degrees* as compared with the 3rd and 4th of a major scale. It is this narrowing of the distance between first note and third that is referred to in the name 'minor.' And it is the main cause of the general 'minor' effect. It brings about a more complex set of vibration-relationships, and its 'concords'[1] have a little of the uneasiness usually associated with 'discords.'[1] (See Fig. 8.)

There is one great advantage which the major and minor 'modes' possess as compared with the ecclesiastical modes. You can alternate between them, and you can easily change the key. In the Middle Ages, once you were in a certain mode you tended to stay there. Nowadays, by borrowing a note from some alien key, and introducing it into a melody at a good, strategic moment, we find the tune heading for a changed keynote. This process is called 'modulation.' If indulged in freely it creates an effect of restlessness—an effect of visiting rather than of being at home.

CHAPTER V

Notation

THE foregoing chapter swiftly summarizes a process that took centuries to work out. The process would not have continued at all had not the growing power of the Church made urgent the solution of the problem of notation. Throughout the earlier Middle Ages, the Church, which could stage-manage complex ritual, administer vast possessions, maintain a code of laws, build monasteries and places

[1] *Concord and discord* will be discussed in connection with harmony.

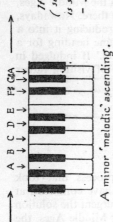

A minor 'melodic' ascending.

If C were sharp also, this would be equivalent to A major, (see page 29). The fact that C is nearer A than C sharp, is sufficient to make the whole scale 'minor' in character.
— Just that one, narrowed interval ...

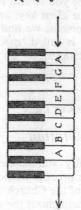

A minor 'melodic' descending.

This is exactly equivalent to the old Aeolian mode, and determines the "key signature" (to be discussed in a later chapter.) It has the same notes as C major.

A minor 'harmonic' ascending and descending.

Semitones :— B C, E F, G sharp A.
Tone plus semitone gap :— F G sharp.

(# = sharp indicating a semitone above a named white note.)

All these versions of the minor scale can be traced along the keyboard beginning on any note, if you preserve the agreed order of tones and semitones.

FIG. 8

of worship, and maintain discipline in a vast multitude of activities, was baffled by the difficulty of securing uniformity in musical method. This seems a small difficulty, but it defied musicians for centuries.

Not until the eleventh century did Guido d'Arezzo devise the series of note-names that are used in Latin countries in place of our alphabetical letters. He taught his choir to sing a Latin hymn that went thus:

	Modern Italian names	English names
Ut queant laxis	(Do) (Ut in French)	C
*Re*sonare fibris	Re	D
*Mi*ra gestorum	Mi	E
*Fa*muli tuorum	Fa	F
*Sol*ve polluti	Sol	G
*La*bii reatum	La	A
*Sa*ncte Ioannes	(Si)	B

and Guido arranged that each line should begin one scale-degree higher than the previous line. Here was the beginning of 'solmisation.' Nowadays the pitch of *do* is fixed by instruments. But, for a singer, *do* could be movable, as it is in the tonic-sol-fa system invented not so long ago in England by Curwen.

From such beginnings as these, musicians went on to build up staff-notation. For a long while they had made do with a system of 'neume'-signs, looking rather like an Oriental alphabet, that served to remind a reader of changes of direction in a tune, provided that, at some time or another, he had learned the tune by heart. It was not accurate or definite: it merely jogged the memory.

Then they conceived the idea that a horizontal line might represent *do*. The outline of a melody could be 'plotted,' much as a sick man's temperature is now plotted on a graph. Guido d'Arezzo put a black line between red and yellow ones. Then he added another black one above. A complete octave of a scale could be indicated thus on a four-line stave.

Do re mi fa sol la si do.

Observe the economical use of lines and spaces, introducing the complication that lower Do is on a line while upper Do is in a space.

Observe also that this system does not distinguish between tones and semitones.

FIG. 9

The principle is really very simple. Wise after the event, we wonder why nobody thought of it sooner. Even as a mere memory reminder, what could be simpler than—to make a frivolous example:

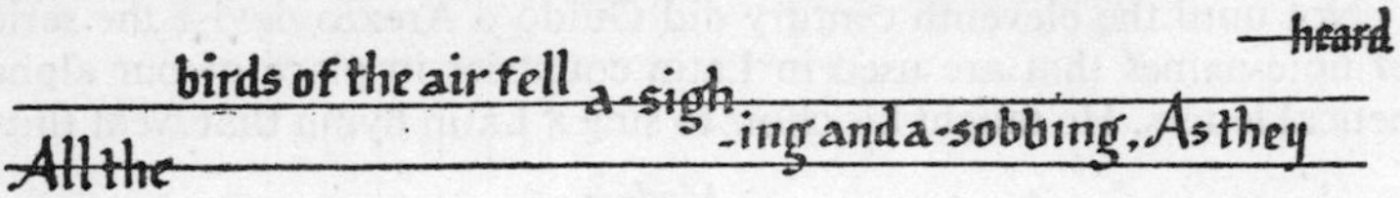

birds of the air fell a-sigh———————————————————————heard

All the ——————————————————————s—ing and a-sobbing. As they

FIG. 10

In principle, there you have pitch notation in a nutshell. As with many other simple principles, long practice is necessary before the principle can be applied at high speed in changing emergencies. What is simpler than tennis *in principle*. Or the flying trapeze?

In due course there evolved an eleven-line Great Staff from which could be extracted five-line staves.[1] These numbers of lines were arrived at quite simply.

Eleven lines are sufficient to cover the range of the human voice if you ignore exceptional notes sung by unusually deep basses or high sopranos. And five lines are generally enough to cover the range of any *one* voice. On those occasions when five lines proved insufficient, the stave could always be temporarily extended by 'leger' lines. (See Fig. 12.)

In order that the performer may know which set of five lines is before him, one line is given a name. If middle-C occurs in a stave, it is indicated by a C-clef. If it does not occur, then other clefs are used. (See Fig. 11.)

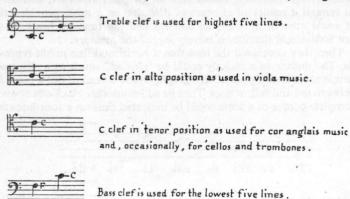

Treble clef is used for highest five lines.

C clef in alto position as used in viola music.

C clef in tenor position as used for cor anglais music and, occasionally, for cellos and trombones.

Bass clef is used for the lowest five lines.

Note the varying positions of middle C. It lies high for a bass, low for a soprano, comfortably for alto and tenor.

FIG. 11

[1] Staff and stave are interchangeable terms.

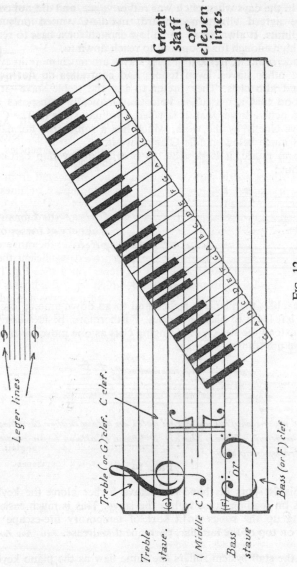

Fig. 12

Even in the days when pitch was rather vague, and did not conform to some agreed vibration-standard, middle-C varied only within narrow limits. It always had to be low enough for a bass to reach up to, and high enough for a soprano to reach down to.

In modern music, treble and bass staves are much more in evidence than the other staves. Even tenors and contraltos do not now use tenor and alto clefs. They prefer to use the treble stave—it being understood that a masculine voice automatically transposes a tune down an octave lower than it is when a woman sings it. The C-clef is kept alive chiefly by the viola, which has a range that normally lies about as much below middle-C as above it.

In piano music, it is possible to provide an overlap between the staves thus:

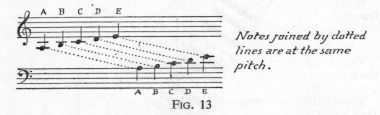

Notes joined by dotted lines are at the same pitch.

FIG. 13

This enables the pianist's right hand to go down among low notes, and his left hand to play high ones. Furthermore, besides using leger lines to extend the staves, or changing clefs as one moves over a wider range, we use transposing signs.

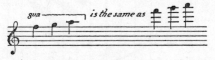

8va .... means play the indicated notes an octave higher than they are written. There is also an 8va bassa ('ottava bassa') indication for transposing down.

FIG. 14

The pianist puts his hand an octave higher along the keyboard, but goes on reading notes within the stave. This is much easier than reckoning up the rungs on a sort of temporary fire-escape ladder perched on top of the familiar, permanent staircase.

Since the staff system suffers the same flaw as the piano keyboard, it needs adjustment in its order of tones and semitones for scales other

than C. This is carried out by signs more frequently corresponding
to the black notes of the piano.

A sign to restore a line or space to white note position is ♮, called a 'natural'.

FIG. 15

In certain circumstances, a note may even be doubly sharpened or
flattened

x = double sharp
$\flat\flat$ = double flat $\Big\}$ occurring in practice on white notes.

This occurs when a composer, who is already using a great many
black notes, wants to transpose by a semitone-shift without abandoning
a certain alphabetical order.

Thus if he has been using D E F♯ G he may find that, later on,
D♯ E♯ Fx G♯ is a convenient notation even though, on the keyboard,
F double sharp is tantamount to an ordinary G.

Furthermore, double sharps sometimes occur in making artificial
leading notes in minor scales that are already mostly on black notes.

To understand and experience notation in all its ramifications, one
must practise music. A complete penetration into the scheme cannot
be achieved by reading a plan in a book. But, just as an example of
complexity, here are alternative ways of writing given pitches (ignoring
names which are purely theoretical but not practicable).

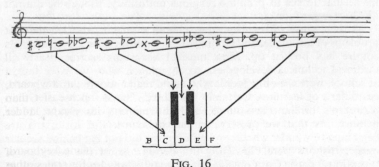

FIG. 16

The notation of rhythm was also investigated by medieval musicians, but their notation underwent considerable change in practice. Rhythm notation assumed modern form under the influence of entertainment music, and will bring itself more urgently to our notice when we come to discuss opera and the dance-forms.

CHAPTER VI

The Medieval Musician

By Charlemagne's time, a measure of order existed over regions that had been a chaos in the third, fourth, and fifth centuries. The Benedictines were building and cultivating and teaching. Many of the small, fortified cities of Gaul that replaced the Roman cities became bishoprics. The frontline soldiers of the Church were carrying Christianity far and wide. The music and ritual that so impressed Charlemagne in Rome when he was crowned there began to be familiar. ('Let all men be compelled to learn the Creed and the Lord's Prayer. . . . And if any man know them not now, let him be either beaten or abstain from all drink except water until he can fully repeat them.')

We have seen that plainsong was firstly 'responsorial'—the chanting of a phrase by a single voice answered either by the congregation or by a choir. As the Church's resources and skill grew there evolved the 'antiphonal' chant that depended on the existence of trained choirs. Music is indebted to a great number of anonymous choirmasters who tried to develop a style of music worthy of the Church's growing dignity. As far back as Charlemagne's time, the emperor employed his secular forces to promote religious uniformity, though he did not much care for monks.

As their sense of security grew, church musicians tackled the first problems of technique, and continued for centuries after Charlemagne's empire had broken up. Most musical historians ascribe nearly all medieval technical development to churchmen who, we were taught at school, were the only people who could read and write and were the custodians of learning. Certainly the Church made full use of Guido d'Arezzo's brilliant inventions, and the monasteries produced the manuscripts that we preserve in our museums. But historians are beginning to wonder whether religious music did not lag behind secular music. Bishops were constantly thundering against the adoption of 'licentious' music from outside which, maybe, was leading the way in new ideas. Church music may represent the simpler forms of then current music. The monks, who had a monopoly of the process of notation, would not devote it to profane music. If this be true, then most histories are misleading. Certainly their summaries of musical evolution are suspiciously simple—too simple to sound like real history.

According to them, the tenth century was largely occupied with plainsong, and the eleventh with the development of modes. By the twelfth, musicians had established the beginnings of a notation of rhythm, monotonously repeating the time patterns that exist in verse. The monotony of verse rhythms is not very apparent in speech unless an unintelligent speaker delivers doggerel in a jog-trot fashion. But in music, with its stricter beat, the 'rhythmic modes' soon began to become unbearable. However, musicians went on and learned how to change from mode to mode until, by the thirteenth century, they were experimenting with the combining of several melodies in several rhythms, thus arriving at true counterpoint.

Even those historians who are content with this version admit that the Church was not a perfect patron of music. The heads of the Church were often abusive. John of Salisbury in the twelfth century said: 'Music defiles the service of religion. For the admiring simple souls of the congregation are of necessity depraved—in the very presence of the Lord . . . —by the riot of the wantoning voice, by its eager ostentation, by its womanish affectations. . . .' Two centuries later, Pope John XIV, writing from Avignon, declared: 'Their voices are incessantly running to and fro, intoxicating the ear. . . . As a consequence of all this, devotion, the true end of worship, is little thought of, and wantonness, which ought to be eschewed, increases.' Pope John actually set out a schedule of permissible intervals.

Unfortunately the musicians were not sufficiently concerned with developing a kind of music that might minister to the humble people who came to church on Sundays. Their cunning, in defeating the reactionaries, was devoted to the pursuit of technique, technique, and more technique, until it took them to a dead-end.

When they first tried to get away from the endless unison singing—yet without allowing themselves a minstrel's freedom of experiment—they tried to combine two sets of voices by maintaining the strict distance of a fifth between firsts and seconds. (Imagine trebles beginning a tune on G, and altos singing the same tune beginning on C below.) Then they tried a fourth. (Either method sounds unpleasant to modern ears.) They tried other intervals (of which more in the chapter on counterpoint). They discussed time-patterns, and decided to call three-time perfect because of its association with the Trinity, and two-time imperfect. They indicated the one by a circle and the other by a half-circle. (We now pretend that the half-circle is a C, and we teach children to say 'C for Common Time.')

They devised the *Motet* (not to be confused with later forms under the same title) in which various voices might have different words at the same time; the *Rota* in which they had the same words but at different times; the *Conductus* in which only some parts had words at all. In the later Middle Ages they devised musical puzzles of a fantastic complexity. The average practising musician does not know what to think of this music. It is scarcely ever performed, and only by long training can one learn to hear it with the mind's ear after studying the score. Some authorities tell us that it is arid and unattractive, of interest only to research workers. Others assert that the modern world scandalously neglects some of the greatest masterpieces ever written. The older histories are responsible for the story that this music became so full of unnecessary ingenuities that the Church was on the verge of banning it all and was only deterred from doing so by the magnificent music of Palestrina. The newer critics think that, though many works were undoubtedly mere dry-as-dust puzzles, there is an unbroken evolution towards Palestrina's masterpieces.

The ordinary listener remains unmoved by this controversy. He is willing to be interested in some of the triumphs of the medieval Church. He can get a romantic thrill out of its gothic cathedrals, its stained glass windows, its illuminated manuscripts. A monk is a figure in a pageant; a nun is a sweet lady dispensing charity and hospitality. But the church musician is a shadowy figure.

The most popular story about him—one that contains some truth but has been much exaggerated—is that he developed the habit of borrowing tavern songs, around which he elaborated contrapuntal parts, and that congregations would sing the original, obscene words on Sundays instead of the Latin text. Some irreverent murmuring of this kind may in fact have occurred among those whose ears were quick enough to perceive a somewhat altered tune buried in the middle of a tangle of counterpoint. And this sort of thing was listed among the abuses which the Church remedied during the Counter-Reformation (of which more later). But the truth is that medieval musicians working for the Church professed a certain contempt for mere tune-mongers. *They* were scholars prepared to transform mere tunes into something worth while. In working on the 'Ordinarium' of the Mass, for example, where there was no harm in letting the oft-repeated words get lost, they borrowed secular tunes and wrapped them up in a multitude of parts. The Masses came to be known by the titles of the borrowed tunes: 'Rosa Bella' or 'The Man at Arms' or 'Gentle Memory.' This was not as reprehensible a practice as some histories describe it to be, but it certainly was not the best way to gain the reverent attention of the man-in-the-street. He may have got some pleasure from the works of the first great Flemish composers, from Dufay's rather vague and dreamy music. But the next school of composers, led by Okeghem, tended towards a more and more scholastic manner. And by the time Josquin des Prés crowned the work of the third school, the common man was rather out of sympathy with his church.

He preferred the music of minstrels; and we, listening for strains of music from a distant past, agree with him in finding the minstrel a more exciting, picturesque, and glamorous person than his clerical rival.

The very word 'minstrelsy' has a romantic sound. There is cause for confusion, however, in the fact that Minstrel as often meant poet as musician, and the word Song was used where we should say Poem. Writers have allowed Minstrel to cover the old Celtic bards, the Troubadours who regarded poetry as a proper exercise for knights, the Jongleurs who were their humble accompanists, the fair-ground entertainers, and a host of others. The art of minstrelsy did indeed include the activities of all these people and its social-historical influence was enormous.

The organ and the elephant and the little luxuries that the Caliph of Baghdad had sent to Charlemagne were among the first items of evidence that informed Europe of Eastern standards of living. As time went on, the younger sons of the feudal lords, having no prospects from inheritance, found their desire to discover new sources of wealth supported by the Church's desire to rid the Holy Land of the Infidel. The feudal lords themselves, whose occupation was fighting, were not unwilling to abandon the sporting contests of the tourney for the more serious business of crusading. And the art of minstrelsy, with its Songs of Deeds (*Chansons de Geste*), helped to cast glamour over the successive crusades that set out on various schemes of conquest, whether against the Saracens in the East, or heretics in the West, or the Byzantium Church; or that merely set out. . . .

The poetry of chivalry is of a splendid magnificence. Under its influence we are persuaded to forget the endless miseries—slaughter, pestilence, and famine—suffered by the common people. Time, and the magic of poetry, have cast an enchantment even over the passages of horror. The characters—Roland of the fine limbs, or Charles with the grey beard—are seen through the mists arising from Merlin the Magician's cauldron.

> *There was great carpentry with swords,*
> *And the earth is clothed with pagans.*

When knights rode in company they loved to sing.

> *Aallard and Guichard began a song;*
> *— Of Gascony were the words and of Limousin the tune,*
> *And Richard sang well the bass.*

On the battlefield the knights are encouraged by songs about the heroes of old. As the Normans charged against the Saxons at the Battle of Hastings, their warrior-singer, Taillefer, chanted a passage from the Song of Roland—Roland who fell fighting against paynims in the Pyrenean ambush of Roncevaux before Charlemagne could rescue him.

> Roland returns to the fray. He does great execution. He weakens. His temples are burst by his blowing of the horn, which once more he sounds. The French host approaching replies with a fanfare of sixty thousand trumpets.

Such minstrelsy was written *by* the fighting, ruling caste *for* the fighting, ruling caste. It consists of an extraordinary amalgam. The mysteries of religion are entangled with the mystifications of sorcery; the reverent worship of womanhood and a thousand devout references to the Virgin do not forbid jovial tales about deceived husbands; priests are often derided yet the old Celtic legends are Christianized. King Arthur dominates the Welsh and Breton stories, but the story of Lancelot is also to be found in Provence. Tristan and Yseult figure in a Cornish legend: the story became a favourite in Germany.

In peace time, at 'courts of love,' the knights debated the nature of love. 'Who loves most? He who cannot resist the desire to speak to his lady, or he who resists and thinks in silence?' Lays and ballads, villanelles and roundelays were composed in Provence by such men as the Duke of Aquitaine, then farther north by such as Thibaut of Champagne. Richard Cœur de Lion and William IX of Poitiers were troubadours.

The order of chivalry flourished with especial brilliance in Provence. Provence had suffered less than most of Europe in the Dark Ages. Its soil was fertile. Its products—wine and olive oil—were in ready demand abroad. Its main port, Marseilles, was magnificently situated. A stream of crusaders and pilgrims enriched it. Its language evolved into a vehicle for subtle verse—verse with the musical rhythms impossible in Latin. Manners grew gay, and thinking became free. The Church and the northern barons decided on action. The minstrels did not compose a Chanson de Geste about the expedition under

Simon de Montfort which 'liquidated' the heresies of Albi and crusaded against the wine and olive oil of Languedoc. The radiance of Romance faded in Provence, and the glare of burning faggots lighted the souls of a too-gay people to damnation.

The troubadours of southern France had their counterparts in the *trovatori* of Italy, the *trouvères* of northern France, and the *minnesingers* of Germany. The poet-musicians whose names derive from 'trobar' (Provençal for 'invent') were supposed to be gifted improvisatores; but actually they composed their works with care, and engaged musicians of lowly birth, called *jongleurs*, to accompany them. The little music that was written and that survives sounds more modern than the Church music of that time. It has more 'appeal.' Most of it is simple and repetitive—even that of Adam de la Hale, one of the few professionals who (like professionals in first-class cricket) were permitted to regard themselves as worthy to practise the same art as the gentlemen on the same championship field.

The *Minnesingers* of Germany—Walther von der Vogelweide, Wulfram of Eschenbach, Gottfried of Strasbourg, etc.—who wrote such stories as 'Parsifal,' 'Tristan und Isolde,' and the 'Epic of the Nibelungs,' were rather less gay than the chivalrous poets of France. They sang more of sacred than of profane love, and their minstrelsy contests were more earnest. Tannhäuser was one of their champions.

If we wished to reconstruct and perform the music of chivalry—even if the works were numerous and the texts clear—we should have the greatest difficulty in reviving the spirit of the style.[1] If it is difficult for a British orchestra to render a Viennese waltz with the right verve or for a gypsy band to play a Harlem blues, we may well give up as almost hopeless the attempt to revive a tourney of song. Wagner's operas, based on the old stories, must continue to serve.

What of the common people? A kind of Merrie-England glamour has been provided for them by poets and opera composers, by religious writers anxious to compare a materialistic age unfavourably with the ages of faith, and by the fairy tales we read as children, in which handsome young knights and beautiful daughters of woodcutters and never quite invincible dragons recall the romances which the humbler minstrels delighted to invent for their exalted patrons. The satirical and critical elements in the humbler kinds of minstrelsy tend to be

[1] Gustav Reese in his *Music in the Middle Ages* tells us that the poetry has survived much better than the music. We have the words of 2,600 troubadour songs but only 240 melodies. As for *chansons de geste*, the only authentic melody we have is one incorporated in Adam de la Hale's play *Le Jeu de Robin et Marion*.

forgotten, but these help us to realize that the poor lived desperately hard lives. As St. Peter Damian said, directly two nobles quarrel the poor man's thatch goes up in flame; and the nobles of the Middle Ages were always quarrelling. The rubicund monk of Christmas-Annual fiction was often in fact a grasping landlord; and, as for his music, it was often completely unintelligible to an audience to whom he scarcely bothered to teach the elements of his religion, much less the appreciation of art. The poor man's lowbrow attitude to this music, before the spirit of the Renaissance brought a new humanity to it, is expressed in a play where the character Ygnoraunce, complaining about Church music, says:

> Is God well pleasyd, trowst thou, thereby?
> Nay, nay, for there is no reason why:
> For is it not as good to say plainly
>   Gyf me a spade?
> As Gyf me a spa, ve, va, ve, va, vade?
> But if thou wylt have a song that is gode,
> I have one of Robin Hode
> The best that ever was made.

The minstrels of the humbler sort travelled the roads in the later Middle Ages, to towns where trade and industry were beginning to make fissures in the feudal structure, singing in market-place and tavern. Carrying the songs of one neighbourhood to another, they are said to have helped bring about a sense of national unity in France. They did not always sing of knightly heroes. They provided a kind of Marseillaise for the peasants who revolted against Duke Richard I of Normandy.

> We are men as they,
> Members have we as they,
> We have as great heart as they.

They are also said to have founded songs on 'Piers Plowman' during the English peasant revolt of 1381.

The accomplishments of a wandering minstrel are quoted in Funck-Brentano's *The Middle Ages* (whence the preceding quotations of *chansons de geste* are taken).

You must know how to compose songs, to jump high, to speak easily, and propose competitions. You must know how to play the tambourine, the castanets . . . how to throw and catch apples with two knives, the songs of birds and marionettes. You must know how to play the guitar and the mandoline and to jump through hoops. You will have a red beard, and make a dog jump over a stick and stand on two paws.

On the whole, the Church was repressive to all sports and pastimes, unwilling to see the word *geste* change its meaning into jest, or *jongleur* into juggler. The Bishop of Salisbury has words on the subject: 'Some haunt public drinkings and wanton assemblies, where they sing divers songs to move men to wantonness; and such are to be damned like the rest. But there are others called *jongleurs*, who sing the deeds of princes and the lives of saints . . . and do not those innumerable base deeds which are done by dancing-men and dancing-women . . . and make men see a certain show of phantasms by enchantment.'

No doubt the Church had grounds for complaint against our rude forefathers, but the suppression of games in England and dancing in Germany was brutally irksome to people whose recreations were few. The Church musicians were hardly in a position to complain if their congregations did sing bawdy words to a 'canto fermo' which the choir was rendering in Latin.

The priests would leave their flocks untaught, and then complain if the old pagan dances were still practised in secret. Joan of Arc's trial is informative on this point. It betrays a great neglect of religious education in her district and the survival of scraps of musical incantation from a dim antiquity. Joan's evidence about her childhood runs: 'I heard oftentimes from old folk . . . that the Fairy Ladies haunted there . . . I have seen girls hanging garlands on the boughs of that tree and I have sometimes done so with them . . . I may well have danced there with the boys and girls and I sang there more than I danced.'

The minstrels still continued to entertain lords and ladies. Sometimes two companies of minstrels would arrive at a castle together, pretend to quarrel about their rival merits, and stage a minstrelsy contest before the lord of the locality.

There were even minstrels in minor holy orders who travelled among the monasteries, entertaining the less disciplined of the brethren with songs of wine and women. And the Church, when in due course it began to stage miracle plays and 'mysteries,' had need of companies of Passion Players. But, on the whole, minstrels became, as theatricals still are, a people apart, forming themselves into guilds, attending international conferences during Lent (which was their slack season), and passing resolutions against 'part time' performers who threatened their livelihood.

The guilds of minstrels must not be confused with the guilds of singers that grew up in the great trading towns of Germany. As the

Middle Ages drew to a close, and the merchant began to oust the baron and the abbot from positions of authority, the burghers of the Hanseatic towns, and the tradesmen of Cologne, Nuremberg, Augsburg, and so on, took upon themselves the encouragement of art. They did not become such fine connoisseurs as their Italian rivals, the Venetian shipowners or the Florentine bankers. But they encouraged music, and endeavoured to promote a kind of domestic minstrelsy among the townsfolk. There grew up guilds of singers—the Mastersingers—who met on winter evenings to practise songs written according to pedantic rule. Imitating the Minnesingers, one of whom had started their movement, they held contests—not tourneys of song, but prosaic examinations. Much as at a modern competition festival, four judges decided on such points as Faithfulness to Holy Writ, Prosody, Rhyme, and Melody. Hans Sachs, a cobbler of Nuremberg, was the most famous of the singers. Wagner's comic character, Beckmesser, portrays the more unimaginative of them. Pedantry was their undoing. Imagine a song, the first words of which are: 'The fifth chapter of Romans tells us . . .' The 'Volkslied' flourished while mastersinging decayed.

Secular music was encroaching on church music, just as secular power and criticism were encroaching on ecclesiastical and feudal authority. That secular tunes should have been borrowed to lie at the heart of many contrapuntal works for the Church, is symbolic. For counterpoint was the last of the great technical developments that the Church may claim to have provided for music.

CHAPTER VII

Counterpoint

LIKE notation, counterpoint seems obvious once it is put before us. Like notation, it makes us wonder why nobody thought of it sooner, since it can occur by accident in the course of a sing-song. Two people, each starting on a different tune, find that their two tunes go together quite pleasantly. Finding simple tunes that may be paired off in this way is not very difficult, especially if the two singers connive at a little adjustment here and there. The most lowbrow of concert-party pianists amuses his seaside audience by playing the 'latest hit' with his right hand accompanied by an 'old favourite' with his left.

And the trick of making a tune accompany itself, as in a 'canon,' is an ancient one. The first singer begins by himself. A phrase later the second singer begins the same tune. Another phrase later the third singer joins in. . . . Everyone has sung that special 'circular' kind of canon called a 'round.'

1 London's burning, London's burning,	2 Look yonder! Look yonder! London's burning, London's burning,
[Pour on water. Pour on water] [FIRE! FIRE! [Look yonder! Look yonder!]	[Pour on water. Pour on water) [FIRE! FIRE!]
3 FIRE! FIRE! Look yonder! Look yonder! London's burning, London's burning,	4 Pour on water. Pour on water. FIRE! FIRE! Look yonder! Look yonder! London's burning, London's burning.
[Pour on water. Pour on water]	

The chance of happy accident that exists in all contrapuntal composition explains why the earliest examples of scholarly counterpoint vary so much in quality. When musicians first began to make a science of counterpoint, their compositions sounded like a species of musical jigsaw. Yet even in the very early examples there are fragments that tempt one to vary the metaphor and to describe the woven melodies as flowers intertwined in a garland. An early success in the art was scored in a round called 'Summer is icumen in,' supposed to have been written by one John of Fornsete, of Reading Abbey. It was composed more than a hundred years earlier than Chaucer's first poems, not long after the signing of Magna Charta.

The chief defect of the happy accident type of counterpoint is that it lasts only for a phrase or two. Therefore musicians set themselves the task of working out a set of rules whereby they could manufacture secondary melodies and rhythms to run in company with a given one. They took a slow-moving 'canto fermo,' often a modified quotation of a song, and arranged other notes about it at the distances they decided were satisfactory and in various 'species' of rhythm (two notes against one; four against one; a rhythm in which one voice seemed always to be lagging a beat behind the others . . .). The secondary melodies were rarely first-rate tunes in themselves, but they attempted to proceed in a reasonably graceful line.

Just as a river determines many of the features of the valley in which it flows, so a series of notes creates a sort of musical environment which determines the distances at which other notes may stand. Men may build a road on one side of the river and a railway on the other; but it is only rarely that all three will run in strictly parallel lines. The river was there first, and scoured out its own channel. Railway and road must wind about on such paths as the river has made possible. Yet they form one general system of transport, which is marked at the towns where the railway station, the landing-stage, and *place de la ville* adjoin. In the course of centuries a fund of knowedge is at the disposal of civil engineers in a science called surveying.

The rules of counterpoint are a musical version of the same process. They attempt to guide the musician in plotting the course of subsidiary melodies, winding their way through the environment which a given melody creates above and below itself. The trouble with early counterpoint was that the rules were too few and too strict. Where technique is undeveloped, a surveyor must choose only the most obvious routes.

We observed that medieval musicians worked out the several fixed distances which notes, sung simultaneously, had to maintain between one another. They experimented at first with those intervals which have a very simple vibration relationship. For instance, $\frac{G}{C}$ is such an interval, vibrating in a $\frac{3}{2}$ relationship. It sounds excellent by itself. But, in progression

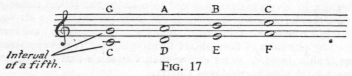

FIG. 17

is an unsatisfactory series; and 'organum' (as the system was called) died out. As in the case of octave intervals, successive fifths attach the two melodies together in too inflexible a binding.

Thirds and sixths were much better. For example:

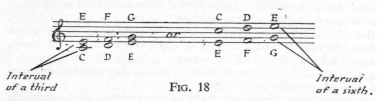

FIG. 18

And the reason why they are not 'rigid' is this. We have already observed the semitones in a scale. Their presence constantly causes the width of intervals-of-a-third to vary.

major minor minor major major minor

Minor intervals shaded   FIG. 19

Yet both the wider (major) third, and the narrower (minor) third are pleasant to the ear. Sixths behave similarly. (Fifths do not vary except between B and F; and that narrower 5th is discordant.) A row of 6ths and 3rds in succession has an effect of comparative elasticity and freedom. By using short series of these intervals, and diversifying them with odd 5ths and octaves, it is possible straightway to manufacture a rudimentary two-voice counterpoint. The main melody need not be the higher one. It can be the lower, and have a 'descant' above it.

6th 5 3 6 6 3 3 5 8 (octave)

In academic counterpoint octaves and fifths have to be employed one at a time — never in series.

FIG. 20

This kind of exercise is fascinating—as fascinating as the problems (with a catch in them) set by a schoolmaster to his mathematics class. Musicians went on to write multi-voice 'polyphony.' Time has preserved only the best examples of the polyphonic style. Few people know how tiresome some of the others were. A trained listener finds it difficult enough to keep track of three or four melodies going on at once. He becomes quite lost in a tangle of ten or a dozen. Furthermore, multi-voice writing increases the difficulty of keeping to the rules of the old 'strict' counterpoint, unless the composer adopts a very monotonous scheme of combinations. And, when one adds to these considerations the fact that medieval musicians were addicted to a great use of 'devices,' the extreme dryness of some of their music becomes easily understandable. The chief of these devices was the 'canon' (a round is a special kind of repeating canon). We have observed that it consists of making a tune accompany itself. But suppose that Tom sings the tune normally; Dick, lagging a beat behind Tom, sings it backwards; and Harry, a beat behind Dick, sings it upside down, his version going up wherever the original one went down. All these performances going on at once! Some of the early contrapuntists wrote a tune, and indicated in a set of instructions what was to be done to it by the various voices. They did not disguise that their interest was in making puzzles, for they wrote enigma-canons and provided clues as guides to a solution. Such compositions were no more music than a crossword is literature.

Nevertheless, out of all these attempts there did at last emerge truly magnificent music. Once it had been demonstrated that the puzzle devices could be used (abstemiously) to heighten a climax, to make beautiful patterns (not merely ingenious ones), and to enhance a singer's interest in his part, counterpoint became music.

In lectures on the Appreciation of Music we are bidden to take delight in the purity and austerity of polyphonic religious music and are assured that we shall fail to understand it if we listen as we do to the 'sensational' music of later centuries. Comparisons are made between this music and the beauties of illuminated manuscripts and stained-glass windows.

It was, however, in the days when printed books had replaced manuscripts, and Renaissance architecture ousted the Gothic, that polyphonic music came to its climax. Its masterpieces were produced when the Middle Ages were at an end, when the frontiers of the Roman Catholic world no longer embraced all Christendom. It may be true that the medieval spirit was here making a supreme effort in the presence of challenging Protestantism, but this is not to say that the music is therefore unemotional. If it *seems* so, as stained-glass and illuminated manuscripts and tapestries sometimes do, the fault lies in us—in our inability to think ourselves back into the centuries when religious beliefs were held fiercely, and Heaven and Hell were more real to most people than Cathay or Eldorado.

If further proof is needed that polyphonic music was imbued with the adventurous spirit of the Renaissance, before the Renaissance produced its own new style of music, we have only to listen to the non-religious works, especially the madrigals. Many of these have plenty of movement and narrative interest. If *they* also sometimes seem too restrained, it is because they are so often performed with excessive primness or in a too academic spirit.

We shall see later how, after more than a century of further development, a new kind of counterpoint, no longer 'strict,' achieved triumphs in the works of Bach and Handel. But by their time there was a new harmony. The technique of musical surveying was on a new basis.

In listening to a choir singing polyphonic music one must always endeavour to hear it as the singers themselves hear it. They are floating along on a river carrying several processions of craft, diverging, converging, lagging behind, catching up. . . . Seeing the pageant from within a boat is a very different thing from standing on the bank and looking across the stream. This latter is the *harmonic* standpoint, for looking across and seeing how many boats are abreast of you is like hearing exactly how many notes are being sounded at a given moment —what the chord is. Looking *along*, and seeing the mazy movements of the flowing currents, is like hearing the side-by-side flowing of separate melodies.

Of course, no music is exclusively contrapuntal. There is no denying that counterpoint *implies* harmony, for, if three voices are singing, they must, at a given moment, produce a three-note chord. But to extract the full savour from music conceived primarily in the contrapuntal way, one must adopt the composer's and the choir's standpoint. Then one will hear, not a series of chords, but a woven texture of melodic strands.

CHAPTER VIII

The Renaissance

THE minstrel's audiences were becoming more prosperous. In earlier days he must have regarded the serf-population as unprofitable, and serfs must have resigned themselves to being unable to afford many entertainments. But after the Black Death labour became scarce and serfs grew rebellious. From the twelfth century onwards there were more and more lords who found it best to sell freedom to their servile communities on the grounds that willing wage-earners were more productive than unwilling serfs.

The gradual disappearance of serfs, particularly in England, meant a relative increase in the number of workmen; and the continuing growth of trade fostered the development of yet more townships. The itinerant musician found himself with fresh places of call on his journeys. And the more settled type of professional found that there were a greater number of permanent posts to apply for. For example, towns employed municipal trumpeters to perform the fanfares which were granted by Royal permission to be an audible counterpart to a coat of arms; and town governors debated the passing of by-laws to control the use of music at weddings—so many trumpeters at a rich wedding, so many pipers at a modest one, so many (or so few) instruments of a plebeian kind for a wedding that was beneath special notice.

The new-rich of many countries looked towards Italy and learned how to design a new way of living, for in Italy there was no art from architecture to cooking, or poetry to dress-making, that was not undergoing development at a hastening tempo. Music certainly was not neglected. By Boccaccio's time the Florentine people were making much of entertainments by music after meals, the young people dancing and singing to lute and viol. And in Venice, when a new Doge was elected, they would arrange great pageants and processions of boats, each craft and guild being accompanied by its own band of musicians.

It is difficult to imagine what their music can have sounded like. Inevitably when we think of pageants and processions our imaginations tend at first to provide an accompaniment of military band music and community singing. Boccaccio's after-dinner lutes and viols do not strike us as effective instruments for the open air, and there was as yet no science of orchestration to allow other instruments to be arranged into what we should regard as satisfactory orchestras. But we may gain some idea of an assembly of instruments, even as early as the fourteenth century, from the twelve sculptures in the minstrel gallery at Exeter Cathedral. Twelve angels are playing: a lute (roughly resembling a guitar), a bagpipe, a shawm (a primitive oboe), a rebec (something like a violin), a harp, a jew's harp, a trumpet, a portative organ (small enough to be rested on the knee), a gittern (again a little like a guitar), a flute-à-bec, a timbrel (of the tambourine family), and cymbals.

Other instruments foreshadowed our modern ones—the sackbut (a kind of trombone), the bombard (a species of bassoon, though the name bombard was later applied to a deep brass instrument), the recorder (a flute of sorts but not played, as modern ones are, across the mouth). There were yet others of a lowlier kind: the one-hand flute played in conjunction with a small drum, the two together being called pipe-and-tabor; the hurdy-gurdy; the fool's-flute.

Venice, more perhaps than any other city, led the way towards the Renaissance manner of living. Powerful and independent, the Venetians made themselves richer and richer by trade. Caravans brought treasure from the Far and Middle East—such treasures as are set forth in Flecker's *Hassan* by the draper and the grocer setting out on the Golden Road to Samarkand.

> THE DRAPER:
>
> *Have we not Indian carpets dark as wine,*
> *Turbans and sashes, gowns and veils,*
> *And broideries of intricate design,*
> *And printed hangings in enormous bales?*

> THE GROCER:
>
> *We have rose-candy, we have spikenard,*
> *Mastic and terebinth and oil and spice,*
> *And such sweet jams meticulously jarred*
> *As God's Own Prophet eats in Paradise.*

In Northern Europe the cities of the Rhine and Danube and the North Sea ports of England and Flanders were trading with merchants from the Baltic—merchants even from the Volga and beyond.

Whereas in earlier times the merchants did not fit in with the feudal and ecclesiastical scheme of society, now the Church failed to adapt itself to the merchant's world. The greater churchmen, it is true, did lead lives according to some of the new standards—too often the standards of luxury and indiscipline—and many lesser churchmen followed their example; but the official attitude towards the common folk made no allowance for new knowledge and the new mood of people who were no longer serfs.

Chaucer's Prioress, Madame Eglentyne, continued to sing music that meant little to the unlearned.

> *Ful wel she song the service divyne*
> *Entuned in hir nose ful semely.*

Dr. Eileen Power tells us of the nuns that they sometimes gabbled through their services, 'they omitted the dipsalma or pause between two verses, so that one side of the choir was beginning the second half before the other side had finished the first; they skipped sentences . . . and altogether they made a terrible mess of the stately plainsong.' They were officially forbidden 'all manner of minstrelsy, interludes, dancing, or revelling,' but the man-in-the-street observed that church people did not always obey their own laws. The records of the Diocese of Lincoln, for instance, report a nun who 'did pass the night with the Austin friars at Northampton and did dance and play the lute with them . . . until midnight, and on the following night she passed the night with the Friars' preachers . . . luting and dancing in like manner.'

These glimpses from a musician's point of view, even if they reveal exceptional events, help to illustrate the great changes which led many men to challenge the Church—its secular power and its doctrine. In the Mediterranean countries the challenge to doctrine was not strong, for the Church and the merchants were as one. Where a Medici, one of a family of Florentine bankers, could be Pope, there would be a little criticism against Church doctrine. And where merchants and cardinals were agreed to patronize art lavishly there would be no attack on the prelate's extravagant standards of living. This extravagance certainly did no harm to art directly; and indirectly it helped by encouraging the search for yet more wealth to spend on art.

Thus when Islam spread itself in Asia, and lay as a barrier across the old trading routes, the rich men of the Mediterranean, eager to find new sources of treasure, could be persuaded to support the mathematicians and astronomers and navigators who asserted that one might find new routes to the East via the West. In this, as in the patronage of art, the Church, after a spell of anti-scientific activity and with a certain reluctance, came to terms with the merchants. And when Columbus discovered America it fostered their interests by dividing the new continent between Spain and Portugal. The Italian states, it is true, were not direct beneficiaries from this scheme, but at least trade still flowed into the Mediterranean.

From the West and South there began to come the treasure galleons, for it was not long after Columbus's voyages that Vasco da Gama sailed round Africa, Magellan sailed round the world, Pizarro invaded Peru—all in the space of about forty years.

From the Near East there had already arrived a store of artistic material—histories and myths and dramas brought by Greek refugee scholars after the Moslem conquest of Constantinople. The Italians began to be interested in reviving the glories of the ancient world—classic Greece and Imperial Rome as revealed by these scholars. All the arts were more and more given to developing classic themes. It seems easy and natural to revive Roman ideas in architecture or to use Greek myth as a subject for paintings. But what of music? Music apparently was missing. The Venetians learned, however, that Greek drama was performed in ancient days with a great deal of singing and chanting. If Greek music were lost, they would make good the omission by writing fresh music in—as far as they could guess it—the Greek Style.

The result was Opera.

All these splendid activities went on in the Mediterranean countries without any struggle between the merchants and the prelates. Out in America, it is true, a trader or soldier might be at loggerheads with a missionary, but in southern Europe the bankers and the cardinals were able to live together in agreement.

But in northern Europe there was no such identity between merchant and prelate nor, quite often, between the man-in-the-street and his priest. The merchants of England and Flanders saw that only by fighting could they partake in the trade that came across the Atlantic or up from Africa. The merchants of Germany, their trade declining, could not patronize art as lavishly as the Italians did; but the Germans were leaders in the craft of printing, and printing is the foster-mother of heresy. The peasants and townspeople were not interested in the churchmen's Venetian palaces, Florentine paintings, and Roman cathedrals that they would never see but which they had to pay for. And as we have already observed, they did not care for the arid puzzle-music which had been their chief experience of 'serious' art. The newer developments in music as yet did not reach them, for only Venice was modern enough and rich enough to experiment with Opera. The madrigal, it is true, was growing in beauty, particularly in England. But for poor men the folk-song was the most powerful musical influence.

Particularly was this so in Germany. Therefore, when Luther, providing simple verses to these tunes and writing new tunes himself, gave to Germany the 'chorale'—the hymn in the plain man's own language—he set free a force which was an enormously powerful aid to the economic and religious forces producing the Reformation.

There is no country where Renaissance and Reformation can be more clearly seen influencing the course of music than England. Ever since the days of the Battle of Agincourt, when Dunstable went abroad to carry English influence into France and Belgium, English musicians had been among the most progressive in Europe. In return they learned much from the French and Flemish musicians who, curiously enough, were often in advance of the Italians in the development of choral music. But all these musicians—Dunstable, Okeghem, Dufay, and even the more human Josquin des Prés—were too much given to ingenuities in music.

The English composers, however, were particularly attracted to the madrigal, and from Henry VIII's time onwards they turned to it more and more as the demand for church music declined with the dissolution of the monasteries, and they showed themselves fully the equals of the Italian masters in this style. The character of the madrigal—which may roughly be defined as a small polyphonic work for a few voices—was more popular than that of church music. However carefully and ingeniously the parts were wrought, the work usually seemed to retain something of folk-song's tuneful character; and the words—generally something about shepherdesses and swains and sweet lasses and amorous youths—were concerned with such matters as anyone may understand. In the madrigal, polyphonic music, which had developed within the Church, went out into the countryside and showed that it could come down to earth without damage.

Church music in England did not die, for, even when hatred of Catholicism was at its height, Byrd continued courageously to write music according to the old faith. But certainly the new English Church was as yet a comparatively unimportant patron. It is true that Christopher Tye managed to write a kind of church music that was recognizably Anglican. But in the days of increasing wealth, most of the other Tudor composers found more generous patrons than the Church, and turned to writing for the lute and for that then new instrument, the virginals, providing entertainment-music in conformity with such standards of living as were never known in pre-Tudor times.

Particularly there was a great cultivation of dance music. The Elizabethan gentlefolk danced the saraband, which had been denounced by one Spanish Church authority as wreaking more mischief than the plague; they displayed themselves in the pavane, which was used 'by kings and princes and great lords, to display themselves . . . with their fine mantles and robes . . . and the great ladies accompany them with the long trains of their dresses let down and trailing behind them, or sometimes carried by damsels.' They daringly danced the volte, a kind of galliard, in which 'after having turned for as many cadences as it pleases you, restore the damsel to her place . . . her head full of giddy whirlings . . . I leave you to consider if it be a proper thing for a young girl to make such large steps and separations of the legs; and whether in the Volte both honour and health are not concerned and threatened.'

The religious struggles of Elizabethan times, the wars with Spain, and the influx of Lutheran and Calvinist doctrine, are reflected in music and in the lives of musicians. Morley is said to have varied the composing of madrigals with secret-service spying on Catholics. Dowland, an internationally famous lute-player and composer of many lovely songs, changed his old religion to Protestantism, having found association with English Catholic exiles in Florence dangerous. Byrd was watched. The owner of the famous 'Virginal Book' (now in the Fitzwilliam Museum at Cambridge)—a rich Catholic who collected this marvellous anthology—had his property confiscated, and died in exile.

The titles in the book reveal some of the variety of the Tudor scene. There are the dances—galliards, pavanes, corrantos, almans, and gigges —that foreshadow Bach's suites for harpsichord. There are The King's Hunt, The Carman's Whistle, The Bells, Pawles Wharfe, Bony Sweet Robin, Giles Farnaby's Dreame (by Giles Farnaby), the Duchess of Brunswicke's Toye, and hosts of others, belonging to the days when humble folk whistled tunes (each man according to his trade) and great folk devised dances and masques, and were expected to be able to sight-read a part in a madrigal, and a king might be a composer as well as a huntsman, and a queen might practise the virginals as well as the art of diplomacy.

The tradition of the minstrels was still alive as pedlars sold political ballads up and down the country. It is said that some of our nursery rhymes derive from these, after many transformations. For example,

Little Jack Horner is supposed to refer to the kitchen boy who found the title-deeds of the Abbey of Glastonbury hidden in a pie and became a landowner after the Abbey's dissolution.

The course of the religious struggle may be traced in the successive editions of the Psalter, one of the most important being compiled during Catholic Mary's reign by Protestant exiles in Calvin's city, Geneva. The 1560 edition was described as 'very mete to be used of all sorts of people privately for their godly solace and comfort, laying aparte all ungodly songes and ballades, which tende only to the nourishing of vice, and corrupting of youth.' There is a puritan accent in these references to songs, some of which are now treasured folk-songs.

The Church did not suffer the reformers' challenge without responding to it. When the Council of Trent met in the fifteen-forties and fifties, it found occasion to include music in its agenda. The Council's object was to support the counter-Reformation, to underpin and repair the structure of the Roman Church, and to rally the faithful. The Church needed music as a missionary force, as it had needed it centuries before in the presence of the Frankish barbarians.

Four men in four countries produced the required masterpieces, and produced them appropriately in the polyphonic style. The kind of music that the Church fostered was not abandoned for something new and experimental any more than were the teachings of Catholicism. But, like the teachings, polyphony underwent a cleansing process and reappeared informed with new humanity. The four composers were Palestrina in Italy, Orlando di Lassus in Germany, Vittoria in Spain, and Byrd in Protestant England.[1]

None of these was a churchman in the medieval sense. All wrote some secular music. All depended to some extent on the patronage of princes. Even their predecessor, Josquin des Prés, who died before Palestrina was born, had belonged sufficiently to the modern world to enjoy the patronage of such rulers as Lorenzo in Florence, Louis XII in Paris, and Maximilian I in Flanders. And the four composers of the counter-Reformation all felt the influences of life outside the Church.

Lassus, for example, was director of music to Albert V in Bavaria and found, even in Germany, where prosperity was declining, a sufficiency of entertainment work according to Renaissance standards of extravagance. Palestrina enjoyed the patronage of the Duke of Mantua. Vittoria was for a while at the Court of Madrid. And Byrd shared with Thomas Tallis a monopoly by royal patent of all music-printing in England. (It was not profitable.)

[1] Palestrina, 1525–1595; Lassus, 1520–1594; Vittoria, 1540–1608; Byrd, 1542/3–1623.

TIME CHART

	Religion	Art and Science	Politics and Economics	Music
1450		First printed books 1443		
1460		Leonardo da Vinci born 1452		Josquin des Prés born 1455
1470		Malory's *Morte d'Arthur* completed		
1480		Durer born 1471 Copernicus born 1473 Michael Angelo born 1475		
1490		Titian born 1482 Raphael born 1483 Rabelais born 1490		
1500		Correggio born 1494 Holbein born 1497	1492 Columbus discovers America 1498 Vasco da Gama round Africa	
1510	Calvin born 1509	Botticelli died		
1520	Controversy between Pope Leo X and Martin Luther	Palladio born 1518, da Vinci died 1519	Magellan's world voyage	Movable music-type invented 1502 Orlando di Lassus born 1519 or 1520 Tallis born
1530	Henry VIII quarrels with Pope		Pizarro invades Peru	Josquin des Prés died 1525 Palestrina born 1525
1540	Society of Jesus founded			Vittoria born 1540

Wm. Byrd born 1542

Date	Wars of Religion / History	Arts & Letters	Exploration	Music: Development of masses, motets, magnificats, anthems, madrigals / Development of instruments: harpsichords (virginals), clavichords, viols, etc. / Development of dance music
1550	Council of Trent	Holbein died. El Greco born 1545 Cervantes born 1547		
1560	Calvin died 1564 Elizabeth excommunicated 1570	Rabelais died; Galileo born. Shakespeare born 1564	Exploration in north-eastern waters opens up trade with Russia	Morley born (approx. date); Dowland born 1562 Palestrina's 'Missa Papae Marce' 1565. Monteverde born 1568
1570	Massacre of Huguenots in Paris 1572			
1580	WARS OF RELIGION IN FRANCE AND HOLLAND	Titian died 1576, Rubens born 1577 Franz Hals born	Attempt to found colony in Virginia 1584 Spanish Armada 1588	
1590		Montaigne died 1592		Byrd published book of anthems 1589; Palestrina and di Lassus died 1594 Morley publishes book of madrigals Opera begins 1597 Opera 'Euridice' at Florence Oratorio begins
1600		Van Dyck and Velazquez born 1599	Dutch East India Company founded 1601	Madrigals by Byrd, Bull, and Gibbons published 1601
1610		Rembrandt born 1607 Milton born 1608	Holland independent 1609 Exploration of Hudson Straits	Vittoria died 1608
1620	Thirty Years War begins	Shakespeare and Cervantes died 1615		Byrd died 1623
1630				Lully born 1633

Byrd, though openly a Catholic, held a post as organist at the Chapel Royal in London. Queen Elizabeth would not lose a good musician merely because he was obstinate in religion. When his other work permitted—when he was not writing songs, and madrigals, and dance pieces—he continued to compose great Masses and Motets in readiness for the time when, as he thought, the old faith would return.

In Germany the works of Lassus and the hymns of Luther confronted one another as the storm-clouds of the Thirty Years War massed on the horizon.

In Spain Vittoria seemed to express the anti-modern feeling of a people who, with all the wealth of El Dorado pouring into their treasury, never learned the trading technique that made England and the Netherlands powerful.

And in Italy Palestrina provided the Pope with patterns of church music for all Catholic Christendom. The legend that it was only the beauty of his Masses that persuaded the Council of Trent to continue with its work of reforming church music is no longer believed. The Council did not really contemplate abandoning church music altogether; and its mention of obscene and lascivious themes was no more than an emphatic warning, in the language of the times, not to borrow too many popular melodies. (We have already observed how congregations were uncomfortably eager to remember the wrong sort of words whenever a disguised street-song turned up as the 'canto fermo' of a piece of counterpoint.) Nevertheless, the old legend about Palestrina's influence with the Council of Trent has this much truth in it, that he was regarded as a model composer and his Mass of Pope Marcellus as a model work.

The Elizabethan spectacle, strangely compounded of prosaic fact and poetic fancy, appears vividly in Thomas Weelke's madrigal, *Thule, the Period of Cosmography*.

> *The Andalusian merchant that returns,*
> *Laden with cochineal and China dishes,*
> *Reports in Spain how strangely Fogo burns*
> *Amidst an ocean full of flying fishes;*
> *These things seem wondrous, yet more wondrous I,*
> *Whose heart with fear doth freeze, with love doth fry.*

CHAPTER IX

Opera

NECESSITY, the mother of invention, was the grandmother of Opera. Necessity gave birth to the seamen who discovered the New World, the astronomers who made ocean navigation possible, the ordnance designers who adapted warfare to new conditions. These things seem remote from music and drama. But Galileo, studying the laws of motion, observed not only the stars but also the conduct of violin strings; and cannon manufacturers studying the speed of sound gave new knowledge to musical instrument-makers.

Leonardo da Vinci, turning from art to military engineering, as he sometimes did, forged a link between the theatre of spectacle and the theatre of war. We must not be misled by Shakespeare's Globe Theatre, with its limited resources, into believing that Renaissance entertainments were all poetry and little show, for the Globe was a commercial proposition with a mixed audience, and had to show a profit. Renaissance entertainments for the nobility, especially in Italy, could be very magnificent. And although the realistic 'props' of later times were not yet in existence, Palladio, the architect, had already begun to devise scenery to make some sort of fake world on the stage.

Necessity's children assembled the material resources for Opera. Tyranny's victims, the exiles fleeing from Turkish conquests, had its subject-matter packed away in their portfolios; and scholarly colleagues were digging up information about the old Roman playhouses.

Resources and subject-matter were brought together and mated in a marriage that followed several good examples. There was the sacred example of the miracle and mystery plays of the Church. There was the profane example of the 'Masque,' an entertainment based on mythical stories that probably began, almost in the spirit of charade, at the masked balls that were popular among rich people. (Fancy dress and masks are powerful remedies against inhibition and stage fright when amateurs set out to be other than themselves.) There was the example set in Rome by St. Philip Neri who, at hospital prayer-meetings, used to present biblical stories accompanied by music. (The word 'oratorio' means a place of prayer: here perhaps is the origin of the term.)

A pioneer of Opera proper was Galileo's father, Vincenzo Galilei. He was one of a group of earnest amateurs who used to meet at the house of a rich Florentine banker, Giovanni Bardi, Count of Vernio.

They conceived the idea of reproducing ancient Greek tragedy; and knowing vaguely that it ought to have music, they produced in 'Dafne' (a poetic drama by Rinucci) a fake Greek play, with music by Peri. Knowing vaguely (we are still vague) that many of the passages in Greek drama were chanted, the Florentines invented a kind of declamatory melodic line called 'recitative'—an almost conversational kind of singing accompanied by simple harmonies. This pedantic attempt to reproduce Greek conditions led towards new methods, and composers soon forgot all about the Greeks. Before long there grew up a convention, surviving to the nineteenth century, which decreed that recitative should quickly describe events, making such explanations as would help the plot, while set songs called 'arias' should express the chief characters' feelings and sentiments.

In 1600, three years after 'Dafne,' the Bardi group produced 'Eurydice,' of which the text still survives. Both Peri and Caccini wrote music for this. And at about the same time a friend of theirs, Cavalieri, devised a kind of religious opera in Rome—the 'Story of the Body and Soul.' Madrigals, which we think of as delicate little works for a few unaccompanied voices, were sometimes provided with accompaniments and reshaped into some kind of dramatic form, and rudimentary orchestral organization began to appear. Madrigals, however, were not satisfactory as material for drama. Polyphonic music is not narrative enough: it is not sufficiently interested in 'getting the words over.' The new enthusiasts were all in favour of 'homophonic' music—tune with supporting chords—and they led the way to a kind of formula-harmony that allowed later composers to sketch out a harmonization by just jotting down a bass line and a few numbers in a system called 'figured bass.' (We shall touch upon it in dealing with Harmony.)

The early amateurish efforts in Opera paved the way for Monteverdi. Having made some reputation with madrigals that introduce discords without warning, he produced 'Arianna' to celebrate a royal wedding. This established the new genre firmly. Monteverdi became one of the most sought after composers of the day. He was a great innovator, and such a work as his 'Orfeo,' though not now performed, remains a musical landmark. In it he practically founded the science of orchestrating for effect instead of just collecting whatever instruments were available and letting each play whatever part lay within its range. He is said to have invented such dramatic effects as 'tremolo' and 'pizzicato' and to have indulged in violent contrasts of tone.

At first Opera was for the rich. While tortured Indians toiled in the mines of South America, and questing sailors endured storms and scurvy and hunger to load the treasuries of Europe with yet more plunder, the Venetians and Florentines did not foresee that the

Mediterranean was destined to become a mere lake (until the building of the Suez Canal), and that the Atlantic was to be the highway of the future. They could, and did, spend—we must allow for the exaggerations always to be found in chronicles of kings—in the grand manner.

Later, of course, Opera became commercial. Some unknown pioneer, surely the progenitor of the race of operatic impresarios, promoted an 'ambulant opera house'—masked performers on a cart during the Roman carnival of 1606—and from such beginnings there arose the idea of entertaining the not-so-rich, at a distance, in regular opera houses. The first opened in Venice some thirty years after the cart incident, and by the end of the century the Venetians had eleven.

Yet despite this slow democratization of Opera, we do witness in Renaissance Italy a kind of class cleavage in the musical world. Opera was not always to be confined to the rich, but it *was* confined to the richer towns. The peasant is shut out, and he does not reappear until the nineteenth century, when the romantics, washing his face and teaching him manners, featured him as purveyor of folk-songs and dance-tune themes for nationalistic works.

Opera in its early days appealed greatly to ardent intellectuals who loved theorizing about the future, and also to the public who liked to be entertained. The more staid music-lovers thought it amateurish (as it was) compared with the polyphonic works. They did not like Monteverdi's 'sensationalism.' They were not beguiled by the rhythmic melodies of Cavalli who, disinclined to be pedantic about ancient Greek principles, reduced the amount of recitative and fostered the development of aria. They did not realize that the old polyphony was at the end of its development and that only when Opera had enriched composers' technique would choral music achieve fresh triumphs.

But, at any rate, if they condemned Opera, they did not do so, as many people do nowadays, on the ground that it is 'artificial.' In those days, nobody had yet heard of 'realism,' and all kinds of combinations of acting, reciting, singing, and dancing had been in existence since man was first an artist. If Opera seems slightly absurd to us, it is because we forget the many backgrounds against which it has been projected in the last three centuries.

It began as a fake Greek tragedy. It turned to Roman history as it became more popular. It adopted elements from the comedy of masks. It became a pageant and a spectacle. All this in its early years. We shall see later how in the days of Grand Monarchy it became bound by etiquette and formality, later redeemed by wit, elegance, and touches of profound humanity. Anyone who ranges throughout Opera repertoire must remember that this composer was a child of the French

Revolution, and that one an Italian Nationalist, and the other a Russian mystic. He must endure librettos, kept alive by music, which as plays would have died together with the other works of their writers. (Who would remember Gilbert but for Sullivan?)

The appeal of Opera to composers lies in its endless capacity for transformation. Every schoolboy who has wrestled with permutations knows that if there are half a dozen people with half a dozen vehicles on half a dozen routes, the possibilities of chopping and changing the transport arrangements run into unexpected thousands. Opera is inexhaustible in possibilities of arrangement of its many elements. With men and women singers, solo or in chorus; appealing to an audience in poetry, prose, or gesture; with actors appearing as types and symbols or as ordinary people; conjuring up history with either new or period music; frankly confessing to artificiality or disguising it in some 'realistic' form; placing chief reliance on the singing, or on the orchestral playing, or on the ingenuities of plot, or on a message from the Spirit of the Age; alternating between perfunctory, explanatory recitatives and formal arias (with applause at the end of each song) or carrying on a continual action; relying on a hundred musicians for a climax or on silence; writing intimately and swiftly in a style that does not survive the translation of the words, or grandiloquently, one-syllable-a-minute; reviving romantic chivalry or insisting on stark misery; killing the principals or marrying them off in a happy-ever-after fashion . . . composers, devising Grand Opera, Comic Opera, Operetta, Musical Comedy, and now in the same tradition, film 'musicals,' are never at the end of their resources. Wagner sought to supplant Opera with . . . music-drama. It was a case of *le roi est mort, vive le roi*; and the Opera dynasty is not yet sterile.

Opera is of particular interest to the historian for it is expensive and therefore reveals what resources were available—to whom they were available, when, and where. We shall have a number of occasions to observe these things later on.

The first opera house was opened to the public in Venice in 1637. Other Italian cities followed suit; but outside Italy, the main centres of Opera grew up in Vienna, Paris, London, and Hamburg. Many years later, St. Petersburg and New York joined the group of operatic centres, which meanwhile had become numerous, since many a princeling, for pride's sake, had his own opera.

Romain Rolland in *A Musical Tour through the Land of the Past* gives us a picture of an Italian opera house in the eighteenth century. The public was noisy and inattentive. Gentle-folk went from box to box during the performance, paying visits. Some people played cards. Since dramatic truth was so often sacrificed to passionate intensity, nobody bothered to pay much attention until moments of climax. Then, however, there was sudden silence and appreciative attention.

This was particularly true in Naples and Venice where vocal music flourished. Turin and Milan favoured instrumental music. Everywhere the most rigorous training was applied to young musicians, and already there existed a kind of concert-agency for supplying foreign courts with performers. There were even women's orchestras. 'Nothing could be more delightful than to see a young and pretty nun in a white habit, with a bunch of pomegranate flowers over one ear, conduct the orchestra, and beat time with all the grace and accuracy imaginable.'

Oratorio, from being a kind of religious opera, deserted the theatre. If a big work for chorus, orchestra, and soloists had a biblical text, the word oratorio came to be regarded as its proper description. For a similar work with secular words, the word cantata was used; and if the words were religious, but not necessarily from the Bible, the correct title was sacred cantata. But not until Victorian days was it considered downright improper for a sacred work to reveal theatrical influence, reacting from the earlier view that a theatrical style would (according to Mattheson in 1728) 'excite virtuous emotions' more satisfactorily than a contrapuntal style.

(Words like cantata and sonata and sinfonia were used very indefinitely at first. Cantata could mean anything sung: sonata anything played; but gradually they acquired specific meanings. Opera is another such word. Literally it means 'a work' like the Latin word 'opus' which we use in cataloguing compositions in chronological order. 'Melodrama' much better deserved to survive as a correct title.)

CHAPTER X

Rhythm

THE new music moved to more involved rhythms than did the old church music. The rhythms were not more subtle: in some respects they were more mechanical, as dance rhythm is as compared with the rhythm of prose speech. But they were precise in time, as geometrical patterns are in space; and they were thus more under the control of the composer and less dependent on the performer's whims than declamation was.

And speed was an important factor. Notes, which had formerly been regarded as swift, became the long notes of the new dispensation.

The very word semibreve, the name of our longest note, actually means half-brief: the word minim (our next longest note) suggests something tiny. The new note-durations had their lengths as carefully related as the values in a metric coinage, and they ousted the old notes that had heads shaped like the 'diamonds' in a pack of cards.

Coinage gives us a valuable means of comparison in explaining the principles of rhythm-notation to those who have never learned music. A currency varies in total value as times change, buying more goods in peace-time than in war-time. Similarly note-durations vary from piece to piece, 'buying' more time in a funeral march than in a galop. Then again, although we regard the pound-sterling as our standard monetary value, we can reckon our small change according to any unit, counting it in shillings or pennies or farthings. By a mental adjustment we abandon the counting of pound notes and say 'let a penny count as one unit.'

Similarly we abandon the attempt to count in whole notes (semibreves) and may decide to reckon a quarter-note (crotchet) as one beat. There is no denying that this is confusing; and some people, after learning music for years, are as unable to read a complex rhythm at sight as others are to reckon a money sum in their heads. But anyone can understand the *principle* on which the system is based.

Before setting out a schedule of relative note-lengths we must realize that durations are measured by a kind of internal clock mechanism, which most people possess, called the sense of rhythm. This sense is delicate in many people, and highly cultivated in accomplished musicians. Hardly anyone is quite without it, for it is a factor in all actions of skill, and governs many of our bodily functions. When you march behind a band, the time that elapses between a left-step and a right-step may be regarded as a beat-length, although the word beat is often applied not to a length, but to the moment of striking the ground with your foot. And every child who recites a nursery rhyme brings out the sing-song pulsation thus:

HUMPty DUMPty SAT on a WALL.

Now for the schedule of note-values (omitting rare notes). (See g. 21.)

Reckoning a long note is easy. For example, a semibreve may be said to last for four steps (left-right left-right). If the piece is a funeral march, marked *lento*, you step slowly; if a galop, marked *presto*, you step 'at the double.' Notes which are 2 beats or 1 beat, will be allotted their correct number of steps. But how to reckon fractions of beats?

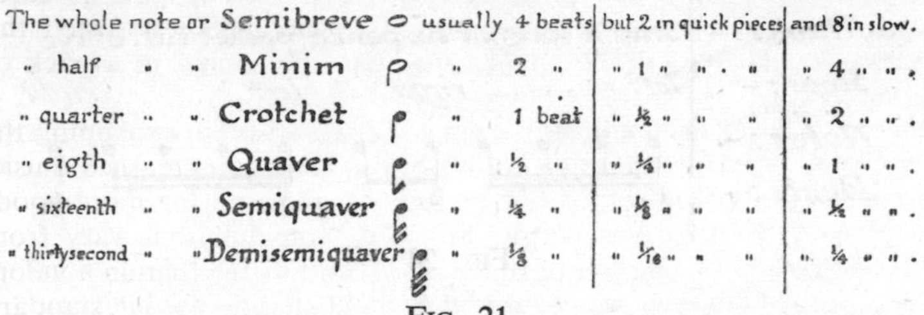

The whole note or Semibreve ○	usually	4 beats	but 2 in quick pieces	and 8 in slow.
" half " " Minim ♩	"	2 "	" 1 " " "	" 4 " "
" quarter " " Crotchet ♩	"	1 beat	" ½ " "	" 2 " "
" eigth " " Quaver ♪	"	½ "	" ¼ " "	" 1 " "
" sixteenth " " Semiquaver ♬	"	¼ "	" ⅛ " "	" ½ " "
" thirtysecond " " Demisemiquaver ♬	"	⅛ "	" 1/16 " "	" ¼ " "

FIG. 21

The *method* is simple. (Its application at high speed may, of course, tax the resources of a Liszt.) Here is an example. Take the following couplet. Say it slowly giving a step to each syllable:

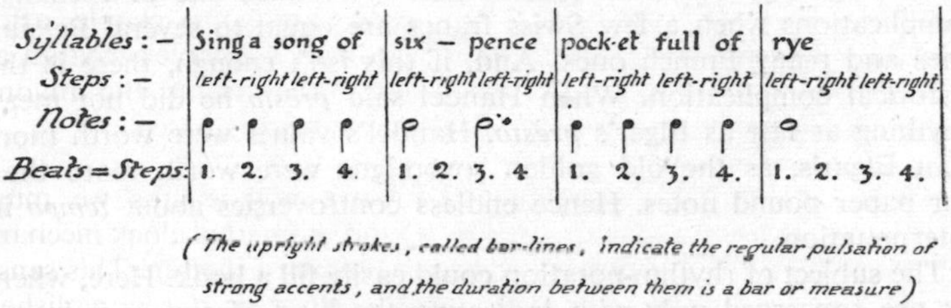

Syllables : -	Sing a song of	six — pence	pock-et full of	rye
Steps : -	left-right left-right	left-right left-right	left-right left-right	left-right left-right
Notes : -	♩ ♩ ♩ ♩	♩ ♩ ♩.	♩ ♩ ♩ ♩	○
Beats = Steps:	1. 2. 3. 4.	1. 2. 3. 4	1. 2. 3. 4.	1. 2. 3. 4.

(The upright strokes, called bar-lines, indicate the regular pulsation of

strong accents, and the duration between them is a bar or measure)

FIG. 22

Now speak more quickly:

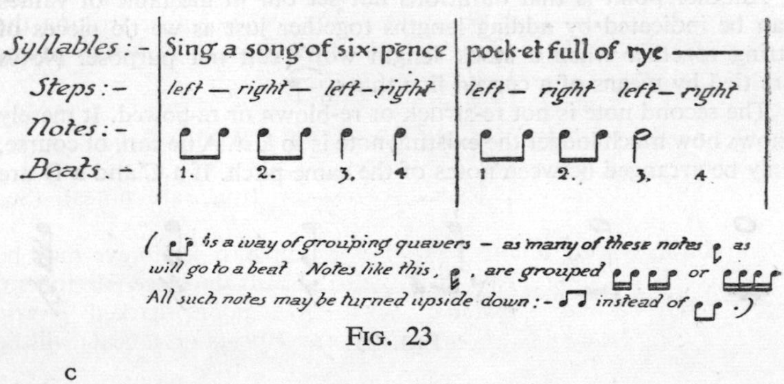

Syllables : -	Sing a song of six-pence	pock-et full of rye ———
Steps : -	left — right — left-right	left — right left — right
Notes : -	♫ ♩ ♫ ♩	♫ ♫ ♩
Beats . -	1. 2. 3. 4	1. 2. 3. 4

(♫ is a way of grouping quavers — as many of these notes ♪ as
will go to a beat. Notes like this, ♪, are grouped ♫♫ or ♬
All such notes may be turned upside down : - ♫ instead of ♫ .)

FIG. 23

C

Now speak still more quickly:

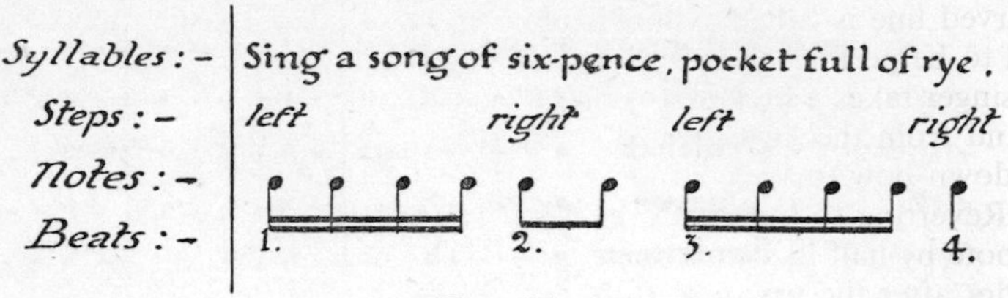

Syllables : – | Sing a song of six-pence, pocket full of rye .

Steps : – | *left*   *right*   *left*   *right*

Notes : –

Beats : – | 1.   2.   3.   4.

FIG. 24

Four *sixteenths* followed by two *eighths* is only a speeded up version of 4 beats followed by 2 double-beats.

One important complication must be noted. If the first version be marked *allegro*, and, in consequence, you step lively, you will get the same effect as if the last version were marked *andante* and you stroll languidly. This is a real bother. It reminds one of exchange complications when a few Swiss francs are equal to several Belgian ones and many French ones. And, if this isn't enough, there is the historical complication. When Handel said *presto* he did not mean anything as fast as Elgar's *presto*. Handel's values were worth more than Elgar's, as the old golden sovereigns were worth more than our paper pound notes. Hence endless controversies about *tempo* in interpretation.

The subject of rhythm-notation could easily fill a book. Here, where we are concerned only with indicating the kind of system it is, we shall observe only a few more points. One is that silences have to be measured as carefully as sounds. For every note-value there is a corresponding 'rest.' (See Fig. 25.)

Another point is that durations not set out in the table of values can be indicated by adding lengths together just as we tie pieces of string together when a stock length won't suit our purpose. Notes are tied by means of a curved line thus: ♩‿♩

The second note is not re-struck or re-blown or re-bowed. It merely shows how much longer the existing note is to last. A tie can, of course, only be arranged between notes of the same pitch. If a C and a D are

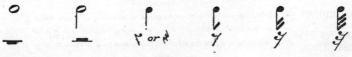

FIG. 25

joined by a curved line there can be no question of a tie. In that case, we proceed as smoothly as possible from one to the other. This kind of curved line is called a slur. It may run across several notes which are all to be performed in a joined-together fashion: at the end of a slur, a singer takes a breath, a wind player does likewise, a pianist raises his hand from the keyboard, a string player changes from an up-bow to a down-bow (or vice-versa).

Reverting to tied notes, we find that we frequently need to prolong a note by half its own value. Instead of tying ♪ to ♪ or ♩ to ♩, we put a dot after the first note (♪· or ♩·).

Such dotted notes are sometimes used as beats. For example:

One	two
Buckle my	shoe
Three	four
Knock at the	door

'Buckle-my' and 'knock-at-the' are groups of three syllables equivalent to one beat. An ordinary crochet beat, for example, equals *two* quavers. But if we dot it, extending it by half, it will equal *three*.

There are two main beats in the bar, but we can mentally divide each beat in three thus :—

Fig. 26

This kind of dotted-beat time involves a complication when we attempt to state the rhythm in the form of an arithmetical fraction. In ordinary time ('Simple time') we can state four crochets in a bar as four quarter-notes $\frac{4}{4}$; or three quavers as three eighth-notes $\frac{3}{8}$; or two minims as two half-notes $\frac{2}{2}$. In dotted-beat time ('Compound' time) we have to divide each dotted beat into a group of three smaller notes. Thus, two dotted crochets (as in Fig. 26) must be divided into quaver groups, and we must state the time as six eighth-notes $\frac{6}{8}$. Three dotted minims would be divided into crochet groups giving us $\frac{9}{4}$. And four dotted quavers would be divided into semiquaver groups giving us $\frac{12}{16}$.

These fractions—shorthand statements of rhythm—are called time-signatures.

It is important to remember in compound time that the main beats of the bar are the original dotted beats, not the smaller notes into which they are divided. Thus *moderato* applied to $\frac{6}{8}$ time does not mean 'count six quavers moderately.' It means 'count two dotted crochets moderately'—an altogether faster *tempo*. Occasionally we meet rhythms where beats are divided in halves at one moment and in thirds at another:

> Three   four
> Knock at the   door
> Five   six
> Pick up   sticks

If we chose ordinary beats, then 'knock-at-the' is a problem. If we have dotted beats then 'Pick up' is awkward. We fall back on 'arbitrary' groups, indicating the abnormal ones specially. (Fig. 27.)

This effect, by the way, is not syncopation. Syncopation occurs when (*a*) there is an accent where the pulsation is normally weak or (*b*) where the normally strong beat is suppressed but yet allowed for. The second effect was amusingly imitated in verse some years ago in

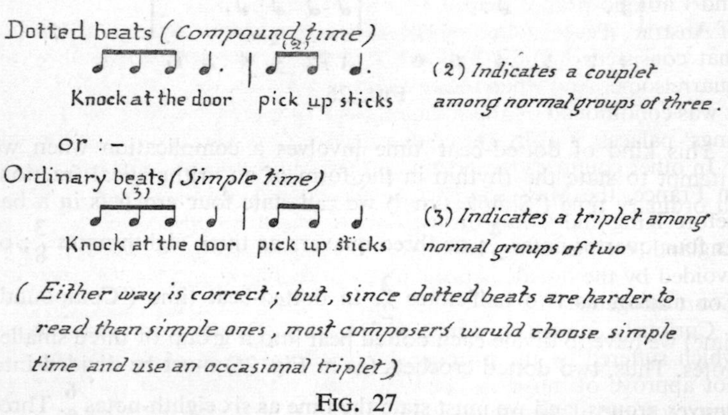

Dotted beats *(Compound time)*

Knock at the door   pick up sticks   (2) *Indicates a couplet among normal groups of three.*

or :—

Ordinary beats *(Simple time)*

Knock at the door   pick up sticks   (3) *Indicates a triplet among normal groups of two*

(Either way is correct ; but, since dotted beats are harder to read than simple ones, most composers would choose simple time and use an occasional triplet)

FIG. 27

a book of nursery rhymes, edited to show the evil effects of censorship. One example began:

> Solomon Grundy
> — on Monday
> — on Tuesday
> — on Wednesday. . . .

The reader allows time for the suppressed accent, but does not utter it.

As in the case of pitch notation, the reader who desires to understand rhythm must practise it—experiencing it, and then setting out his experiences in a system. But this chapter may explain to the uninstructed listener the general method—the basic nature of the system; how it associates itself with verse rhythms; how, guiding the dancer and being guided by the conductor, it links up with movement and gesture.

CHAPTER XI

The Grand Monarch

THE struggle between the German Hymn and the Latin Mass was fought out in blood and treasure. The Thirty Years' War reduced Germany from a position of leadership and left it sunk in misery. Neither side was victorious, and at the end of the war there was unresolved discord. Calvinists were found who quarrelled with Lutherans; and Catholic France helped Protestant Sweden to restrain the power of Austria. 'Peace' found hardly any artistic activity left in a Germany that consisted of three hundred and fifty states—exhausted but still quarrelsome. And when music again became a force in German affairs it was conditioned by the standards of living to be found at the princelings' palaces, and by the material poverty of the Lutheran Church.

In other countries the Hymn and the Mass did not come to a truce. In France, the Mass was victorious and was always duly celebrated before King and Court turned their attention to opera and ballet. In England, on the other hand, the threatened return of the Mass was avoided by the drastic expedient of abolishing King Charles I and his Court altogether.

Curiously enough, in England it was the Hymn rather than Opera which suffered by the process. The Puritans were Calvinists and did not approve of music in church. A few extremists went so far as to destroy some of the organs in places of worship, and a certain number of musicians—those employed in churches and those patronized by the nobility—fell out of work. But music *out* of church was permissible. Indeed Cromwell and Bunyan were both enthusiastic music lovers. Opera actually received its first performances in London under the Commonwealth, and collections of popular music were sold widely. For example, Playford, the publisher, was very successful with *The Dancing Master*—a treasury of the nation's tunes—and he followed it with an *Introduction to the Skill of Music*. Henry Lawes composed several sets of songs which gave Milton great satisfaction. And psalm-singing (which had crossed the Atlantic in the *Mayflower*) flourished.

Nevertheless, although England was not musically sterile, it was not really favourable soil. The middle classes had not yet arrived at the point where they could be patrons of art, and neither Church nor King was available.

In France both were available, but the Church, in the person of Cardinal Richelieu and, later, Cardinal Mazarin, had been busy building up the power of the State; so that when Louis XIV came to the throne he was in an excellent position to become a despot—and such a patron of the arts as the world rarely sees. Sustained by an efficient civil service, defended by an often victorious army, and un-challenged by the nobility (who seemed quite prepared to dwindle into mere courtiers), Louis became an artist in magnificence. His palace, Versailles, is almost insanely splendid. Health and comfort were both sacrificed to splendour. But the Court attracted all men of talent—great artists (architects, dramatists, painters, composers) and lesser artists (landscape gardeners, pastrycooks, dancing masters . . .). And though the inhabitants of the palace could amount to ten thousand at a time, it was found possible to make sure that all the artists were conforming royalists. Louis insisted on the outward forms of homage and gravely accepted all the set pieces dedicated to him. He promoted art and science—but only if subject to censorship. In founding institutes and academies of all kinds he had no intention of assembling the intellectual fuel that was destined to make the French Revolution so great a conflagration. He did not foresee that revolution would happen despite censorship. He made it impossible for Descartes to publish the writings which are a milestone in the history of philosophy. Drama could speak freely only if well seasoned by the palatable wit of Molière. Even music, though it cannot strictly be censored, conformed to the despotic code. Thus art became a kind of defence, shielding the Court from knowing by what methods taxes were raised, and war-with-splendour paid for. The strains of minuet and gavotte and *passe-pied* shut out the whisper of Mazarinades and gave no prophetic hint of the quick-march of the Marseillaise.

Louis patronized the art of façade-building during most of a reign that lasted for seventy-two years.

The chief musical figure of Louis' reign was Lully. He had come from Florence to France as a page boy in the retinue of Mlle de Montpensier, a niece of the King, and arrived at a Court where Cardinal Mazarin had been trying to foster Italian Opera for political reasons. At the age of fifteen, Lully became one of the King's Twenty-four Royal Violinists. Soon he had his own little orchestra. He studied hard, he dissipated, he intrigued, he flattered the King. In 1662 he was commissioned as Music Master to the Royal Family. He enjoyed a Royal income of 30,000 livres per annum and married another 20,000. He collaborated with Molière. He intrigued his way into the position of master of the theatre in place of the director of the Academy of Music. He was in a position to pay a tame poet 4,000 livres a year to provide librettos for operas. He seems never to have displeased Louis. And his Royal master forbade any theatre other than Lully's to employ more than two voices or six violins except by Sieur Lully's permission (penalty 500 livres). When Lully died in 1687 he left four houses and a large sum of money.

His music is rarely performed nowadays, and for most musicians his operas—the first French operas of any consequence—are only history-book knowledge. Most of them began with a prologue of gods and goddesses singing Louis' praises, and continued in a manner calculated to suit a Court tied up in the purple tape of etiquette. Considering the musical resources available, they have a grand manner, and employ both ballet and chorus freely. The grand manner was then much to the public taste, and not only at Versailles. It is said that an opera performed in Padua (Freschi's 'Berenice') included in its cast 12 minstrels, 2 elephants, 6 charioteers, various wild animals, and— 100 virgins and 100 soldiers.

Lully's pieces for dancing became models. The vigorous and sometimes unseemly dances of Renaissance times, some of them of peasant origin, were tamed and polished. The mincing steps of the minuet inspired a style of music that remained in the ascendant until the bourgeois waltz swept it out of the ballroom. Dancing and deportment —the bowings and curtseyings and paradings and finger-tip contacts calculated to a nicety by the arbiters of these elegancies—became prime occupations for gentlemen whose titles had been won by ancestors skilled in the conduct of lance and battle-axe. The ideas of 'good form' established at Versailles were an influence in the development of musical style: the ideas of artistic style were an influence in the evolution of the musical form that we shall discuss when we come to Haydn and Mozart.

CHAPTER XII

The Merry Monarch

LOUIS' Court became a pattern for Royal establishments. Before long, every monarch with pretensions to culture had to provide himself with as grandiose an imitation of Versailles as his unfortunate subjects could be driven to pay for. All the stupidities of empty ceremony, all the extravagances of gilt and tapestry decoration, all the unjoyous 'gaiety' of the fashionable world were reproduced in every palace and *residenz* and *schloss* and *château*.

This influence in the courts of Germany and Austria in the eighteenth century is always fully dealt with in musical histories. But it exerted itself before then in England. When Cromwell's Commonwealth came to an end, and the restoration of the Stuarts permitted those who could afford to entertain themselves to be as gay as they pleased, Charles II promoted the fashions he had learned during exile in France. Charles was connected by marriage, policy, and religious belief with the French Court, and his methods of patronizing art and science were according to the French manner.

If it is a mistake to imagine the Cromwellians as suppressing all merriment, it is equally a mistake to think of the Restoration only in terms of Nell Gwynn and almost unprintable plays, or to remember only the profligacy and extravagance that prevailed at Court.

The Merrie Monarch, like the Grand Monarch, was a patron of art and science. He gave a charter to the Royal Society which, to this day, enjoys as great a prestige as any body of scientists in the world. He sent Pelham Humphrey to study music with Lully, spending £450 of secret service money on doing it. He made Purcell one of the Composers in Ordinary for the Violins of His Majesty.

Purcell, who was organist of the Chapel Royal in 1682, found himself subject to very diverse influences during his musical life. There was the French influence, but without the strict etiquette that existed in Paris. There was the Italian operatic influence of Alessandro Scarlatti, but little native tradition with which it might be mixed. There was the Royal influence, but much more limited by the power of the noble families than was the case in France. There was the Church influence, arising from his post as organist of Westminster Abbey, a superficial influence in an age when Charles was a secret Catholic, his brother and successor (James II) an avowed one, and *his* successors (William of Orange and Mary) defenders of the Protestant faith.

Unlike the Vicar of Bray, who changed his doctrines with every change of government, Purcell found it possible to write one kind of music for all his monarchs, coronation music for James *and* for William, and funeral music for Mary. He wrote a great many anthems for the Abbey and also some official music—odes of welcome and such pieces —for the Court. But his interest lay largely in the theatre. In his day the theatre was active, and he did not lack work to do. Some of his music was incidental to plays now forgotten. One work—his operatic masterpiece 'Dido and Aeneas'—was composed for a girl's school in Chelsea. There were collaborations with Dryden. And there was 'The Fairy Queen,' so freely adapted from 'A Midsummer Night's Dream' that not a word of Shakespeare is to be found in any of the songs. Dryden said in a preface to his 'King Arthur' that music had 'arriv'd to a greater perfection in England than ever formerly; especially passing through the artful hands of Mr *Purcel*, who has compos'd it with so great a genius, that he has nothing to fear but an ignorant ill-judging audience.' Dryden was prepared to adapt his verses, 'and make them rugged to the hearer' if it would help Purcell, since 'in reason my art on this occasion ought to be subservient to his.'

Purcell died (1695) of consumption before he was forty. He was buried in Westminster Abbey, not merely because he had been organist there, but because in his short life he had shown himself to be perhaps the greatest musician then alive.

Though interest in his works has grown, and 'Dido and Aeneas' is no longer a museum piece, much is likely to remain neglected. For example, 'King Arthur,' though usually described as an opera, employs music only as an adjunct to the play. The singing parts are not given to the chief personages of the drama, and much of the music has the character of *intermezzi*. The result is that only a few (but very lovely) songs and short instrumental excerpts are really familiar to concert-goers.

The Grand Monarch was Lully's patron: the Merrie Monarch Purcell's. Queen Christina of Sweden was Alessandro Scarlatti's. This was after she had abdicated and was living in Rome. She had always fostered learning in her own, then somewhat barbarous country. Now she devoted herself to art and to the Catholic religion to which she had been converted. It is interesting to observe the continuing association of Opera with royalty—how composers flocked towards a ruler and how rulers regarded Opera as a splendidly suitable expression of their magnificance. Queen Christina did not continue her direct patronage of Scarlatti, but, later in life, he became a member of the somewhat fantastic Arcadian Academy which derived from her Clementine

Academy. Artists, scientists, and political thinkers (each calling himself by the name of some Arcadian shepherd) met to discuss current problems, and at these gatherings Scarlatti made the acquaintance of Corelli, the founder of violin playing as we now understand it.

Alessandro Scarlatti is remembered largely for his technical advances in Opera. He used strings to accompany recitative, instead of relying on the harpsichord. He standardized the form of the aria, dividing it into three sections, of which the third was an exact repetition of the first. (At the end of the second section he merely wrote the words 'da capo,' and the singer obediently went back to the beginning and sang as far as the finishing-point, marked 'fine.') He devised those concerted items in which a number of characters, each concerned with his own problems, sing all at once in an 'ensemble of perplexity.'

Whether in Versailles, Rome or London, composers were hard at work on many problems of technique. The 'ensemble of perplexity' meant a revival of interest in counterpoint. The elaboration of accompaniments meant fresh ideas in orchestration—learning from Corelli how to write for the superb violins which the families of Guarnerius, Amati, and Stradivarius were turning out at Cremona in Lombardy. If peasant dance tunes could be transmogrified into courtly suites of dances by Couperin and Rameau, then (according to Burney) 'the melody of tunes sung by carriers, muleteers, and common people' could be delicately adapted by Scarlatti's son, Domenico, in little virtuoso pieces which in those days were called sonatas. Domenico Scarlatti and Couperin, though they both wrote choral and operatic works, are chiefly remembered for their pieces for harpsichord (clavecin).

The problems of harmony received special attention. Rameau, who was Lully's most distinguished successor, wrote a treatise on the subject. But Purcell was dead, and Alessandro Scarlatti and Couperin were old men before this book, with all the defects of a pioneer work, made its appearance. In those days, as always, theory lagged behind practice, for there is nothing amateurish about the practical harmony of Rameau or of Domenico Scarlatti.

There is nothing amateurish about the harmony of their contemporaries, Bach and Handel.

CHAPTER XIII

Harmony

HARMONY begins with the observation that certain notes can be pleasantly sounded together. We have already observed the most fundamental of these arrangements. The 'common chord,' part of the harmonic series which the Greeks investigated, vibrates in the relationship 4, 5, 6; and the simplest example of it on the piano keyboard is (starting from the bottom of the chord) C, E, G.

The student learning formal harmony first becomes familiar with this arrangement in all keys. The next step is to arrange this 3-note chord so that it shall be sung by *four* voices.

Why four? There are two good reasons. The first is that the human voice is found in four grades of pitch. (The second reason will reveal itself later.)

WOMEN:

    SOPRANO (or boy's treble) .   .   . High
    (mezzo soprano)
    CONTRALTO (or alto)   .   .   . Low

MEN:

    TENOR .   .   .   .   .   . High ⎧ octave below
    (baritone)   ⎪ the correspond-
    BASS .   .   .   .   .   . Low ⎨ ing women's
                                    ⎩ voices.

Similar divisions are found among instruments. The string quartet (two violins, viola, and cello); the wood wind quartet (flute, oboe, clarinet, bassoon); the quartet of horns found in the larger orchestras, and their confrères the 2-trumpet 2-trombone quartet—all these may be roughly compared with the vocal quartet.

What is the best way of arranging three notes for four voices? Usually it is the root note that is sung by two of the voices; but, of course, there are occasions when the middle note (the '3rd' of the scale) or the top note (the '5th') are 'doubled.' This brings the student to the problem of spacing the notes. Here are some of the solutions he arrives at for C-major chord.

Experiment shows that the two men's voices may be widely spaced. In fact, they should not be close together unless they are both fairly

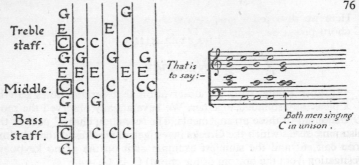

FIG. 28

high. Other voices, however, should not usually be more than an octave apart.

Spacing must be studied in all keys. For example, in C major, a bass has a choice of two C's; but in E major, if he has a decent range, he might sing any of three E's (the one below the stave, the one in its middle, and the one above middle C).

In the examples given above C is always the bottom note. So long as this is so, and no matter how the other notes are spaced, the chord is said to be in its root position. If E were the bottom note, the chord would be in the first 'inversion'; and if G were the bottom note we should have reached the second inversion. Each inversion has its own problems of spacing and doubling, and the use of the minor key introduces further rules to learn.

But chords are not static. They proceed. One chord fades-out and another fades-in. The student has to learn the laws of progression. Here is an example. The C E G chord and the G B D chord have G in common. By careful arrangement we arrive at:

FIG. 29

The voice that sang G at the top simply repeats it. Each other voice moves down one note.

Here is another example, with C standing still and the other two voices moving *up* a step.

Here we discover a new complication. The chords to which the
C chord progressed were G B D and F A C—the common chord of

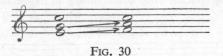

FIG. 30

G major and the common chord of F major. But these chords are
also part of C major for, after all, they consist entirely of white notes.
You can go to a G chord without going into G key. On further investigation we find that there are five common chords, some major,
some minor, which can be regarded as belonging to a given major
scale as well as to their own keys. Here they are in C major:

D   E   F   G   A   B *cannot produce a common*
Minor Minor Major Major Minor   *chord on white notes.*

FIG. 31

If it be true that five chords other than C are available *in* C, then
it is equally true that C chord may be borrowed in five other keys.

Several chapters are devoted in the standard harmony books to
tracing the connections between all these chords in all keys, and in all
inversions. The student who survives these chapters is then called upon
to study discords. The first to be observed is the one that *looks* like a
common chord on B (b.d.f.). The distance between B and F turns out,
however, to be a semitone too narrow, and the chord seems to demand
to be followed quickly by something else. All discords have this restless
quality. You cannot, according to traditional rule, bring a piece to
an end on one. The chord into which a discord melts is called its
resolution.

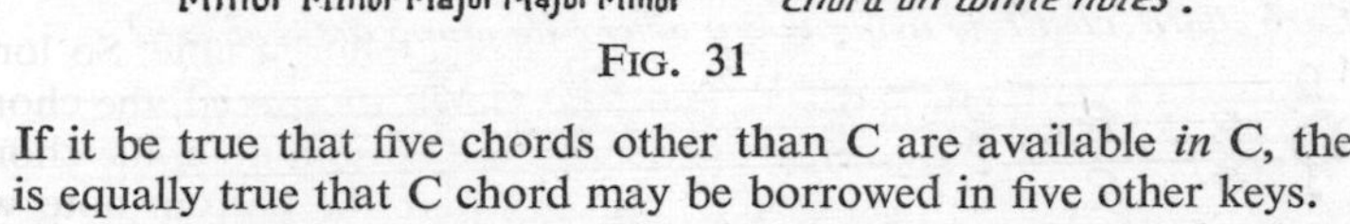

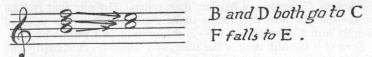

*B and D both go to C
F falls to E.*

FIG. 32

If a composer is bent on maintaining a restless mood, he delays
resolution. He hangs on to his discords, or sideslips on to other discords, constantly putting off resolution on to a concord.

Three-note discords in their root positions are usually rather like common chords in appearance, but their outer notes are too widely or too narrowly spaced. They occur mostly in minor keys:

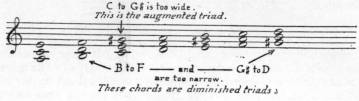

C to G♯ is too wide.
This is the augmented triad.

B to F ——— and ——— G♯ to D
are too narrow.
These chords are diminished triads.

FIG. 33

But most useful discords consist of *four* notes. And with the realization that this is so, we understand the second reason for studying four-part harmony.

Let us build up some 4-note chords by adding another story on each triad-edifice.

Each chord is built by using every other note along the keyboard.

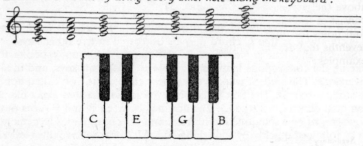

C   E   G   B

FIG. 34

All these chords-of-the-seventh (they are seven notes wide) are in the key of C. Some are harsher than others. The one that is least harsh—the one also that seems to be most anxious to be resolved directly into C common chord—is the seventh that stands on G.

Now G is the fifth note of the scale, and musicians customarily call the fifth note in any scale 'the dominant' of the key. The chord G B D F is, then, the 'dominant seventh.' This chord, and the analogous dominant seventh chord in each other key, is the most important of discords. And since it has so strong a tendency to resolve directly on to the common chord, it is very useful as a way of leading into a new key when we are modulating. Composers of 'musical switches' having ended one 'favourite number,' and wishing to introduce another, often simply blare out the dominant seventh of the new key, hold it for a moment, and then proceed. The characteristic resolution of the dominant seventh is:

Root notes in parenthesis.

FIG. 35

As it has four notes, it has three inversions. Fortunately the chord does not alter in the minor key. But its resolution does—slightly.

The question now arises: if we can add a note on top of a triad to make a seventh, can we add further notes above *that*. The answer is: yes. We can make ninths, elevenths, and thirteenths. Nothing further is possible, since, at the fifteenth, we reach a note two octaves above the root note, and have to start over again. These new chords consist of too many notes to be very useful *in toto*. And if we take out four notes for our four voices, we find that we have those secondary sevenths that are the brothers of the dominant seventh. Here are some examples:

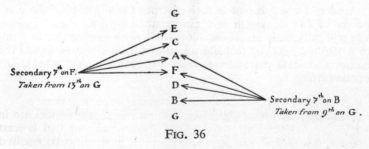

FIG. 36

There are only two more kinds of chord-progression to observe. One is the 'suspension' in which only some of the notes of a discord are resolved, while others are left standing . . . to be resolved a beat or two later. The other is the chromatic chord progression, in which notes foreign to a key are used cunningly *without* causing a modulation. Here are simple examples of both.

Suspension.

*B and F are resolved
two beats late.*

Chromatic chord.

*C chord is on either side of
a chord containing two flats.*

FIG. 37

In all chord progressions the rules of *counterpoint* are observed—the rules about consecutive fifths and octaves, for example. We observed in the chapter on counterpoint that a succession of fifths was unsatisfactory. Fifths remain unsatisfactory even if obscured by other notes.

Fifths.

FIG. 38

To be more precise, they are unsatisfactory in simple harmony of an academic kind. They are nearly always unsatisfactory when they are written inadvertently. Written deliberately and appropriately by a man who is a born composer, they may make a magnificent effect.

Academic counterpoint is derived from the practice of the composers of the eighteenth and nineteenth centuries, when harmony was still sufficiently orderly to allow students to analyse chords down to a 'figured bass' or to build up chords *from* a figured bass. (The numbers indicate characteristic intervals, common chords being left unnumbered.)

*Händel, Bach, and their contemporaries would "rough out"
an accompaniment by jotting down a figured bass.
The performer was expected to improvise the upper parts.*

FIG. 39

There are two modern tendencies to be noted, however. One is to ignore the discord's desire to resolve. As a modernist, you regard the discord, not as an arrangement of four sounds, but as *one* sound. You follow it by other sounds, without tracing connections along the tenor-line or the alto-line. A chord is under no sort of compulsion to choose between two or three possible resolutions. Debussy is the father of this kind of harmony. He refused to listen to his chords half contrapuntally. According to him the dominant seventh was a pedantic abstraction. Play it on the piano deep in the bass and it suggests one emotion. Play it high in the treble and it means something different. Score it for wood wind very softly, then for brass muted-yet-loud, and you have virtually two different chords. For Debussy the question of timbre—quality of tone—was all-important.

The other modern tendency is to go to the other extreme and to give each voice or each instrument in the orchestra so independent an existence as almost to shatter any idea of harmony altogether. With 'polytonality' they may play in different keys at once. With 'atonality' they so completely abandon any connection with a keynote as to make the effect of being in no key at all.

CHAPTER XIV

Bach and Handel

WITH John Sebastian Bach and George Frederick Handel, music makes, for many people, a beginning—as history makes a beginning with William the Conqueror. Their birth-date, 1685, is, so to speak, the 1066 of music. Anything before that is ancient and only rarely performed.

Music-lovers who have never bothered about dates are astonished when they realize that their Old Masters are so recent. From the 'year dot' until the fifteenth century of the Christian era there emerged only a few specimens of performable music. From the next three centuries the average listener can cull a few madrigals, a few folk-tunes, and, if he be a Roman Catholic, some Palestrina and Byrd. He may know a little Purcell. The eighteenth century has already begun before Bach and Handel are old enough to start composing in earnest.

They were both South Germans. Bach was one of a family that had practised music for generations. Handel was the son of a barber-surgeon, who, having got on in the world, wanted his boy to do something 'better' than music—law, for instance. Bach was an orphan at the age of ten, but an elder brother took him away from Eisenach, his birthplace, to Ohrdruf, not far away, and saw that he got a decent education in a religious and musical environment. At the age of fifteen Bach was earning his own living as a choir-boy at Lüneberg, a couple of hundred miles from home. And it was while he was in his 'teens that he formed the habit of walking—journeys of up to sixty miles— to hear the best organists in other towns, or the French band at the Court of Celle, so that the style learned from German composers like Pachelbel and Buxtehude should be diversified by that of Couperin. By the time he was eighteen he had a job as choirmaster and organist at a new church (at Arnstadt) at a salary roughly equivalent to a modern sixty pounds a year. Bach went straight into the musical profession, and earned his living as his forefathers and relations had done.

Handel, on the other hand, endured a certain amount of opposition from his father. In those days a musician was, socially, of no great account. If he were a church organist his pay was wretchedly poor. If he were a court musician he was only a lackey. Artistically, either kind of appointment *might* be good if one's immediate employer were enthusiastic. But one could not be sure. Some of the little princelings really loved music. Some merely wanted to be imitation *Rois Soleils*, showing off a fine band headed by a distinguished *Kapellmeister*, as a millionaire might show off a racing stable that could boast a Derby winner. Some merely kept up appearances on the cheap, for few were as rich as they pretended to be.

Handel, like Bach, was orphaned while still a child. After a brief course at university, he accepted the post of organist at Moritzburg Cathedral and held it for a year. By the time he was eighteen he had left his birthplace, Halle, for good, except for some fleeting visits.

Bach and Handel were soon set on different roads. Bach was a domestic type. He married young. His first wife bore him four children: his second, sixteen. He travelled only occasionally. Handel was a bachelor. He travelled a great deal, was a man of the world, later making and losing large sums of money in theatrical ventures—but not in Germany.

To understand the difference between Bach's career and Handel's one must compare Germany with England, for Handel in due course became a naturalized Englishman.

Germany had not yet fully emerged from the Middle Ages. She had been held back by war—the bitter Thirty Years' War and then the War of Spanish Succession. Her trade had declined as the Atlantic trade grew. There was still a great deal of feudalism in her social scheme, and there was as yet no sign of democratic representation. Religion and music both tended to keep Bach and his contemporaries in medieval ways of thought. This may seem a curious statement about the Reformation states. But Lutheranism, though it attacked the old church, was not a religion of 'progressive' tendencies.[1] Luther desired to recall a spirit which he thought Rome had forgotten. He desired what R. H. Tawney (in his *Religion and the Rise of Capitalism*) calls 'the arraignment of a degenerate civilization before the majestic bar of an uncorrupted past . . . Renouncing the prizes and struggles which make the heart sick, society must be converted into a band of brothers, performing in patient cheerfulness the round of simple toil which is the common lot of the descendants of Adam.' Tawney might almost be writing of Bach when he states Lutheran doctrine thus: 'Christians should earn their living in the sweat of their brow, take no thought for the morrow, marry young, and trust Heaven to provide for its own'; for Bach, who was twice married, had twenty children, and his widow died in poverty.

If the religion of the Bach family was one that medieval people could have been made to understand, so was their music. It is true that in the Protestant states, the Hymn had conquered the Catholic Mass. But the Lutherans devised a kind of Mass for themselves, of which Bach's B minor Mass is an example; and the German musicians, unlike the Italians, the French, and the English, maintained the practice of elaborate counterpoint. They were not, of course, ignorant of Italian opera or French ballet, but for typical German music one must turn to the contrapuntal pieces, woven around a hymn tune, which are called Chorale Preludes. Some of the old scholasticism had, it is true, departed from counterpoint. Much of the new harmony had filtered in. But Germany had lain outside the track of the operatic maelstrom that had set music topsy-turvy in the Mediterranean and Atlantic countries. And so it came about that the Lutherans—the reformers—preserved a habit of thought that the Catholic countries largely abandoned.

By contrast with Lutheranism, the other fiercely Protestant religion was thoroughly anti-medieval. There was an element in it that appealed to merchants and tradesmen and industrialists. ('Whence do the merchant's profits come, except from his own diligence and industry?' asked Calvin in one of his letters.) In the big merchant cities—in Geneva, the headquarters of Calvinism, in Antwerp, the richest city in Europe, and in the City of London, which had supported Cromwell —Calvinism evolved from a religion of militant Puritanism into one

[1] Luther sided with the princes during the Peasants' Revolt.

that encouraged the gaining of wealth, provided that it arose from
the exercise of such Christian virtues as thrift, sobriety, and indus-
triousness. There have been times when, precisely by the exercise of
these virtues, a man might become rich; when an industry begun on
one man's savings did not have to compete with concerns founded
on shareholders' capital reckoned in millions. Increasing wealth often
confirmed a man's idea that he was one of God's elect. The poverty
of others called for little compassion because they were probably
pre-ordained to damnation.

The big merchant cities that had once been Calvinist could afford
to import Opera for a select clientèle, as they imported so many com-
modities; and when Handel arrived in London he exploited Italian
music and English business methods. His music did not lay emphasis
on his German origin until, in later years, in the presence of misfortune, he remembered his religion, and remembered that its customary musical speech for him was counterpoint, as cultivated by
Bach and other German musicians.

At Arnstadt, Bach had a good organ. Here he wrote the first of his
three hundred cantatas and some fugues and virtuoso pieces for the
organ. (A Toccata is a piece to display touch and agility.) But a good
organ was not enough. He must hear good organists. So he walked
a couple of hundred miles to Lübeck to hear Buxtehude and, in the
course of his pilgrimage, overstayed his leave by three months. His
employers were displeased, naturally enough, and reminded him that
as choirmaster he had exerted too little discipline, while as organist
he had let his fancy stray too much. They did not dismiss him; but
by the time he was twenty-three he had nevertheless moved to Mülhausen, where he married a cousin who had sung in the Arnstadt
choir. (A girl in the choir was one of the examples of his indiscipline.)
At Mülhausen the newly-weds had an income of 85 gulden in money,
3 measures of corn, 2 trusses of wood, and 6 trusses of faggots delivered
at their door.

Mülhausen, however, was infested with the same sort of Puritans
as, in Cromwell's day, had piously wrecked the organs in English
churches; and before long Bach had moved again, to become organist
and second-in-command concert-master to the Court of Saxe-Weimar.
Though the Prince there called himself a Royal and Serene Highness,
and was relatively generous to Bach, he was compelled to employ his
musicians in a very economical spirit. One of them was 'groom of the
apartments and trumpeter'; another was 'court secretary, master of
the page boys, and bass-player.' However, Weimar provided Bach
with excellent opportunities, and here he wrote, besides more organ

music, some concertos. He had an orchestra of about twenty and such regular work to do as writing one cantata per month and providing music for Royal births, marriages, and deaths. His fame grew, in a local fashion. He was invited to play on other people's organs, and his playing was sufficiently notorious to scare away the famous French organist, Marchand, who had thought of competing with him in a public musicianship-contest. Nevertheless when the post of *Kapellmeister* fell vacant, Bach did not get it, and at the age of thirty-two he went on to be *Kapellmeister* to the Duke of Anhalt-Cöthen, after being 'ungraciously allowed to resign' by his former employer. (A princely patron, when annoyed, was apt to remember that his pet artist was after all only a servant in livery.)

Handel's early manhood provides a very different tale. With little money in his pocket, he set off for Italy, at the instigation of a dissipated young Medici who had admired his music in Hamburg. Italy was still a Mecca for musicians. Her prosperity was slowly declining, it is true; but patronage was still in the grand manner, and standards were high. The best operas and singers were here; the best violins and violinists; the newest ideas on the planning of instrumental forms. Corelli and Alessandro Scarlatti were among the great men of the day. Domenico Scarlatti was one of the promising youngsters.

The time was coming when music, instead of being an art to spend money *on*, would become an exportable commodity to gain money *with*. With increasing poverty in Italy, musicians would take their art and their voices to all those foreign cities that desired to import culture. Handel, though a German, was in fact one of the first to show the way. An Italian reputation stood him in good stead when he came to London.

How Handel, an unknown, honest Saxon, steered his way to fame amid the intrigues of Italian Courts is a mystery. But in his early twenties he was well received in Florence, Rome, and Venice. In the first city he wrote an opera, and in the second (where Opera was banned by the Pope) some church music. In the third he was urged to visit England by the British Ambassador. In Rome again he gained the patronage of a Cardinal and a Prince; in Naples that of the Viceroy of the Court of Spain.

Nevertheless, when the chance occurred to become *Kapellmeister* to the Elector of Hanover, Handel accepted the post, though his opera 'Agrippina' was the rage in Venice. Ten thousand thalers per annum in a settled job was balanced against Latin enthusiasm. And the new job did not prevent him from making an early visit to London.

Here he was as immediately successful as in Italy—with a new opera called 'Rinaldo'—and after a year back in Hanover, he obtained leave for a second visit. Like Bach he overstayed his time—two years as against Bach's three months. And while he was still in London his employer, the Elector of Hanover, became . . . George I of England. Much can happen during a two years' leave.

During that two years Queen Anne had granted Handel a pension of £200 a year (and pounds were worth a great deal more than they are now). And King George was so quickly reconciled with his truant *Kapellmeister* that he granted him an extra £200. Queen Anne's gift is more remarkable than George's, for George spent English money freely on his German followers. Handel's ability to make noble friends and enemies was prodigious. His restoration at Court is said to have been brought about by the charming expedient of composing some special 'Water Music' for a Royal procession down the Thames, and having it played by some musicians in a barge following the King's boat.[1] Evidently there was a diplomatist hidden behind the bluff exterior of the Saxon.

Bach and Handel were now both at Court; but Bach was a Court servant, whereas Handel was a quasi-independent impresario serving the nobility of England under the sign of a Royal appointment. Cöthen turned Bach away from religious music to chamber music. Some of the new works were exercises in foreign dance idioms—the French and English Suites and the Italian Partitas. Bach had to bow to the spirit of Versailles and compile sets of Allemandes, Courantes, Sarabandes, Minuets, and Gigues. Did anyone dance to them? Few of these dances make the impression of being practical ballroom music. In Cöthen, too, he wrote the Brandenburg Concertos—not, as in the modern fashion, for soloist and orchestra, but rather for a *group* of soloists, themselves members of the band, accompanied by the rest of the orchestra. But most important were twenty-four preludes and fugues for either clavichord or harpsichord.

Ever since the days of antiquity, musicians had been bothered by the 'Comma of Pythagoras'—arthimetic's failure to make 12 fifths tally up to exactly the same number of vibrations as 7 octaves. Many schemes had been tried, all of them beginning with certain notes in tune and attempting to make the best of a bad job with the others. Bach was strongly attracted to a new idea (he did not originate it), which consisted of making *all* notes out of tune. Just as a tax, if levied on the whole community, falls lightly on the individual, so an adjustment of tuning, if applied equally to every note, is hardly perceptible. The

[1] This all too romantic story is usually ascribed to the year 1715, but according to documents quoted by Newman Flower the music belongs to 1717 and to a different procession, long after the royal displeasure had evaporated.

'equal temperament' system divides each octave into 12 exactly similar semitones. No interval except the octave is *quite* in tune, but all notes are equal in importance: no key takes precedence over the others. To demonstrate the point, Bach wrote a prelude and fugue in every one of the 24 (major and minor) keys, and called the set 'Das Wohltemperirte (well tuned) Clavier.' Twenty-two years later, he added a companion 24 pieces to make up 'The Forty-eight Preludes and Fugues.'

Bach remained at Cöthen until he was thirty-eight. He was now married for the second time, his first wife having died. His second wife, gracious Anna Magdalena, served him devotedly until he died. It was for her that he wrote the Clavierbüchlein that is still a child's introduction to Bach. Despite the appalling infant mortality in eighteenth-century South Germany, she managed to bring up enough of her own and her step-children to form a small orchestra, learning to play and to copy her husband's music in her spare time.

The family moved to Leipzig, where Bach remained as Cantor of St. Thomas's Church until he died.

Handel did experience a short appointment on Cöthen lines. For three years during his early thirties he was master of music to the Duke of Chandos at Canons, Edgware. The Duke, as Paymaster to the Forces, had made a vast fortune (public life was terribly corrupt) and he set himself up in a palace that was an English equivalent to a continental *Residenz*, and there Handel wrote his first English oratorio 'Esther.' But Handel was soon back in London as chief of an operatic venture.

Those were days of fantastic speculation and gambling. Rich people flung their money about (Charles James Fox gambled away £11,000 in a single sitting) and set an example to many poorer people who were persuaded to invest in wild-cat schemes. Where did the money come from? Some came from far away, by way of the East India Company and from the islands of the Pacific. This kind of merchant trading led to the notorious boom and slump known as the 'South Sea Bubble.' A little wealth, too, was beginning to arise from manufacture and mining. Most came from robbing the peasant of his land, by a system of enclosures, and applying to the new estates the latest ideas in agriculture. Religion and morality were at a low ebb, there was the sharpest contrast between wealth and poverty, and crime was rampant. Oliver Goldsmith's *Deserted Village* is apt.

> *Ill fares the land, to hast'ning ills a prey*
> *Where wealth accumulates, and men decay.*
> *. . . . But times are alter'd; trade's unfeeling train*
> *Usurp the land and dispossess the swain.*

Along the lawn, where scatter'd hamlets rose,
Unwieldy wealth, and cumb'rous pomp repose;
. . . While, scourged by famine from the smiling land,
The mournful peasant leads his humble band;
And while he sinks, without one arm to save,
The country blooms—a garden and a grave.

Handel's new 'Royal Academy of Music,' a title borrowed from the Paris Opéra, was capitalized to the tune of £50,000 with several peers on the board. Its career was enlivened by the famous rivalry between Handel and another composer named Bononcini. Bononcini was supported by the great houses of Rutland, Queensberry, Sunderland, and Marlborough; and the noble gentlemen were not dismayed when Handel's superiority was demonstrated in an opera to which each composer contributed one act.

Some say, compared to Bononcini
That Mynheer Handel's but a ninny;
Others aver that he to Handel
Is scarcely fit to hold a candle.
Strange, all this difference should be
Twixt Tweedledum and Tweedledee!

said a wit of the day.

During the eight years of the Royal Academy, Handel wrote a series of operas that are now never performed, though they contain much fine music. By modern standards they are dull dramatically— each a kind of vocal concert in which the items are sung in costume and strung together by a thin story to which the ill-mannered audience paid little attention. A concert system had not yet arisen. (Such a gathering as regularly took place in a loft above a warehouse, on the premises of Thomas Britton, 'the small-coal dealer,' was only a prophetic glimpse of concert seasons.) And operas were good enough if they were concerts in disguise.

Furthermore, the heroic parts were sung by male sopranos—singers who, having undergone a barbarous operation while they were children, preserved a treble voice into manhood. Nobody is now available to sing their music. These *castrati* were extravagantly admired and earned enormous sums. One of them, Farinelli, later became attached to the Court of Spain, where he was paid a large salary to sing the same four songs every evening to the melancholy King. (When he retired to Italy, he ironically called his palatial residence 'The English Folly.') Evidently these monsters were magnificent singers. Apart from the evidence of contemporary raptures, we have the music that was written for them. It is not easy.

Castrati and *prima donnas* were always quarrelling. Business methods were neither businesslike nor methodical. But the final blow was delivered by the production of John Gay's flippant extravaganza on criminal themes, 'The Beggar's Opera.' The 'quality' were entertained to see on the stage the *habitués* of Newgate Prison, the squalid mobs who infest great cities when a brutal law is administered without efficiency. The new opera, with its Hogarthian humour and its fine tunes borrowed from all kinds of sources (one from Handel himself), quite eclipsed the Italian opera.

Handel's second operatic venture, financed by his own savings (he possessed £10,000), ended in bankruptcy. The Prince of Wales being at loggerheads with the King (George II), the Prince's friends set out to ruin the King's musician, and put their money and influence into a rival operatic company. They engaged Farinelli and they succeeded in their purpose. The upshot was ironic. *Both* ventures went bankrupt . . . and Handel was reconciled to the Prince of Wales. A new opera by Handel, 'Serse' (Xerxes), from which the world-famous 'Largo' is extracted, helped to pay a few debts, but was not really successful.

Bach's Leipzig period produced the great choral masterpieces— the St. Matthew Passion, the St. John Passion, the Christmas Oratorio, and the B minor Mass. These were the outcome of stupendous labour, for many a man would have found the routine tasks of his post enough. Bach had to cope with choir-boys, a dictatorial rector, the Town Council that governed St. Thomas's School, and the University that ran the Musical Society. The income was about £70. Making allowances for alterations in monetary values and purchasing power, Bach was about as prosperous as the headmaster of an elementary school of to-day.

He was famous enough in his later years to be invited to Potsdam by Frederick the Great (who played the flute) to try the latest keyboard instruments and display his musicianship. On returning to Leipzig he sent to Frederick a 'Musical Offering'—exercises on a theme set by the King. He never lost interest in technical problems, as The Forty-Eight and the 'Art of Fugue' show, yet he was rarely dry-as-dust. He could be astonishingly rhapsodic and lyrical. He could be serene, he could be gay.

He was blind shortly before he died—he had over-used his eyes. He left no means to support his widow. His sons appear to have forgotten their duty to her. The highly gifted Friedemann Bach was, it is true, only her stepchild and something of a ne'er-do-well. Carl Philip Emmanuel was also a child of the first Frau Bach. But John

Christian, successful as composer and teacher in London, should have sent his mother some help.

Handel's last period was noteworthy for his abandonment of opera in favour of oratorio. An attempt to return to opera was barred by his aristocratic enemies, who were determined to sabotage, by hired violence if necessary, any theatrical venture.

Two oratorios had had only a little success; and, with everything against him, Handel wrote the 'Messiah'—in twenty-four days. Then, at the end of a successful season of concerts in Dublin, where he had been invited by the Lord-Lieutenant of Ireland, Handel produced his new work with great success.

In London he was again beset by titled enemies. This time they resented the success of his new oratorio ('Samson') as against the failure of their opera season. They resented his 'bobbing up,' his honourable repayment of debts in full to his creditors. The 'Messiah' was not so successful as 'Samson,' even though the King visited it and inaugurated the now time-honoured custom of standing during the Hallelujah chorus. In the upshot, the new season ended in failure.

Nevertheless, Handel persevered. A new work 'Judas Maccabaeus' succeeded because (a) it seemed somehow apt during the victories over the Scottish Jacobites; (b) because it pleased the Jews among Handel's London supporters, and (c) because Handel put the performances on a new basis, opening them to the general, unfashionable public, who have continued to love their Handel to this day. Revivals of earlier oratorios and presentations of new ones brought new prosperity, and Handel, ever generous, presented an organ to the Foundling Hospital, and arranged performances in aid of the charity which brought in some £11,000.

It was in this year that Bach died. The two men never met. They had just missed meeting when Bach was at Cöthen, and Handel was travelling in the neighbourhood in search of singers for London.

Handel lived for another nine years, for the last six of which he, too, was blind. With the help of a secretary he continued to work, revising earlier work and directing performances. When he died he was buried with great pomp in Westminster Abbey. Had *he* left a widow she would probably have enjoyed a little private means.

Handel's choral works differ from Bach's in being more simple and direct and easier for the singers. Bach, although he wrote many fugues—and fugues are choral in essence—was so much under the influence of instrumental technique that his choral writing was influenced thereby. . . . But fugue demands a chapter to itself.

One final reflection suggests itself. Both men's lives show that a great artist need not be a Bohemian, or live in a garret, or die young. They refute the belief that an artist must undergo extravagant ecstasies and harrowing despairs or must lead the kind of private life that cannot be discussed in print. Handel, it is true, went through a few short bouts of mental instability when his fortunes were at a low ebb. But excepting for Handel's borrowings without acknowledgment from other men's work when he was in a hurry, there is little for the iconoclast to discover in either man's life in an effort to 'debunk' the great.

To us, Bach's music often seems daringly progressive. Its harmonies, for instance, are more modern than those of many of his successors, its modulations more free. Yet to his contemporaries he was old-fashioned, full of pious reverence for the traditions of the German school of organist-composers among whom his own ancestors had played an honourable rôle. The younger men of his day were abandoning counterpoint for the simpler melodic styles of southern Europe. They saw no reason why, if Bach wanted to glorify religious themes, he should not employ the resources of the new operatic manner. They recognized him to be a great man, but he was never a fashionable composer.

G. K. Chesterton was fond of observing that when a man accepted a dogma he became, not enslaved, but free. It is the freethinker who is a slave—to doubt and perplexity. Bach's music suggests that this argument may perhaps contain more than a paradox. The Christian dogma and the fugal dogma seemed to confer on Bach a certainty and freedom of movement that make us forget that he accepted limitations. Not that he simply accepted his beliefs. They were part of the stuff of which he was made. He was never guilty of that humbugging, Sunday-clothes piety that is often nauseating in other men's religious music. There was no ostentation in his brilliant technical accomplishments. He could be tedious at times, spinning out pages that were deliveries of required music according to schedule. But his music is never cheap and nasty, never gross or sensational, never flippant or superficially elegant. Like Milton's poetry, it speaks of Paradise and angelic hosts and the forces of darkness. Even more than Milton's poetry it is concerned with the common man and woman who are Adam and Eve.

Handel, by contrast, was a fashionable, progressive composer writing, for a metropolitan audience, pieces in the most admired Italian style. Yet, by historical chance, he is regarded almost as Bach's brother. If only his theatrical music were more performed, the comparison would no longer be made. But since it is his oratorios that are now remembered, and since they, like Bach's, are religious in spirit and contrapuntal in style, we tend to look for resemblances. We notice the eighteenth-century formulae which were common to both. Handel's choral style is simpler, more singable than Bach's, his piety more English and 'hearty.' But for the ordinary listener the impression will probably remain that there is an affinity between the two men. And, though this impression is somewhat superficial, it is by no means entirely false.

CHAPTER XV

Fugue

THE sopranos are singing a tune. It is not in itself a very engaging tune. It sounds a little artificial and contrived, for it is not only a 'subject' but also, in a sense, the clue to a puzzle. When they have finished their little theme, they hear that the contraltos have taken up the tune . . . the same tune but set four notes lower down to suit the lower voice. Transposed thus to the dominant key, the tune is now described as an 'answer.' The sopranos, however, do not stop singing. They continue—to supply a counterpoint—a counter subject —above the answer. The two voices, after a modulation that switches back to the original (tonic) key, are then joined by the tenors, who proceed to sing the subject once again, but an octave lower than the soprano version. And it is the contraltos who now sing the counter-subject, while the sopranos supply a free part on top. Finally, in come the basses, singing the answer an octave lower than the contralto version. The tenors sing the counter-subject above *them*, and the two female counterpoints are free.

This brings the fugue to the end of the exposition. (See Fig. 40.)

The development now begins. The subject crops up as a whole or in fragments, sung now by one voice, now by another, while modula-

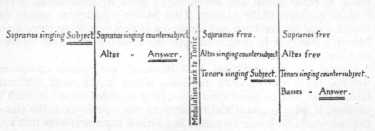

FIG. 40

tions take them through several keys. Sometimes the subject is nowhere to be heard. The voices are passing through an 'episode.' Sometimes one voice will begin the subject before another has ended it, and the one tune will be occurring in two parts, but out of step. Thus, for example:

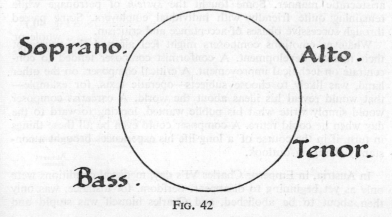

Fig. 41

As a climax to this development section, *all* the parts tread on one another's heels in a grand 'stretto' which ushers in a return to the original key. A short restatement of the subject (final section) in the tonic key brings the work to an end.

The foregoing describes *a* fugue. Let us observe alternative possibilities.

(*a*) The number of voices may vary from two upwards. In actual practice five is about as many as a composer can conveniently manage or a listener follow.

(*b*) There need not be a countersubject. All voices can be free once they have sung their subject or answer.

(*c*) The voices need not enter in the order already given. But they usually go round the circle (clockwise or anti-clockwise) and not across it.

Soprano.   Alto.

Tenor.

Bass.

Fig. 42

(*d*) There may be two subjects—two expositions perhaps—in a 'double fugue.'

In the chapter on counterpoint we discussed such devices as augmentation (double-length notes), diminution (half-length notes), inversion (melody going up by as many notes as it previously went down, and vice versa). Such devices are to be found in fugue from time to time. Bach was one of the select few composers who could devise a really involved fugue containing all these tricks and a few others too, and yet produce music. It is almost as though a writer should invent a double acrostic, and thereby produce a poem.

CHAPTER XVI

Aristocratic Patronage Reaches Its Climax

Gluck, Haydn, Mozart

THERE were various ways of responding to aristocratic patronage. One was the old-retainer method. Like a butler or a gardener, a composer could identify himself with his employers, taking pride in the work of the estate on which he lived, assisting in entertaining visitors, celebrating the births and marriages of the young masters and mistresses with cantatas and serenades, and preparing for Court consumption the best home-reared symphonies.

By no means did all composers accept this status happily. Some quarrelled with their patrons on personal grounds, disliking the aristocratic manner. Some fought the *system* of patronage while remaining quite friendly with individual employers. Some passed through successive phases of acceptance and criticism.

Whatever emotions composers might feel affected the course of their musical development. A conformist composer tended to concentrate on technical improvement. A critical composer, on the other hand, was likely to choose subjects—operatic texts, for example—that would reveal his ideas about the world. A careerist composer would simply write what his public wanted, looking forward to the day when he could retire. A composer could even be all these things in turn, if in the course of a long life his experiences brought a constantly changing outlook.

In Austria, in Emperor Charles VI's day, medieval conditions were only as yet beginning to disappear. Serfdom, for instance, was only then about to be abolished, and Charles himself was stupid and reactionary. His successors, it is true, were less stupid, and liked to regard themselves as enlightened monarchs; but they were unreliable patrons for a man with genuinely new ideas. A reputation at the Court of the Hapsburgs was, of course, much sought after, and occasionally the Court would live up to its reputation for discernment. But neither Gluck nor Mozart were destined to receive true understanding or full support in Vienna.

In Prussia, the Hohenzollerns were ceaselessly concerned with the military virtues. Frederick the Great wrote of his father: 'The capital became the stronghold of Mars. All the industries which serve the needs of armies prospered . . . Society took a military turn. . . . The age of gallantry passed away. . . . Ladies fled the society of men and the latter compensated themselves with carousals, tobacco, and buffoonery.' We have seen that Frederick himself attempted to restore a measure of culture at his Court and that he invited Bach to play to him. Nevertheless, Berlin and Potsdam, for all their veneer of art and philosophy, were even less satisfactory as musical centres than Vienna, for Vienna, even if it were reactionary, sustained a great musical activity. A success in Vienna was an important event in a man's career. And, as for despotism, music without a text cannot, after all, be censored by the police. In the German-speaking countries, a composer was most lucky if (a) he were uninterested in social relationships and (b) he could find a generous and enlightened patron. Haydn was lucky in this fashion.

England, one feels, ought to have been a great centre of musical development, for it was the richest and most progressive country in Europe. (Handel was not the only foreign musician to be attracted by London's opportunities.) But two circumstances forbade a great development of composition in England. One was the capriciousness of Nature, which is apt to produce musical geniuses in countries that are hardly able to nourish them while withholding them from countries where every resource is available. (Compare rich America at the beginning of this century with any poverty-stricken Slavonic country.) The other was England's concentration on commerce and industry.

During the lifetimes of Gluck, Haydn, and Mozart, industry in England was revolutionized by the inventions of spinning machines—the devices of Hargreaves and Arkwright—and the improvement of Newcomen's crude stream-engine by James Watt. Roads were so much improved by Telford and Macadam that the stage-coach brought hitherto unimagined swiftness, before it was swept away by the railway. (The London-Manchester journey seemed very swift when it took no longer than modern steamer crossings between Southampton and New York.)

Foreign musicians came to England to make money. Gluck did as a young man. Haydn did as an old man. Mozart intended to renew acquaintanceships he had made as a child prodigy, but died too soon. London to the eighteenth-century musician was as New York to the early twentieth. It was the place for box-office successes rather than experiments.

Paradoxically, it was in reactionary France that a man might most certainly find an audience for new ideas—an audience, too, that was likely to include a sprinkling of nobilities and royalties. And in understanding how this came to be, we understand in part how the music of Gluck, Haydn, and Mozart prepared for that of Beethoven.

The condition of France at the death of Louis XIV made many people doubt whether *Le Roi Soleil* was as great a monarch as his flatterers had declared. And the condition of France continued to decline. The artists of Paris were no longer under the patronage of a man who, to do him justice, would have attained eminence even if he had been born in a slum. They were ruled over by a man who would probably have sunk into squalor had he not been born in a Royal palace. It was not enough to flatter Louis XV; one had to pay court to Madame de Pompadour and Madame du Barry. And when the Dauphin grew up and got married, there was his Austrian wife, Marie Antoinette, to bring further irrelevant influence to bear on state affairs.

The writers and artists of Paris were perturbed. They saw their country first an enemy of Austria and then her ally. They saw Frederick of Prussia, however he might be hammered, fight on to eventual victory. They saw England, subsidizing Frederick, take advantage of the continental wars to make herself mistress of India and Canada, driving out the Frenchmen who were left almost unsupported by their own government, and acquiring territories that inspired the machine inventors to provide an ever-increasing stream of trading goods.

The writers and artists of Paris began to consider social conditions. Voltaire attacked the evils around him with brilliant satire. Montesquieu investigated the nature of law and government, and propounded a system based on liberty and equality. Rousseau proclaimed the importance of virtue and the right of anybody, however humble, to a measure of happiness. And the Encyclopædists, directed by Diderot, undertook to assemble the scientific information that should allow their country to reorganize itself on a basis of prosperity and justice.

The writers and artists found the Court almost solidly against them. Yet it was true that at one of the most reactionary Courts in Europe there assembled an audience for the most reformist operatic music. If to Mozart as a child prodigy Paris was a city where one sat on the

Queen's lap or evoked sighs of admiration in Madame de Pompadour's *salon*, to Gluck as a grown man it was a favourable strategic point for a campaign for operatic reform. Not because the Court liked his music. Not because his patroness, Marie Antoinette, understood it. Only that Marie Antoinette enjoyed pitting her power against those who hated the 'barbarian invasion' from her country. What was good enough for Vienna, she felt, should be good enough for Paris. Gluck profited by her wilfulness, produced the newest ideas to die-hard reactionaries . . . and was accordingly attacked by progressives. In such ironical circumstances his battle for a more free style of opera prospered.

Gluck's ideas on this subject are more important than the details of his life. He had great influence on later composers. A performance of one of his operas is now relatively rare, but it always somehow ranks as an important occasion.

As a young man he had known the empty satisfaction of writing fashionable pieces in Vienna, Venice, and Milan, and he had learned how much more there was to achieve by measuring these things against such works of Handel's as he heard on a visit to London. He had gained successes in all the principal capitals of musical Europe and, by the time he was forty (1754), had become *Kapellmeister* to the Court Opera of Empress Maria Theresa in Vienna. He had taken the trouble to add to his scanty education until he had become an accomplished, well-informed man of culture, acquainted with the world around him and well instructed in ancient history and classic mythology. But fashionable success was not enough.

In 1761, when he was forty-seven years of age, Gluck produced his 'Orfeo' in Vienna. It introduced new practices into the composition of operas. The recitatives were now accompanied by the orchestra instead of by a harpsichord and, instead of being sharply contrasted with the set arias, were made to be part of a work that could claim a certain dramatic continuity. The chorus assumed greater importance. Opera, which originally had begun with free declamation and then become excessively formal, threw off some of its chains. Gluck was paving the way for Weber and Wagner.

Vienna was not sure at first whether it liked 'Orfeo.' The work did indeed become a success, but Gluck refrained from embarking on another reformist work until he was fifty-three. Then, in the preface to 'Alceste,' he declared that he sought for beauty in simplicity and sacrificed academic rule for the sake of dramatic effect. He deplored that nobody seemed ready to follow him in destroying the abuses from which Italian art suffered.

D

It was at this moment that a Frenchman in Vienna, an attaché at the Embassy, urged Gluck to write a work for Paris. This Monsieur Bailly du Roullet gave practical effect to his advice by arranging a libretto drawn from Racine's 'Iphigénie en Aulide'; and Gluck obtained an invitation to Paris from Marie Antoinette, to whom he had given music lessons in Vienna before she became the wife of that French Dauphin who was soon to be Louis XVI.

Gluck in Paris, in the city of advanced thinkers, found a Court antagonistic to him—merely obedient to the princess's commands. This probably surprised him. In the age of such great despots as Catherine the Great, Frederick the Great, Maria Theresa (and her son who was to become Joseph II of Austria), there was at least a measure of polite welcome for new ideas at the Courts of St. Petersburg, Potsdam, and Schönbrunn, since the despots considered themselves enlightened. In the city of Voltaire and Rousseau, Gluck might well have expected to find immediate understanding. In actual fact he found both greater enthusiasm and greater opposition than in Vienna, and found both in unexpected quarters.

Perhaps this was because Gluck was practising an art that does not explicitly state the opinions of its creator. People cannot easily tell by listening to a melody whether its composer is pietist or atheist, republican or monarchist. It is only by considering the whole body of a man's work, after a new kind of music has associated itself with certain happenings, that we can discern a man's opinions in his music just as we can in his conversation. Music lends itself to many interpretations—as we can see whenever a visiting royalty is received in Paris by the strains of the 'Marseillaise,' a song that seems to sound the death-knell of royalism.[1] On such occasions as these, and recalling how medieval musicians had incorporated tavern songs in sacred motets, we can well understand why musical historians in the past have concentrated most of their attention on the private lives of composers and only perfunctorily referred to the course of external affairs. The meaning of music has seemed too elusive and changeable to be related to world events.

Some people, indeed, have persuaded themselves that music must have no meaning at all—that it is an exercise in 'pure' beauty. But if we go further than merely listening to individual melodies, and try to observe a man's music as a whole, observing his favourite texts, observing his bad works as well as his good, and observing the faults that sometimes help to explain the virtues, we experience a growing

[1] Its composer, Rouget de Lisle, was not a revolutionary, but the course of events and the temper of the Men of Marseilles changed a patriotic song (originally for the French Army of the Rhine) into a hymn of defiance.

conviction that, to mention only a few examples, Bach's fugues and Bach's Lutheranism, Schubert's songs and Schubert's Vienna, Wagner's epics and Wagner's social philosophy . . . hang together.

Gluck's operatic reforms belong to a time of reformist and revolutionary discussion. But because Gluck spoke in the language of music, the pamphleteers did not immediately realize that he was trying to agree with them. We have the peculiar spectacle of Rousseau championing Italian Opera against Gluck's, and being persuaded to be a supporter only after a while. We observe Marie Antoinette, doomed as an anti-progressive to die on the guillotine, granting her *cher* Gluck 6000 francs (from France's empty treasury) for every fresh work he should produce for the French stage.

'Iphigénie' provoked much debate in Paris. So did the revised 'Orfeo.' Only a few years earlier, Paris had witnessed a 'war of the Buffons' waged over Pergolesi's pioneer comic opera, 'La Serva Padrona.' Now the kind of warfare that had blazed then (remember Handel and Bononcini) was to be staged between Gluck and a certain Piccinni. There were many political intrigues behind this conflict; also personal dislike between the dowager royal mistress, Madame du Barry, and France's Austrian queen.

Gluck, however, gained successes with 'Alceste' and 'Armide' and 'Iphigénie en Tauride,' and finally returned to Vienna to enjoy a certain ease and considerable prosperity during his last years. (He died in 1787.) He had had his cake *and* eaten it. He had placed himself among the forerunners of the French Revolution and had made a fortune.

Hadyn, fourteen years younger than Gluck, never seems to have taken notice of the new ideas that were transforming life in his day.

His parents, a wheelwright and a cook in an Austrian village near the Hungarian frontier, seem to have encouraged his musical gifts; and by good fortune young Joseph was carried off to sing in the choir of St. Stephen's Cathedral in Vienna. The organist-choirmaster of the Cathedral had been travelling through the village scouting for fresh talent.

At the age of seventeen, his voice broken, Haydn was unemployed; but a little help from a fellow-choirboy, a few pupils, an attic furnished with an old clavier, and a little music soon put him on his feet. Before long he was acting as valet-accompanist to Porpora, one of the greatest singing teachers ever known. And this engagement led to his becoming violinist in the household of Karl von Fürnberg. One more step—a post with the Emperor's Chamberlain and Privy Councillor—and Haydn found himself under the wing of Prince Anton

Esterhazy. And with the Esterhazy family he remained connected for the rest of his long life.

The discerning, generous patronage of the Esterhazy family is so well known as to cast a glamour over the whole system of patronage. People remember Haydn and his prince, they remember his position of security and the recognition of his talent, they remember the happy anecdote associated with the Farewell Symphony, and they sigh for the 'great days' . . . in which Handel and Gluck had constantly to scheme and intrigue against nobleman-enemies and Mozart was allowed to die in poverty.

Prince Anton was succeeded by Prince Nicholas; and, in 1766, Prince Nicholas finished building himself a palace. The Esterhazys always lived in the grand manner. The first prince had helped deliver Vienna from the Turks, and then had devoted himself to curtailing the freedom of the Magyars. Nicholas's grandson appears in later history as founder of an art collection and provider of a regiment of a thousand men against Napoleon—enterprises that involved the family in debt for two generations. Nicholas himself established his estate to the tune of eleven million gulden. Sums of money expressed in foreign and now-abandoned currencies do not perhaps convey much meaning. But Schloss Esterház included, besides the palace (126 rooms), the park, and the gardens (not to mention temples and grottoes and summer-houses), a theatre for living actors and another for marionettes. There was a standing orchestra and a company of singers. Visiting actors and virtuosi swelled the artistic establishment.

A cavalcade of noble visitors carried away memories of splendid entertainment, of art collections, of the diamond-covered uniform of a charming and cultured host. And of Haydn's music.

Schloss Esterház was thirty miles from Vienna, remote from the distractions of the city, yet in touch with its artistic life. The estate was self-contained. Haydn was not just a magnificent possession— a 'lion' well spoken of in Leipzig, Paris, Amsterdam, and London— he was an artist, treated as such by his patron. Haydn himself said: 'My prince was always satisfied with my works; I not only had the encouragement of constant approval, but as conductor of an orchestra I could make experiments, observe what produced an effect and what weakened it, and was thus in a position to improve, alter, make additions or omissions, and be as bold as I pleased; I was cut off from the world, there was no one to confuse or torment me, and I was forced to become original.' (The only person who confused and tormented Haydn was his wife.)

What form did his originality assume? As far as the *craft* of music is concerned, his chief contribution consists of establishing sonata-form in its classic perfection. (This structure will appear in the chapter on Form.) The reason for Haydn's interest in it lies largely in the conditions under which he worked. The whole system of patronage tended to lay emphasis on style, symmetry, elegance, and proportion, and the existence of established orchestras at the various Courts persuaded composers to write instrumental movements on a large scale. Several distinguished composers had already worked out some of the principles of lay-out and arrangement. Corelli and Tartini for the violin, and Bach's sons (Carl Philip Emmanuel and John Christian) for the clavier, had set out something like the sequences of themes and devices of development that were to serve Haydn. They learned to contrast a severe theme, devised for discussion, with a more tuneful melody, devised for contrast. They planned their phrase-lengths and introduced their modulations as cunningly as a landscape gardener plans his vistas and designs his pathways. The comparison is permissible, for these were the first signs of that feeling for nature which would arrive at full musical expression in the next generation. Much of the music that now seems formal was then held to be natural. Technical development was in accordance with the improvement in instrument-making, the increasing complexity of the orchestra, and the demand for music of a non-dramatic kind to interest a small, 'hand-picked' audience; and it was animated by the aristocratic spirit.

The details of Haydn's earlier life need not long detain us, for they tell us little about his times or his music. The histories tell how much he admired and loved his young rival Mozart, though he rarely met him; how various Royalties commissioned this symphony or that quartet and sent presents of diamond-studded snuff boxes as marks of their pleasure; how Haydn obtained a holiday for his musicians by composing a Farewell Symphony, in the last movement of which each player in turn blows out his candle and steals away from his desk until nobody is left playing—an amusing and charming method of voicing the request.

The details of Haydn's later life are perhaps more significant. But throughout a long career (he died at the age of seventy-seven) Haydn remained a composer of the old school. The French Revolution and the Napoleonic Wars, it is true, evoked one patriotic melody for Austria. But neither they, nor the west wind of democracy that came blowing from America, affected his music as they were destined to affect Beethoven's. We shall see how Haydn's fame and fortune held out in the days when younger artists were in rebellion against the kind of music favoured by the aristocrats. Perhaps this was because Haydn's works, though they move with perfect deportment and a good deal of formality, were neither cold nor pernickety. They were not over-bred: they retained a peasant's vitality; and their genial good nature earned the affection that has caused generations of musicians to speak of 'Papa' Haydn. They remained vitally alive when the next generation of composers were busy in a campaign for artistic freedom.

America was the refuge of people seeking freedom from various kinds of European tyranny. The colonists, it is true, ignored Red Indian rights and imported African slaves, but for white men they cherished ideals of freedom and independence that made them unruly children of their mother countries, and endeared them to the younger artists. If the Americans were independent in spirit it was perhaps because they had opportunities to be independent in fact, for where there is virgin country to be seized by resolute people, anyone who is unwilling to be a servant may set up on his own. But to European idealists, particularly to the 'advanced' artists and philosophers in Paris, they seemed to be people pointing the way to a new kind of society. And indeed it was true that although in the bigger American towns there were something like European gradations of status, many a colonist felt himself anybody's match and beholden to none.

As in the days of the Tudor composers, so now in the lifetimes of Gluck, Haydn, and Mozart, America exerts a roundabout influence by imposing a strain on existing European institutions. In both eras, the effect is to make artists break away from old traditions. In both eras there is a 'romantic' movement.

The artists of Europe saw that even England—England who seemed to build up an empire in a few years while other people's backs were turned, and was always on the winning side—even England could be compelled to give up her American colonies when these colonies fought for their independence. The rights and wrongs of the struggle were of less importance from the writers' point of view than the fact that the free pioneers could win.

Revolutionary ideas in France received fresh impetus. By a strange irony, Louis XVI and Marie Antoinette, actuated by jealousy of England, helped the American republicans. They did not stay to realize that they were encouraging French republicanism and further undermining their own finances.

The romantic literary movement was beginning in England and Germany. In the latter country we have particularly to observe the works of Goethe, Lessing, Klopstock, Wieland, and Herder, because their poetry paved the way for Weber's operas and Schubert's *Lieder*, and Mendelssohn's Songs without Words. . . .

They paved the way. But music, as always, was the last art to express the new ideas. Not until Beethoven's day did it learn to address its audiences in the new romantic spirit of Liberty, Equality, and Fraternity.

But in Mozart's music the current is perhaps setting in. Still waters run deep; and beneath the unruffled, polished surface of Mozart's music many critics claim to have plumbed down to where the European maelstrom was assembling its forces.

The idea that Mozart was merely an inspired child is fading. He has been compared with Shelley, who to some people is only a lovable, wayward adolescent, and to others is a hard-thinking critic of social institutions. On the surface, Mozart's music seems happy, childlike, serene, elegant—never violent or miserable or startling. On the surface his life seems unaffected by wars and empire-building and mechanical inventions. Yet music lovers, once they have discerned the something in Mozart's music which is quite fully adult, when they observe the unerring dramatic gift in his operas, ask themselves what might have happened had one of the greatest geniuses in music not died at the age of thirty-five. Though Haydn outlived Mozart and the two are often bracketed together as musical twins, Haydn was in fact old enough to have been Mozart's father. It is, of course, quite true that a page of Mozart's music is often so much like Haydn's that a radio listener, switching on in the middle of a performance, cannot decide whose music he is listening to. Yet there are deep differences too in the greater works, where each man gets away from eighteenth-century conventionalities. And we find ourselves wondering whether we ought not to bracket Mozart with Beethoven, rather than with Haydn. Mozart was nearer Beethoven's generation. There was little more discrepancy in age between them than between an average husband and wife. The question arises in our minds: If Mozart could influence, as he undoubtedly did, a composer much older than himself, might he not in turn have been influenced by the young Beethoven and by all the storms that swept across artistic Europe? Was he, in fact, already being influenced by the new ideas when an early death carried him away?

The gifts appeared at the age of three. Mozart was composing at the age of five, to the delight of his father, Leopold Mozart, a violinist in the Archbishop of Salzburg's band. Leopold, a man of character and ability, if a little narrowminded, guided young Wolfgang with loving care and attention until the great musical spirit freed itself from leading strings.

Wolfgang's elder sister was an accomplished musician, and the two children were taken on a tour to visit the musical Courts of Vienna, Munich, Paris, and London. Everywhere the gay, high-spirited boy particularly excited incredulous astonishment by his playing at sight and his improvisations—feats much more convincing in a child than the brilliant execution of pieces already learned. And when after four years of travel (financially unsatisfactory) the family returned to Salzburg, the Archbishop was ready with commissions for compositions.

In 1768, when Mozart was only twelve, he was asked to write a work for the Vienna Opera. Gluck approved, but the manager of the Opera was doubtful. Leopold Mozart wrote: '. . . the theatre is leased . . . to Affligio who must pay annually 1000 gulden. . . . The Emperor and his whole family have the right of free entry. Consequently the Court cannot say a word to this Affligio as he takes all the risks.' This then was the glamorous Vienna Opera, where many of the singers were such poor musicians as to have to learn their parts by ear. Emperor Joseph paid Mozart a hundred ducats consolation money . . . 'for the Court cannot say a word to Affligio.'

Leopold, as soon as the Archbishop would grant further leave, took Wolfgang to Italy, still the centre of Opera. And there young Mozart wrote out from memory a 'Miserere' that he heard only once, since no copies were available. (The Papal Choir forbade copies under pain of excommunication.) The Pope decorated the boy with the Order of the Golden Spur. The Philharmonic Society of Bologna, after a severe examination, admitted the thirteen-year-old composer to membership. The Philharmonic Society of Verona followed suit after the production of an opera on the subject of Mithridates, King of Pontus.

Now, with approaching manhood, Mozart found the dull town of Salzburg unattractive. Its people were provincial after London and Paris: its music incompetent after that of Mannheim, where the Elector Karl Theodor was spending a million gulden on an Academy of Science, a National Theatre, the best orchestra in Europe, and a German Society to foster the self-respect of German-speaking people overawed by the arts of France and Italy.

A new Archbishop in Salzburg favoured Italian music and would not promote the Mozarts. Wolfgang, returning from successful visits to Munich and Vienna, found it intolerable to keep menial company at the Archbishop's table and to have a request for leave to go on tour refused. He applied for his discharge . . . and thus the composer who had been a king's favourite as a child became an unemployed musician as a man. Mozart the child had been almost persuaded that he was the equal of princes. He was now reminded that he was not the superior of servants.

It was decided that he should go on tour again, this time with his mother, and that Paris, the centre of modernism, should be his ultimate goal. But on the way, at Munich, Mozart interviewed the Elector of Bavaria.

'I have been in Italy three times, have written three operas, am a member of the Academy of Bologna after a trial accomplished in one hour which has taken many *maestri* four or five hours of hard labour: this may serve as a witness that I am qualified to serve any Court. My only wish is to serve Your Highness, who himself is a great——'

'Yes, my dear young fellow, but there is no vacancy! I am sorry, if only there were a vacancy——'

'I assure Your Highness I should be an honour to Munich.'

'No doubt, no doubt, but there is no vacancy. . . .'

On the way to Paris, Wolfgang lingered in Mannheim because he was in love with a girl . . . whose younger sister he ultimately married and whose eldest sister was the first Queen of the Night in 'The Magic Flute.'

The Paris visit was a failure. Nothing better was offered than an organist's post at Versailles; and, in any case, the Gluck-Piccinni rivalry was making Paris deaf to Mozart's music. Mozart's mother fell ill and died.

Humbly he had to return to Salzburg to the second-rate position of organist. The *Kapellmeistership* went to an Italian.

Once again Mozart found himself too near the cooks at table, too meanly paid, too frequently abused by the Archbishop. Once again he applied for discharge. This time—so it is said—he was kicked out of the Archbishop's house by the high steward. ('No more Salzburg for me! I hate the Archbishop almost to fury.')

And now, at the age of twenty-six he settled down in marriage with Constanze Weber who annually presented him with a new off-spring (only two of whom survived).

An opera 'Entführung aus dem Serail' was seen by the Emperor in Vienna. Still no Court appointment. Six quartets dedicated to Haydn did not stave off the necessity to give uncongenial lessons. The birth of a child did not melt the heart of Leopold, who had disapproved of Constanze. Concerts in Vienna were notable for Gluck's praise and the Emperor's staying to hear the encores. But the Haffner symphony and several concertos still led to no appointment though nine princes and five ambassadors were among the subscribers to the concerts.

And now there appear two circumstances that dispel the innocent child myth. One is Mozart's waning interest in conventional religion and growing attachment to Freemasonry—then a quasi-political move-ment with liberal ideas frowned upon by Church and State. (It still is in many countries.) In Vienna, it is true, the State, in the person of the Emperor, adhered to the Craft; and Frederick the Great was a Mason. But Mozart was not seeking the company of the 'enlightened despots.' Rather we have to think of him as belonging to a fraternity that included Goethe, Herder, and Gluck.

The other circumstance was a meeting with Lorenzo da Ponte, 'an Italian Jew by birth, a priest by profession, and a poet by inclination' as Dyneley Hussey describes him. Da Ponte made a libretto from Beaumarchais' 'The Marriage of Figaro,' a play that appealed to Mozart perhaps because he had good reason to enjoy its anti-aristocratic flavour, perhaps because as a Freemason he liked its political implications, perhaps only because his dramatic instinct was responsive to the story and the characters. The play, *as* a play, had been banned in Vienna; but, modified into a libretto and then illuminated by Mozart's music, it was allowed to achieve performance in a form that softened the satire. (Beaumarchais' Figaro had said of the aristocrats: 'You made the effort to be born, and that is all you have ever done.' Beaumarchais knew his aristocracy for, cynically manipulating the abuses he satirized, he had become what he called a 'self-made aristocrat.' When the Revolution occurred he remarked that though he had always fought for liberty and equality he was not sure that he cared for fraternity.)

'Figaro' was a success. The Emperor had to forbid encores. Still no appointment. 'Don Giovanni' was also a success—in Prague— and did at last bring a post in Vienna—Emperor's Chamber Composer at about eighty pounds per annum, little even in those days when money bought more than it does now. (These successes reconciled old Leopold shortly before he died.)

'Cosi fan tutte' was hindered by the Emperor's death; and to attend the new Emperor's Coronation at Frankfurt, Mozart had to pawn his valuables. Operatic success under eighteenth-century conditions did not mean the financial rewards that are obtainable in these days of commercial publishing, copyright, royalties, etc. At the end of 1790 Mozart's position was desperate, and ill health (his own and Constanze's) caused him to refuse a good offer to visit London. Ill health or no, during his last year of life, he produced two quartets, a pianoforte concerto, and the opera on the subject of Freemasonry— 'The Magic Flute.' The libretto of this, by Schickaneder, is obscure to most audiences, but it purports to be an allegory of man's eternal quest for something beyond and above himself.

The new work was a great success. It established the equality of German Opera with Italian Opera (Mozart had composed to librettos in both languages). There were schemes on foot to provide Mozart with an income, schemes in Holland and in Hungary. But Mozart, busy with his Requiem Mass, was now despondently convinced that the mysterious stranger who had commissioned the work was an ambassador of Death. He was failing and weakening.

When he died, Baron van Swieten made funeral arrangements—on the cheap. On a day of vile weather, Mozart's corpse was committed to a pauper's grave containing nearly a score of coffins. And when Constanze was well enough to visit the cemetery, a new gravedigger could not tell her where her husband was buried. She inherited hardly any money and little furniture. The world inherited an incredibly copious output of operas, symphonies, concertos, overtures, sonatas, chamber works . . . that includes some of the greatest masterpieces ever devised by a human being: works in which a deceptive simplicity conceals an enormous skill, where imagination and technique are perfectly mated, where, even in the lesser pieces that reproduce only the current eighteenth-century formulæ, there is always ease and style.

Mozart had lived, despite his many troubles, with a sense of style. He had worked as a past master works, thinking out his compositions in his head and then writing them down as decisively as though copying them from someone else's score. He maintained a sense of fun and pleasure, not disdaining a little vulgarity, and mated these qualities with a fundamental seriousness. 'I never lie down in bed,' he wrote, 'without considering that, young as I am, perhaps on the morrow I may be no more. Yet not one of those who know me could say that I am morose or melancholy. . . .'

His career seemed to run the wrong way round. It began with success and ended in poverty and early death. The easy, elegant style that seemed to come unbidden to the precocious boy was already habitual when adult problems called for profounder expression. There have been other great composers whose music wins through to ease after years of struggle with the problems of life. Mozart's seems to arrive at the problems of life after years of ease, and to deal with them without doing the least violence to the original qualities of his music.

CHAPTER XVII

Form

FORM grows out of rhythm. In a simple song the arrangement of strong and weak beats into bars leads to the arrangement of strong and weak bars into phrases. Form in song evolved side by side with form in poetry, and we sense a phrase-ending in a song where we sense a line-ending in a stanza of poetry. (See Fig. 43).

On the words 'snow' and 'go' the music, in each case, reaches a 'cadence.' A cadence occurs at the end of a number of notes which,

though they may not be a complete tune, hang together and make
sense. We can make a close comparison with speech. If one says:

> '. . . everything into . . .'

one has virtually said nothing. But if one says:

> 'taking everything into consideration . . .'

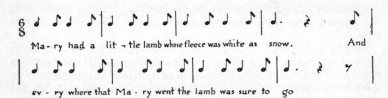

Ma - ry had a lit - tle lamb whose fleece was white as snow.   And

ev - ry where that Ma - ry went the lamb was sure to go

FIG. 43

one has completed a stage in saying something.

In music this sense of completion is partly a matter of rhythm (as
in the example of 'Mary had a little lamb') and partly of harmony,
even if only by implication.

Recall the fact that, in the Middle Ages, the modern scale triumphed
over the modes precisely because its tunes seemed to be attracted
finally towards the tonic. In harmonized music there is an attraction
towards a final tonic chord—an attraction which modern composers,
by the way, sometimes resist.

The art of composing an extended movement consists to some extent
of evading the final tonic chord, putting it off by three devices:

(*a*) by using cadences that do not end on the tonic;

(*b*) by using cadences that end on an inverted form of the tonic
chord;

(*c*) by modulating to fresh keys where a tonic chord, if it does occur,
will not suggest that the movement is at an end.

Is it really important to avoid the direct tonic at a middle cadence?
'God Save the King' provides an answer and a warning.

God save our gracious King, Long live our no - ble King, God save the King.

FIG. 44

At the end of this fragment the tonic chord is so emphatic that many an orchestra, winding up a concert or a meeting or a theatrical performance, does not bother to go any further. A stranger who had never heard the tune before might easily imagine that he had heard the whole of the National Anthem.

On those occasions when the orchestra does intend to go further, it is careful to proceed without stopping to a bridge-passage of four notes thus:

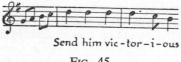

Send him vic - tor - i - ous

FIG. 45

Such a bridge-passage minimises the effect of stoppage; and here we have an elementary example of the extended bridge-passages that link up one subject with another in a big movement.

Cadences are catalogued in the form book under various names. We have already observed the final 'perfect' cadence (or 'full close') ending on the tonic. Here is one ending on the dominant, useful half-way through a simple tune.

This cadence is called the 'imperfect' cadence (or half-close). Then

FIG 46.   Dominant
of C - Key.

there is the 'interrupted' cadence in which the composer seems just about to land on a full close but substitutes an unexpected chord for the tonic. And finally there is the 'plagal' cadence—the two chords usually used in playing *amen* at the end of a hymn or prayer. (All cadences really consist of *two* chords—the chord on which the phrase ends, and the chord which leads up to it. In the 'Annie Laurie' example the dominant chord is preceded by a chromatic seventh-chord.)

The remainder of form consists of learning to manage these devices on a bigger and bigger scale, and also in learning some more or less standardized layouts which have become associated by tradition with such titles as 'symphony' or 'rondo' or 'overture.'

Many simple pieces show the first stage of expanding the scale of operations. Just as the first phrase of a simple tune may end on the dominant chord, so the first *page* of a simple piece may end in the dominant *key*. Although there may be, technically, a full close at this point, the fact that it occurs in a *new* key gives it much the same mental effect as a half-close in the *original* key. Then, balancing the first page (which has proceeded from tonic to dominant) is another, rather similar, proceeding from dominant to tonic. Many of Bach's dance pieces are constructed on this plan ('binary' form).

A more developed arrangement is to state an idea, diverge to a new one, and then restate the first one.

This 'ternary' form occurs on a small scale in tunes like the 'Blue Bells of Scotland.'

Cadences occur at ×——×

Fig. 47

Ternary form occurs in a larger scale in 'Minuet and Trio' form which may be planned thus:

Binary Minuet   Binary 'Trio'   Binary Minuet again

(The word 'trio' survives from the early days of minuets when the middle section of the dance was often accompanied by three instruments.)

Ternary form exists in a still larger scale in 'Sonata Movement,' which has a special prestige among the great accepted forms. At least one movement of a sonata or a symphony or a concerto or a work for a chamber combination is usually in this form (most often the first movement). Here it is in a diagrammatic arrangement:

Introduction is optional: occurs more frequently in symphonies than in sonatas.

EXPOSITION:

PRINCIPAL SUBJECT in tonic key, varies from a few notes—a mere 'motto'—to an extended melody. Usually contrived to be striking and memorable.

BRIDGE modulating to a new key, and ushering in a group of SECOND SUBJECTS. These are usually more melodious and flowing than the first subject. They form a group of secondary ideas with which the first may be contrasted. They conclude with a CODETTA, a little coda ('coda' means tail-piece) in the same key as the second subjects. At the end of the codetta, the movement usually pauses a little. The older composers often indicated a repeat here, but the repeat is frequently ignored nowadays in performance.

DEVELOPMENT:

The foregoing subjects now appear in various disguises. Conventionally, the Principal Subject is developed most, but even the bridge and the codetta may be developed. Beethoven capriciously developed *only* them in some movements. A certain amount of episode—not based on anything in the exposition and not intended to be repeated—is introduced. Beethoven filled some of his development sections almost entirely with episode. Subjects are disguised by reharmonization, alteration of rhythm, contrapuntal elaboration, modulation through fresh keys, fugato, fresh orchestration, extension of short melodies and contraction of long ones, etc. etc.

RECAPITULATION:

PRINCIPAL SUBJECT as before.

BRIDGE modified so as to remain in tonic key.

SECOND SUBJECTS as before except that they are now transposed to tonic key. All the recapitulation is in one key, so that the movement may end in the tonic.

CODA. This may be much the same as the codetta. Usually it is expanded by a few final flourishes, but occasionally it blossoms forth into a whole host of fresh ideas and after-thoughts.

Other standard forms are (1) rondo: Theme, 2nd subject; Theme, 3rd subject; Theme, 4th subject; Theme . . ., etc.; and (2) sonata rondo:

EXPOSITION:

Theme; bridge modulating into new key; 2nd subject in new key; theme again.

EPISODE:

A longish excursion into fresh territory. A few of the features of the exposition may be sighted *en route*.

RECAPITULATION:
Theme; bridge *not* modulating; 2nd subjects in *tonic* key. Coda.

This is a 'cross' between simple 'old' rondo and sonata form, and is often used for last movements.

A total sonata usually consists of three or four movements. The first is most often in sonata form: the last in sonata-rondo. If there is only one middle movement it is a slow one, perhaps on a rather disguised ternary plan. If there are two, the remaining movement is either a minuet-and-trio or a speeded-up, less dancelike, movement called a 'Scherzo.' (The presence of a minuet reminds us that sonatas evolved from dance-suites.)

The listener must be warned that he will encounter sonatas that do not agree with conventional descriptions. He must remember that Domenico Scarlatti and his contemporaries applied the name to simple little binary movements, that Beethoven occasionally wrote only two movements, and that the romantic composers tried various experiments in an attempt to avoid formalism. Two of these experiments are of note, both largely Liszt's work. One was to use one principal theme throughout the whole work, presenting it in a fresh, disguised form (Liszt called it a metamorphosis) in each movement, and linking the movements so that no pause occurred between one and another.

The other, for orchestral works, was to preserve only the roughest semblance of symphonic form and to make the music follow a story or 'programme.' This kind of piece, called 'symphonic poem,' formed a link between the true symphony (which began as 'abstract' music for a small audience) and opera (which contains dramatic music for a big one).

Besides dealing with elementary structure and the bigger standard forms, the textbook attempts to explain certain titles. They tell the student that a Gavotte must begin on the third beat of a quadruple bar, and a Bourrée on the fourth. They discuss the technical features of Courante cadences and Polonaise rhythms. They trace historical changes in the Overture. But the authors are again and again defeated by the caprices of composers who insist on writing rhapsodies that do not rhapsodize, overtures that do not open any specified proceedings, and scherzos that are not playful. The authors are also bothered by the fact that a mere definition of, say, a March conveys little to anyone who has never heard a military band. What is a Variation if you have never heard one? What is the repeated 'ground bass' of a Passacaglia if your ear is not trained to hear a bass line?

A final word must be said about the use of form by those who are intended by Nature to master it.

A given form is like one of Nature's patterns. For example, the year has four seasons; but within the framework of seasonal change there is endless variety. Some years are orderly. The weather is seasonal, the harvest plentiful, men's lives not unduly interfered with by their own folly, and the course of history not diverted by 'acts of God.' Other years are memorable for catastrophes and wars: yet others for advances in civilization. In some, the procession of seasons is hardly observed amidst the alarms of a great public cataclysm. And there are years in an individual life when private emotion turns the attention away from the world.

As one looks back on a year, observing the interplay between Nature's events and Man's actions, there is an appearance of inevitability. Looking back, one says 'it had to be.'

The events in a great symphony present this same appearance of *having* to be just so. They *occupy*, they fill up, the accepted pattern of time and season. Anything that may be unseasonable in a movement one accepts as one accepts a cold spell in June or a green Christmas. It just happened that way on that occasion. . . .

But sonata or symphony form in the hands of a pedant is like a small-town pageant. A series of 'striking' events are arranged in 'effective' order according to a consensus of 'authoritative' opinion, so that there shall be 'no jarring note.'

The result is not history: it is a churchwarden's charade.

CHAPTER XVIII

The Dynasts and the Peoples

Haydn, Beethoven, Weber, and Schubert

THE kings and statesmen of Europe observed England attentively, but few of them foresaw that in their countries, too, towns would assemble themselves around mines and factories, that some of the peasants would become proletarians, that populations would increase and people agitate for reforms, demanding education and votes. Europe did not anticipate these events. 'So far from attending to the faint signals of the coming industrial democracy which were already visible in the sky,' says H. A. L. Fisher, 'it plunged into the wars of the French Revolution and the Empire.'

Beethoven observed both England and France. He was a democrat, he was a parliamentarian, and he was a sympathiser with the French revolutionists and an admirer of Napoleon—until Napoleon sought to found a dynasty of emperors.

The Napoleonic empire, however, lay in the future. Meanwhile, in Vienna, where aristocratic patronage prevailed, Beethoven enjoyed great success. How was this?

The twenty-two-year-old young man—somewhat ill-educated and at times ill-mannered—who came to Vienna from Bonn in 1792, was obviously a musician of great gifts and powerful personality.

The musical aristocracy of Vienna, admirers of Haydn and Mozart, were fortunately as disinclined to rebuke Beethoven because he insisted on being regarded as an equal, as Queen Elizabeth was to discharge Byrd because he insisted on remaining a Catholic. Count Waldstein sponsored the young men, and the Viennese aristocracy forgave Beethoven's 'insolence' because somehow he was brilliant and gay and attractive, despite all his touchiness and clumsiness, because he played the piano like a virtuoso and could improvise astonishingly, and because, a little late as compared with Mozart, he showed signs of becoming a composer of note. (Theirs was the only available patronage, for Vienna had no such concert-going public as Haydn found in London.)

By descent Beethoven was the son of a singer in the choir at the Court of the Elector Archbishop of Cologne. His mother was a cook. His father, who was often drunk, had tried to make the boy into a second Mozartian prodigy and had failed. But young Beethoven had picked up some scraps of education (his arithmetic and his spelling, were always bad) and had learned a great deal of music from the Court organist. He had paid a visit to Vienna when he was sixteen, astonishing Mozart by his gift of extempore playing, he had acquired a little polish by association with understanding friends (particularly a family named Breuning), and he had gained the protection of Waldstein, a rich nobleman hardly older than himself.

Settled in Vienna, he took lessons from Haydn (whom he found too easy-going) and Albrechtsberger, the leading teacher of counterpoint.

The Count's protégé soon became a 'lion' in Vienna, the rival of the greatest pianists, and the teacher of that Czerny whose exercises were to lay the foundations of modern pianism. He toured Prague, Berlin, Dresden, and other cities. Perhaps the arrival of the French Republican army in Bonn, and the flight of the Elector (who was the Emperor's uncle), helped him to decide to stay in Vienna permanently.

The dedications of Beethoven's works read like a page from the Almanach de Gotha. These dedications were paid for by the various counts and dukes and princes in return for the right to possess a piece exclusively for so many months while it was still new. Prince Lichnowsky, when Beethoven was staying with him, instructed the servants to answer Beethoven's bell before they attended to his own summonses. The young man's success, and his air of success, caused Haydn to nickname him 'The Great Mogul.'

Beethoven had not yet left Bonn when he first met Haydn. Haydn was returning to Vienna from a triumphal visit to London. After long service with the Esterhazys, and following the death of Prince Nicholas, he had found himself bound only in name to the family (which continued to support him with a settled income of 1400 florins a year) and was free to accept an invitation from Saloman, the London impresario. Haydn was astonished by the wealth in England. £300 were offered for an opera, £500 for the copyright of half a dozen symphonies, £200 for twenty other pieces, £200 as guaranteed minimum for a benefit concert. 'It is only in England one can make such sums,' said Haydn. It was true. England could quote the words of James Watt's business partner, Matthew Boulton, who, when Boswell visited his steam-engine factory, said 'I sell here, sir, what all the world desires to have—Power!' The profits from the sale of power enabled England to send Haydn back to Vienna with twelve hundred pounds in his pocket, not to mention a pair of socks, embroidered with *motifs* from his symphonies to remind him of a nation of shopkeepers. There were visits to Royalty, Guildhall banquets, the conferring of degrees at Oxford, excursions to the races and the theatres, sittings for portraits.

England was at peace. Austria was preparing for war in defence of Marie Antoinette, whose life was in danger. By the time Haydn, after a brief sojourn in Vienna, had returned to London for a second visit, Louis XVI and Marie Antoinette were dead; and the Republican armies of France were fighting Austria and Prussia and over-running the Netherlands.

Unlike Beethoven, Haydn took little notice of politics, though he was destined to hear Napoleon bombarding Vienna. Under the inspiration of Handel's music, which he heard in London, and adapting texts from Milton and Thomson, he occupied his last years of creative energy in composing 'The Creation' and 'The Seasons'—oratorios which for many years vied in popularity with 'The Messiah' in England.

Beethoven's enthusiasms were unsettled. We do not know what he thought of the Reign of Terror in Paris or of the Austrian decision to war against the Revolution. He composed a farewell song for the Austrian Volunteers in their campaign against Napoleon, who was winning his earliest success in Italy. He wrote a second military song soon after Haydn's patriotic Emperor's Hymn was first performed, (Haydn's one display of interest in public affairs is a fine melody, but a curious counterblast to the 'Marseillaise.')

Beethoven, despite his two songs, seems to have shared the opinion of Goethe, who, witnessing how the ill-equipped French compelled a Prussian army to submit at Valmy, declared that a new era was opening in history. Whatever the brutal excesses of the Paris mob, the French were showing how men will fight for a country that they feel is truly theirs, for an inspiring doctrine, for foreign conquests that take the shape of liberating oppressed peoples. ('We have no quarrel save with the tyrants who enslave you.') The artists of Europe were almost all stirred by the Revolution. Some forgave all its excesses because it seemed to promise an era of brotherhood. Some recoiled violently, feeling themselves bitterly deceived. Some were attracted by Napoleon's decree that careers should be open to talent—that every soldier carries a field-marshal's baton in his knapsack. Napoleon had abandoned the expensive superstition that gentility and ability are one. Among other gestures he opened the gates of the ghettoes—the musical results we shall see later—and earned the gratitude of the Jews. He bestowed ministerial portfolios on scientists, though the Revolution had executed Lavoisier.

Napoleon in this guise appeared to Beethoven as a hero. He appeared as a leader who, saving the revolution from terror and anarchy, had turned it into a crusade for freedom, opportunity, justice, and scientific government. Perhaps, too, Beethoven was uneasy about Austria's conduct, for Austria had dishonourably helped Russia and Prussia to dismember Poland. Busy in Poland, Austria had allowed the French Republic to establish itself. The Austrian Netherlands were now France's; most of the Hapsburg dominions in Italy had fallen; and Napoleon, inviting Austria to accept part of the republic of Venice, offered to make peace.

Certainly Beethoven was not a conventional loyalist. In 1798 he was friendly with the French Ambassador, Bernadotte, and from him is said to have got the idea of writing an heroic symphony in honour of Napoleon.

This was the year when Beethoven first observed that he was getting rather deaf. For the time being he was secretive about it, perhaps because he was sensitively unwilling to confess a weakness, perhaps, as some biographers suggest, because the malady may have had its origin in some disreputable amorous adventure.[1] (That Beethoven was

[1] Romain Rolland argues that the symptoms do not point to such an origin, and suggests that Beethoven's intense concentration damaged his hearing.

something of a Puritan by conviction does not rule out the possi-
bility of a lapse in his moral conduct, especially as he showed a
similar capacity for odd occasional misdemeanours in his financial
transactions.)

Gradually he withdrew from brilliant society. More and more he
devoted himself to composition. For a short while he was in love
with Countess Giulietta Guicciardi. To her he dedicated the Rondo
in G, and then, changing his mind, withdrew it and gave her that
'Sonata quasi una Fantasia' which the public calls 'The Moonlight
Sonata' (Op. 27, No. 2). But his love-affairs always petered out quickly,
and nobody now knows whether the Countess was the 'Immortal
Beloved' to whom was written a passionate love-letter found in Beethoven's desk after his death. Perhaps. There was a medallion portrait
of her among his other effects. But Thayer, Beethoven's most pains-
taking biographer, thought not.

Gradually Beethoven abandoned hope of cure for his deafness.
But he fought the mood of despair. He who would not raise his hat
to a prince unless he knew him personally, would not bow to the
malign fate that was now his too familiar companion. In 1803 he
embarked on Bernadotte's project, the 'Napoleon' symphony.

Napoleon still appeared in a favourable light. In France he defended
his countrymen against further revolution. He defended them against
counter revolution. He brought trophy home and the people enjoyed
unaccustomed prosperity. In a series of codes of legislation he con-
solidated as many of the new schemes for justice, education, and
administration as would not conflict with his ambitions. Much of the
essence of revolutionary philosophy lay preserved in these practical
measures, which promised liberty without endangering order. Even
in England, the most implacable enemy of Napoleon's ambitions, not
everybody shared Burke's horror of the Revolution. Indeed Pitt
thought it best to institute a barrack system in the industrial districts
lest, under the old system of billeting, soldiers should become dis-
affected. But whereas sympathy for Napoleon in England was intermittent, it continued unabated in many countries that had reason to
regard French institutions as infinitely more promising than their
own. And, at the time when Beethoven was at work on his third
symphony, even England had agreed to an uneasy peace (Peace of
Amiens 1802).

But when the symphony was finished, Napoleon, who had already
become First Consul, and then Consul for life, organized a plebiscite
that proclaimed him Emperor. The Pope was compelled to crown him.

Then it was that Beethoven found himself in the company of the
disillusioned. Angrily he tore up the original title-page of his Bonaparte

symphony. To Prince Lobkowitz there went the right to possess the score of the 'Eroica.'

By now Beethoven had published nearly half of the thirty-two sonatas he was destined to write, three of the nine symphonies, some chamber music, three pianoforte concertos. He felt he must write an opera. He was not truly an operatic composer by temperament, and his one essay, 'Fidelio,' has been eclipsed by many works that contain fewer fine passages. It is significant to notice, however, that it is a drama in praise of liberty, an attack on tyranny.

From then until the year when Napoleon embarked on his fatal Russian adventure, Beethoven, withdrawing into the fastnesses of his own mind, produced another five symphonies, the Mass in C, two more concertos for piano and one for violin, the 'Coriolan' and 'Egmont' overtures, the Rasoumovsky quartets (written for the Russian Ambassador), and some of his most famous sonatas. Yet even his deafness and his absorption in work could not decrease his awareness of world events.

His variations on 'Rule Britannia' and 'God save the King' are unimportant as music. But they show (what later evidence confirms) that he looked to London as he had once looked to Paris for leadership and—let it be admitted—for patronage. He saw his own country involved in new warfare and beaten at Ulm and Austerlitz. Austria was humiliated. 'Fidelio' received its first performance while Napoleon was quartered at Schönbrunn. On a visit to Prince Lichnowsky in Silesia, Beethoven found French officers quartered on his host— and he refused to play the piano for them.

The 1809 bombardment of Vienna which drove Beethoven into a cellar in an effort to preserve the remnants of his hearing, found Haydn on his deathbed. He called to his servants: 'Children have no fear; no harm can come to you while Haydn is by.' The last time he touched the piano he played his Emperor's Hymn. Five days later he was dead. The kind, industrious, happy-natured composer, religious, respectful, and affectionate, had outlived his era. The French sent a guard of honour to his funeral.

Beethoven's music, by contrast to Haydn's, is for a great part the music of struggle. He accepted sonata form as he accepted willy-nilly the conditions of the profession of music in Austria, and it is extraordinary that he made few radical experiments in form. He preferred to adapt and patch and mend a structure strained by his romantic, narrative, autobiographical music. No composer before had expressed such romantic emotion, such boisterous humour, such naïve earnestness. No composer, before or since, provides us with so many enigmas as are to be found in the late works of Beethoven's 'third period.'

In the musical world the economic background of the profession was changing. Aristocratic patronage in the future would be only one source of income among many. Publishing was increasing in importance. Härtel, the Leipzig publisher, with Mozart, Haydn, Clementi, and Dussek in his catalogue, was publishing a musical magazine. He introduced the engraving of music on pewter plates. He began to manufacture pianos.

Pianos were now no longer in an experimental stage. The loud-soft 'Fortepiano,' the 'hammer clavier,' which evolved into our modern pianoforte, was ousting the harpsichord. It opened up prospects of new technical feats. It allowed keyboard pieces to make their effects as concert-works, not merely as chamber-works. It supported the singing voice with new effectiveness and promoted the development of the *Lied*.

A wider public was forming. For example, no sooner was Haydn's 'Creation' engraved than choral societies were formed for the express purpose of performing it.

It was as an engraver that Weber, at the age of fourteen, thought of earning his living. (He had learned lithography from its inventor, a minor composer who sought to print works that publishers would not accept.) And before he was finally settled in music as a profession he was fated to earn his keep as a private secretary. But there was never any real danger of his being anything but a musician. The 'von' Webers were of aristocratic descent, but young Carl-Maria's father had knocked about the world as band conductor and director of strolling players, as steward and as soldier. (He was Major Franz Anton von Weber, uncle of the Constanze Weber whom Mozart had married.) From such a father and from family associations, the delicate boy learned something of the world of music and drama, and from a series of excellent teachers he learned his technical skill.

In 1804, when he was seventeen, he became conductor of the Opera at Breslau. This sounds magnificent, but German Opera was in a sad state.

The post lasted two years, during which he was badly paid and badly served by players who disliked the leadership of a youth. A new post helped him escape from dissipation and debt, but the wars compelled Duke Eugen of Württemburg to reduce his musical establishment. The Duke's brother Ludwig offered Weber employment as secretary, to conduct correspondence with another brother, the King of Württemburg. In the midst of family intrigues, Weber indulged in further dissipations, until the conduct of his seventy-year-old father in embezzling some of the Duke's money caused the Major and the composer both to be expelled from the kingdom.

Weber was already the composer of several now-forgotten operas, the latest of which he proceeded to revise. Within a few months of the disgrace which suspended rehearsals in Stuttgart, he saw 'Silvana' produced in Frankfurt before an audience that would have been larger had not many people stayed away to witness the ascent of a balloon (1810).

Weber's cousin-by-marriage, Mozart, had written Italian as well as German Opera. Weber himself (he was a small child when Mozart died) wrote only German works. German nationalism was fed on German folk-lore and poetry; it had been inspired by the patriotism of the first French republican armies; and now it grew stronger as the French seemed transformed from friendly liberators into plundering enemies. Prussia was reorganizing itself after the defeat at Jena, spreading military training beyond the confines of the standing army, abolishing the remnants of serfdom, abating privileges where they interfered with efficiency. This was the Prussian aspect of nationalism; but in all the centres of culture the new romantic ideas—counterpart to the crusading spirit of liberty—were more and more asserting themselves in artistic guise. The younger writers and musicians sought inspiration in nature and in national and racial peculiarities. They cultivated fantastic descriptiveness. It is perhaps difficult for us nowadays, surrounded by railway posters, to realize that a romantic love of the countryside could have been regarded at first as an affectation. Before the romantic movement began, many people regarded the countryside as something to be either disciplined to produce food, or tamed to become a park. To love it for itself, to prefer it wild and rugged, and to seek out the tumbledown, the picturesque, and the quaint, was to declare oneself uncivilized. (One might as well cease to wear a white powdered wig, preferring to be bald if nature so willed it.) Weber was of the new generation.

So was Schubert, who was thirteen years younger than Weber.

Schubert's early years are a tale of poverty against a background of warfare in a Vienna that was far from being the gay city of tradition. His father, a schoolmaster, was ill paid, and there was little luxury at home. The 'Imperial Konvikt School' where Franz was admitted at the age of twelve was on a wartime basis, and the boarders' rations were scanty. Vienna itself, as described by Newman Flower in his

Franz Schubert, was ruled by a brutal government and a servile court, was riddled by police spies, and was populated by a corrupted community that permitted any sexual licence and censored everything but immorality.

The Viennese endured virtual famine at times during Schubert's childhood. They suffered all the evils of an inflated currency when, in 1811, the State went bankrupt.

Schubert, whose voice and musical gifts had won him a choirboy's scholarship at the Konvikt, was often hungry. ('You know from experience,' he wrote to his brother, 'how sometimes one wants to eat a roll and a few apples, and all the more when after a modest dinner one can only look forward to a wretched supper eight and a half hours later.')

Beethoven was too famous to be allowed to go hungry. But publishers were not generous, and patrons were affected by the war. He was in financial difficulties. A few years earlier, an offer had arrived from Jerome Bonaparte that he should become *Kapellmeister* (or rather *Maître-de-chapelle*) at Cassel. Art was evidently held to be apart from war. The dynastic idea that war was a ruler's business in which the peoples acted under orders, uninspired by any nonsense about patriotism or nationalism, was still current except in the two countries which fought most determinedly—France and England. But the dynastic idea was not Beethoven's, and he refused the post. This stimulated three of his most distinguished and far-sighted patrons to club together to guarantee him an income. The Archduke Rudolph, Prince Lobkowitz, and Prince Kinsky arranged for him to receive 4000 florins a year . . . and thereby they put the whole world in their debt.

But the florins declined as the currency lost value. Prince Kinsky died, and Beethoven had to be persuaded to refrain from going to law and to accept a settlement.

Napoleon was at his zenith. Austria was crushed. An Austrian princess was now Empress in Paris in place of divorced Josephine. Marie Louise, whom Napoleon wished to be the mother of a dynasty of Bonapartes, seemed a symbol of her country's humiliation.

CHAPTER XIX

The First Romantics: Post-War in Vienna

Beethoven, Weber, Schubert

THE French republicans who had been transformed from brothers of mankind into patriotic Frenchmen were finding themselves confronted by the patriotisms of other peoples and by a tougher resistance than the will of emperors and kings. England had possessed the patriotic spirit for centuries; it awoke in the German states; it startled Napoleon's marshals in the Spanish Peninsula.

Moscow was the beginning of Napoleon's end. The tone poem '1812' which Tchaikovsky would later write to commemorate the Napoleonic disaster—the battle-piece which is so full of Russian victory that it fails to remind us of the hideous retreat of the Grand Army across endless snows—was a belated contribution to the descriptive pieces that exulted in French defeats.

Beethoven wrote one: a 'Battle Symphony: Wellington's Victory at Vittoria.' He wrote it for a mechanical instrument (the precursor of cinema organs maybe?) invented by Maelzel, who was the originator of metronomes. Originally for this 'Panharmonicon,' but later scored for full orchestra, the battle-piece was performed during the first meetings of the Peace Congress of Vienna.

Six thousand people heard Beethoven's now rarely performed act of war. The Empress of Russia sent the composer £100 towards expenses, and other sovereigns sent presents. Beethoven invested in some shares in the Bank of Austria.

Beethoven, however, had cried victory too soon. Napoleon, in France again, had escaped from Elba.

Another hundred days of warfare showed, however, that France really was beaten. And when Waterloo ended Napoleon's career finally, Weber followed Beethoven's example by coming forward with a cantata 'Battle and Victory.'

It began with an orchestral introduction depicting the horror of the nations hearing of Napoleon's return from Elba. As the composer described it, 'the introduction is of a rugged, stormy, mournful, angry spirit, broken in its accents; rising in force towards the end, and dying in dry, hard, sullen strokes.' There are warlike choruses. The Austrian Grenadiers March is heard in the distance. Spitta describes the battle section: 'A wild march announces the approach of Napoleon's army, while the Germans sing a solemn prayer. The battle, which then commences, is at first left entirely to the orchestra. The day is going against the Allies. The French tune "Ça Ira" is heard shrilling out wildly and triumphantly above the other instruments, while broken ejaculations burst from the Allies scattered about the field. The tumult is just dying away, when lo! the Prussian horns, first faint in the distance, then louder and louder; the Chorus listens, and then bursts into the air of Weber's "Lutzow's Wild Ride." . . . The enemy flies with the victor at his heels, till at last "God Save the King!" peals solemnly forth from the orchestra, and the colossal tone picture is at an end.'

Although this work is now ignored, we observe it, as we observe Beethoven's political pieces, because it illuminates the general change in musical style. Besides this piece, Weber wrote a number of patriotic 'Songs of War and Fatherland' which roused fervid enthusiasm among the youth of Germany. The era of national music had begun.

The new nationalism was quite different from that of Mozart. He had written German works to show that they could be as good as Italian ones. He was not loudly proclaiming that they were better, that they *must* be better *because* they were German. Also he wrote, according to the aristocratic temper of the time, comedies of manners about people of rank that may be compared with the plays of Sheridan, Congreve, and Goldsmith; works that dealt with recognizable people instead of the gods and heroes of Handel's and Gluck's mythological librettos.

The new-style opera, of which Weber was a pioneer, dealt with knights in armour and hapless maidens, demons and fairies, national (not classical) legend. If one must seek a literary counterpart to them one could choose the novels of Walter Scott.

The new style songs—the *Lieder*—which, also at about this time, sprang fully mature from Schubert's fertile mind, were equally characteristic of romantic individualism. They are not gallantries addressed by Count X to the Duchess of Y's lady's-maid. They are the love songs of any anonymous youth and any unknown maid. They are Gretchen at her spinning wheel betrayed by Faust, the child whose spirit is snatched away by the demon Erl King of the forest, the serenader to his mistress, the miller at his water-wheel, the fisherman angling for trout, the skylark at heaven's gate. The *Lied* was destined to become for millions of people the most directly moving of all artistic experiences.

One has sorrowfully to admit that Schubert's limpid lyric compositions ushered in the era of sex-appeal in music and that their degenerate offspring include the drawing-room ballad and the crooner's spineless laments. It was in Schubert's day that youths and maidens, forsaking the finger-tip contacts of the aristocratic minuet, clasped one another in a quasi-embrace, and horrified their elders by inaugurating the long reign of the waltz. Their elders' horror is understandable. Only twenty years—and all the difference between pre-war and post-war.

Before Weber wrote his battle piece, he had wandered across Germany finding commissions wherever he could. A little Arabian Nights opera 'Abu Hassan' pleased the Grand Duke of Hesse and brought in 440 florins. There was work to be found at Prague, Dresden, Leipzig, Saxe-Gotha, and Weimar. Some of these towns were visited and revisited; and at last Prague offered a post—the directorship of the theatre and the task of reorganizing the Opera.

Weber was a man who, however undisciplined might be his private life—he was soon entangled in an amorous intrigue in Prague as he had formerly been in Breslau—was magnificently conscientious where Opera was concerned. He even took the trouble to learn to speak Czech in order to be able to reply to criticism in the language of the critics. Altogether he seems to have sobered in Prague; and before he left his post for the conductorship at Dresden he married the discreet, sensible, and charming Caroline Brandt, who, seven years earlier (when she was only eighteen), had sung the principle rôle in his 'Silvana.'

By this time he had written two piano concertos, several solo works including sonatas, a piano-quartet, and number of songs besides his operas and his patriotic pieces.

Now he faced the task of persuading Dresden, which still exalted Italian Opera above German, to follow the lead of other cities and to establish native art in a worthy fashion (1817).

At the age of sixteen, before leaving school, Schubert finished his first symphony, but he did not immediately become a full-time professional musician. Partly to please his father, with whom he had quarrelled and who was now temporarily reconciled, and partly to escape the seven years' military service which his country demanded, he trained as a teacher. For a while he taught the lowest class in his father's elementary school. But the torrent of his compositions had already begun to flow. In one year he wrote 6 operas (he wasted much energy on unpractical librettos), 2 masses, 2 symphonies, 3 sonatas, and *a hundred and forty-four* songs. He was eighteen years old, he was teaching children for six hours a day, his salary—it seems incredible—was thirty-two shillings a year. The year's songs included 'Gretchen at the Spinning Wheel' and 'The Erl King.' On one day he composed eight songs.

The next year saw another mass, the fourth and fifth symphonies,

110 songs, and other pieces. Not every year of his life was thus productive; but many were; and even the leaner years brought forth
what many another composer would have regarded as a respectable
output. In the year when Weber went to Dresden, Schubert turned
his attention to pianoforte sonatas and attempted to write pieces
worthy to stand beside Beethoven's.

Post-war Vienna was not a happy place for musicians unless, like
Rossini, they had the gift of writing opera in a popular style. Yet
the city was still *the* city of music. Beethoven was its most famous
citizen, and all the musicians of Europe, from the greatest down to
beer-garden singers, continued to regard it as their metropolis.

The battlefields were quiet; and a choice lay before the Congress
of Vienna—a new Europe or an attempt to recall what Talleyrand
called the 'principle of legitimacy' (the principle of tracing a ruler's
descent while ignoring racial or geographical considerations).

Beethoven was outspoken in his views, and he was saved from police
action only by his fame and the protection of Archduke Rudolph.
Not that Rudolph, a son of the late Emperor and a nephew of Marie
Antoinette, approved of democratic opinions; but he loved Beethoven's
music too much to care what the deaf, ageing man might say. The
authorities were persuaded that Beethoven had grown eccentric, that
he was disturbed by quarrels with his nephew. It is true that Beethoven
was disturbed. He was not fitted by temperament to be guardian over
a mettlesome boy, who might well have been better off had he been
left with his widowed mother. (Whatever her moral faults of which
Beethoven disapproved, she would probably have well understood the
boy's waywardness and she could hardly have neglected his food and
clothing more than Beethoven did.)

Beethoven had begun to wonder whether, in defeating Napoleon,
the peoples of Europe had not jumped out of the frying-pan into the
fire. Cipriani Potter (later a principal of the London Royal Academy
of Music) who visited Beethoven in 1817, declared that the composer called the Austrian Government by every sort of insulting
name.

We can construct something of his talk from the conversation-books
in which his friends wrote down their part of discussions that his
deafness made somewhat onesided. Sometimes they came to discuss
what should be done about the nephew who, poor lad, explained
that 'he would like to live with his uncle if he had but a companion,
as his uncle was hard of hearing and he could not talk to him.' They
remained to talk politics, to curse the censorship and the spy-system,
to deride the superficial mysticism which was the reverse side of Vienna's

reckless living, to discuss the growing importance of the financiers, to console one another with the belief that in fifty years Europe would consist only of republics governed by parliaments on the English model.

Beethoven's contempt for post-war Vienna was matched by the fear which Schubert's father felt for young Franz—the fear that a young artist might be contaminated by too reckless a way of life. For the Viennese were allowed nothing by their Government but such amusements as continue to flourish though times are bad. Newspapers, local and foreign, were rigidly censored, clubs were forbidden, even academic philosophy was suspect. Music, of course, could not be censored, but its spirit could be unwelcome. Both Beethoven and Schubert found their artistic lives hindered by the rage for Rossini, whose music—gay, superficial, and belonging by temperament to an earlier age—was perfectly satisfactory to Metternich and the Court. Schubert, particularly, had no friends or patrons among the aristocracy, and he lacked the business acumen to obtain reasonable prices from the publishers. The story of his dealings with them is one of such meanness on their part that one reads the figures again and again, believing that something surely must have been omitted. A quintet was sold to Schott for twenty-five shillings, a trio to Probst for seventeen and six, some songs to Diabelli for tenpence each. Make whatever allowances one may for differences in purchasing power—the prices are shameful.

The fears which Schubert's father felt were justified by events. Biographers have enlarged sentimentally on Schubert's love affairs. Romantic playwrights recall his declarations about Therese Grob: 'For three years I hoped to marry her, but could find no situation, which caused us great sorrow.' But the disease which ultimately killed Schubert was almost certainly due to an adventure in dissipation. Schubert was easygoing, he lived in a time of degeneracy, he had a gay and affectionate disposition, and, once he had given up school-mastering, poverty and uncertainty made marriage impracticable. . . .

Music continued to pour forth from him, and it drew around him a circle of understanding friends who compensated in some measure for lack of rich patronage. They were not titled folk. Had they been, Schubert would have been ill at ease. They were middle-class people, professional men and artists mostly. Among such people Schubert became something more than the Schubert of the sentimental plays.

And in the absence of titled patrons there were other influences. The Society of the Friends of Music elected Schubert a member. This society—not banned by the police since music is no evidence—

reflected the change in social conditions. Its members were bourgeois. Some were well-to-do, but they were not 'quality.'

In the last years of his short life, Schubert enjoyed a little recognition in the midst of troubles that often worried his well-wishers more than him. He was a leading spirit in a circle of young writers and artists, leading in their meetings and discussions about poetry and drama, and not lagging behind when they adjourned to a tavern. He toured as accompanist with the famous singer, Vogl, who introduced his songs to audiences outside Vienna. He was praised by a few discerning critics. But he never attained the settled position he hoped for. Nothing better offered than the post he held intermittently as music teacher to Count Esterhazy's children in Hungary.

In Dresden, Weber found himself regarded as occupying a position inferior to that of his rival, the director of the Italian operas. He found that the King of Saxony, who had unwisely allied himself with Napoleon, was suspicious of a composer whose patriotic songs had exulted in Napoleon's downfall. But Weber was determined to make German opera respected. Many activities delayed the appearance of 'Der Freischütz,'and several works (including the 'Invitation to the Dance') preceded it. It was first produced, not in Dresden, but in Berlin where there was also strong bias in favour of Italian Opera. But though the Berlin director was the distinguished composer, Spontini, and though three of Spontini's operas had been produced with great success, 'Der Freischütz' was a triumph. (The overture was encored before ever the curtain rose.)

It succeeded brilliantly in Vienna, too, and led to a commission from Barbaia (Rossini's impresario) for a new work. Unfortunately the new work, when it did appear, was handicapped by the somewhat ridiculous libretto written by a self-satisfied lady named Helmina von Chezy, and 'Euryanthe' was only moderately successful.

But 'Freischütz' had been to London and had filled Covent Garden, Drury Lane, and the Lyceum simultaneously. And Charles Kemble, directing Covent Garden, was suggesting a visit and offering £1000 for an English opera. ('Only in England,' Haydn had said, 'can one make such sums.')

Weber came to London, and 'Oberon,' a fairy opera, opened successfully, although the aristocracy did not support Weber as, three years earlier, they had patronized Rossini. It resulted in concert giving and other engagements, and these activities kept Weber busy even when 'Oberon' was waning.

All this was too much for a consumptive (he had always limped from an affection of the hip bone), and in June, 1826, Weber died.

He was buried in London. Dresden did not claim his body until 1844 when Wagner was conducting opera there. The prophet was not without honour save in his own theatre.

Weber had set out to further German culture. Until his day it had been possible for a man without wide culture—German or otherwise—to be a great musician. But a Romantic musician had to be sensitive to poetry, susceptible to the magic of faery, regarding national legend not as tales for children but as symbols of the spirit of his race. From such subject matter as frolicsome peasants, spotless maidens, ruined castles, and haunted forests there was to be distilled truly great music —music which provided a way of escape from the grim realities of the political and industrial world.

The typical hero of Romantic spectacle took his magic sword, his inventive genius, and his unsleeping energy and, by sheer merit, married a king's daughter. Such an idea was acceptable to audiences which, more and more, consisted of middle-class people.

In such society, the status of the musician began relatively to improve. Von Weber, a man of good family, educated, travelled, and patriotically devoted to his country's art, set a new standard for musicians. The days when they had to accept patronage servilely were over. A new-style profession of music was being established and would have to come to terms with a commercial and industrial Europe.

In 1827 Schubert acted as torchbearer at Beethoven's funeral. Some of his songs had been shown to Beethoven as the giant lay dying, and they had met with praise. The two men never met.

Beethoven's last years contained much suffering. Some he brought on himself. He continued to be at odds with his nephew who, now at university, desired to visit the mother of whom Beethoven disapproved. Beethoven was hurt and angry: the boy desperate enough to attempt suicide and to injure himself. The young man, once he was allowed to follow his bent and join the army, turned out quite well. He just could not return the fierce affection lavished on him by his uncle who, now in his fifties, and aged by sorrow, was more and more becoming a recluse, wearing clothes so threadbare and untidy that the police once arrested him as a tramp. Beethoven had eye trouble, jaundice, dropsy, and finally, cirrhosis of the liver. He was not a jolly uncle.

For the last ten years of his life he had been producing his final masterpieces, working simultaneously on the Hammerklavier Sonata, which challenges the imagination and technique of the greatest pianists, the Mass in D, and the Ninth Symphony, the last movement of which, a choral setting of Schiller's 'Ode to Joy,' reveals how indomitable Beethoven remained in spirit. The symphony had been commissioned by the London Philharmonic Society (for £50), but Beethoven allowed it to be performed first in Vienna and to be dedicated to the King of Prussia. This was unworthy of him, as was his tendency to be suspicious of the friends whose speech he could not hear. But such occasional lapses did not affect the integrity of his work. The last sonatas and the chamber music that followed them have an awe-inspiring spirituality about them, a quality that places them among the confessions of the saints, a profundity that is the product of years of struggle in the mind of a great genius. Beethoven's spiritual struggles were matched by his technical ones. No composer ever revised and reconsidered his work more than he did. It was as though the wilful spirit of his music had to be fought and compelled to submit to the requirements of proportion and logic.

Yet this man, whose severe face, we are told, could shine with melancholy and goodness, was subject to fits of wild temper. A quarrel with his brother in the country—on the subject of when the nephew should join the army—provoked Beethoven to leave for Vienna in the worst of weather. Pneumonia set in. It seemed to pass, but there was a relapse. The London Philharmonic Society, hearing that he was in need, sent £100, confirming Beethoven's perhaps too idealistic conception of Englishmen.

In March, 1827, he knew he was dying. It seemed appropriate that there was both snow and thunder on the night he died. All Vienna mourned. Nobody could be so frivolous as to ignore so great a loss.

On the first anniversary of the funeral, Schubert gave a concert of his own works. It was the only one. The profit—£32—enabled him to buy a ticket to hear Paganini play the violin.

Shortly afterwards he fell ill with what was perhaps food poisoning. His already enfeebled health could not withstand an attack of typhoid. Had he lived for another three months he would have been—thirty-two.

His 'effects' consisted of some clothes and domestic necessaries, some music, and a bundle of his own unpublished works. The bundle was valued at 8s. 6d. Some obituary notices and a memorial concert showed that at last a few people recognized his worth; but it was quite possible at that time for an intelligent musician in Austria never to have heard of him, though his songs alone totalled some six hundred. Only a few in Vienna mourned. The others could ignore the loss. They had not been informed.

1826, Weber. 1827, Beethoven. 1828, Schubert.

CHAPTER XX

Post-War in Paris

Rossini, Berlioz, Meyerbeer

THE greatest musical minds in Europe were almost solidly antagonistic to the legitimists and reactionaries who tried to restore the *status quo ante*. Almost all the younger men were liberals, progressives, reformists of one kind or another.

There was one distinguished exception. Rossini as a child had seen some of the disadvantages of holding unpopular views: his father had lost a job through being an ardent republican. Perhaps this affected him only unconsciously, but certainly it was not until he wrote his last big work that he seemed to recognize the new spirit that was abroad.

Success came early. A serious opera 'Tancredi,' and a comic one 'L'Italiana in Algeri,' were both written and produced in 1813 (the composer was twenty-one), and both threw Venice into a frenzy of enthusiasm. Having conquered Venice (and a number of Venetian ladies) Rossini succeeded in gaining the interest of a famous impresario in Naples. This Barbaia, who was 'farmer' of the Neapolitan gaming-tables, had a mistress. Man and mistress both were attracted by the gay young man. (Rossini later married the mistress without falling out with Barbaia.)

From Naples, Rossini went on to conquer Rome with his 'Barber of Seville.' Beaumarchais' Figaro seems to have had the gift of inspiring masterpieces of music, and *Il Barbiere* has many of the qualities that Rossini admired in Mozart's work. Figaro had previously inspired yet another composer, Paisiello, whose partisans helped to wreck the first performance. But the Barber, written in two weeks, was soon a success.

Other successes followed. Rossini had the happy knack of slipping away from the wars and revolts that threatened at times to interfere with his career, and in 1822 he was called to Vienna by Barbaia, who was now managing the Kärnthnerthor Theatre. Vienna too he conquered. Some musicians opposed him. For example Weber, who had no sympathy for anything but German music. But Schubert liked Rossini's operas. And Beethoven told him to 'give us plenty of 'Barbers." '

Rossini, who had intensely admired the Eroica, was unafflicted by the sorrow-for-mankind that weighed on Beethoven, but he was not so heartless as to witness unmoved the squalor in which the older man lived. He attempted to raise a subscription for Beethoven. The Viennese indifference that killed the project must have re-established his cynicism.

At about the time when Weber's 'Euryanthe' was being performed at three theatres in London, twenty-three different operas of Rossini's were being performed in different countries, and hardly anything was being performed of Schubert's. (Weber was thirty-seven, Rossini thirty-two, Schubert twenty-six.)

London saw the successful Italian before it invited Weber. The tale of success continued. Rossini sang duets with George IV; he gave concerts for which the aristocracy paid two guineas for a seat; he composed a topical Dirge for the Muses on the Death of Lord Byron; he appeared at soirées at £50 per occasion. At the end of five months he appeared at a concert at the Duke of Wellington's, for which the King especially travelled up from Brighton; and he went off to Paris with £7000 in his pocket.

Paris, which had made few appearances in musical history since the time of Louis XIV, was now to wrest from Vienna the position of musical capital of Europe. French culture had always been highly respected in the Courts of Europe and it continued to hold its own. Austria had no solid contribution to make to European affairs, and despotism was powerful enough to resist fresh ideas. France, on the other hand, was one of the first European powers to follow England's lead towards an industrial and financial system on modern lines. It is true that there was despotism in Paris, too, but it was insecure and uneasy. The Napoleonic regime had protected science and advanced men of talent. In the industrial field, France developed a considerable textile industry. What English inventors had done for cotton, Frenchmen did for silk.

In Paris there began to be assembled musical resources that the Viennese could respect and material wealth that London could not despise.

Rossini sensed the new atmosphere. Though he began as director of the *Théâtre Italien*, he set himself to conquer the French *Opéra*. The campaign could be conducted in comfort because the theatrical directorship was followed by two sinecure posts—Composer to His Majesty and Inspector-General of Singing in France—that brought him 20,000 francs a year. The success of his opera 'Moses' suggested that champions of liberty were acceptable *dramatis personæ*. Rossini followed up the idea, and paved the way for the long succession of operas with such heroes.

Semi-realist opera on historical subjects was really established by his 'William Tell,' a work that has had enormous influence on musicians, though Rossini saw it eclipsed in favour by the works of Meyerbeer. It was produced shortly before the 1830 revolution, which drove Charles X from his throne. The champion of Swiss liberty seemed a topical chief character for an opera at a time when France, grown tired of the still continued attempt to restore a long discarded type of royalism, sought a constitutional monarch. (Beethoven had been dead three years. He had asked for plenty of 'Barbers.' He would have been astonished, but not perhaps displeased, to see Figaro's impudence succeeded by Tell's earnestness.)

Not everyone had Rossini's or Meyerbeer's knack of getting on in a swiftly changing world. Schubert had been neglected in Vienna: Berlioz could find no patron in Paris. Both men, from a worldly point of view, were their own worst enemies.

Berlioz's career is difficult to summarize because he had the habit of reconstructing his works over and over again. Fragments rescued from some discarded early work would be rescued and built up into a new piece under a new title. Something which had been offered in honour of one occasion would be found suitable to commemorate another. His private life was lived in a perpetual state of worry, exaltation, despair, quarrelling, reconciliations. His public life was punctuated by sudden triumphs and disasters.

The son of a physician at La Côte St. André, in the mountains near Grenoble, Berlioz was intended for medicine. But the attempt to pursue curative science made Berlioz ill, and he was soon playing truant from medical school in Paris and frequenting the Opera. In 1823, when he was twenty, he at last succeeded in persuading an angry father that music was the only possible profession, and he was allowed to study in earnest at the Conservatoire, where he was already known as a frequent visitor to the library. His existing musical equipment was slender. He could play the flageolet, the flute, and the guitar, he knew some harmony, and he had experimented with some compositions, fragments of which were destined to reappear later on.

In music, as in life, Berlioz was the pure Romantic. From the days when, as a boy of fifteen, he fell madly in love with a twelve-year-old neighbour named Estelle, to the last years when—he old and weary, and she a grandmother—he called on her to resume old acquaintance, he made his loves and hatreds, his marriages and infidelities, his tours and his sojourns in Paris the subject-matter of his work. He expressed his anguish at parting from Estelle by setting some lines of La Fontaine —and later used the melody in the 'Symphonie Fantastique.' He wrote the 'Symphonie Fantastique' when he was twenty-five because he had fallen madly in love with an Irish actress named Harriet Smithson who was playing Shakespearian rôles during an English season in Paris. (It was the Charles Kemble who had invited Weber to London who took Harriet Smithson to Paris.)

Between these two events Berlioz wrote various highly romantic works and enjoyed a measure of success at two concerts of his works. These pieces, which included the 'Waverley' overture, 'Les Francs Juges,' 'La Révolution Grecque,' part of a Mass, and a fragment destined later for 'La Damnation de Faust,' earned him the title 'The Byron of Music.'

One of the two concerts had been given in the hope of interesting Harriet Smithson, but she remained unaware of Berlioz's existence. He wrote letters to her and she did not answer until, on the point of her departure, she declared his passion hopeless. Distraught at some uncomplimentary tale about his idol, Berlioz became engaged 'on the rebound' to a young pianist named Marie Moke.

Further public performances of his music were given at about this time (at one of them he flung the score at the inefficient musicians who had missed their cue), and now the time had come to take advantage of his 'Prix de Rome' scholarship. This prize, which he had gained after several attempts (the examiners thought his music extravagant and unacademic), entitled him to study in Italy.

His journey, partly by ship from Marseilles, gave him material for 'The Corsair'; and his stay in Rome was later transmuted into 'Harold in Italy'; but he gained little direct satisfaction from his Roman activities at the Villa Medici.

A typical episode interrupted his studies. Not having heard from Marie for a while, he impulsively set out for Paris. At Florence he had tidings from her mother that Marie was married. (Her husband was Pleyel, the piano manufacturer, and as Camille Pleyel she became a celebrated pianist.)

Berlioz determined to 'kill two guilty women and an innocent man.' He even bought women's clothes in which to disguise himself. But he lost the disguise *en route*; delays gave time for second thoughts; and the town of Nice inspired him to write the overture to 'King Lear.' He returned to Rome, to compose 'The Corsair' and 'Rob Roy' overtures.

In Paris again (Autumn, 1832), and living in an apartment once occupied by Harriet Smithson, Berlioz gave another concert. Harriet Smithson who was again in Paris was invited, and she realized that it was herself who was the central character of 'Symphonie Fantastique.' Berlioz's passion was in full blaze once more, and, now that he was something of a celebrity, he more imperiously than ever demanded that she should meet him. She consented. On her part, she had become less of a celebrity. A second season of Shakespeare, this time with her own company, was turning out disastrously. In the following spring she was bankrupt and, to add to her misfortunes, she broke her leg. Berlioz, however, continued to be devoted. Marriage with such a man seemed a risky adventure. He was temperamental. His earnings were small, though he was writing brilliant criticism for the newspapers to supplement his income. But he insisted; they were married at the British Embassy (a couple of months before his thirtieth birthday); and an extremely unhappy partnership was launched.

After 'William Tell,' Rossini practically gave up composing. He was not yet forty. He would live to be sixty-six. In all those latter years he composed only the 'Stabat Mater,' the 'Petite Messe Solenelle,' and the trifles which are now put together as the 'Boutique Fantasque' ballet. As a rich invalid, cared for by his second wife, he fades out of musical history, except as a witty host at those Saturday evening musical parties where some of the greatest musicians in Paris were wont to congregate.

The man of the moment was Meyerbeer. He had the initial advantage of possessing means derived from his Jewish banker father; he had learned German music in Weber's company and had studied the Italian style in Rossini's works. Well-to-do and well equipped, he made a resounding success with French Opera on historical subjects.

The Parisians were ripe for such pieces. Ever since Waterloo they had lived uneasily, first under Louis XVIII, then under his much more autocratic brother, Charles X. 'I would rather chop wood,' said Charles, 'than reign after the fashion of the King of England.' But the fashion of the King of England was in fact the fashion that the new era demanded from royalty. Despotic royalism, Church control of schools and newspapers, and the restriction of the vote to only 80,000 people in all France, was an inappropriate way of government for a developing country. The Parisians looked abroad and observed unrest in Germany, rioting in England, revolutions in Italy and Spain, nationalism in Greece, declarations of independence in Brazil and Peru.

Paris decided the issue for all France. Charles fled and was replaced by Louis Philippe. The new King had known poverty, he understood the bourgeoisie, and he had no ambitions to be a *grand monarque*. Not he but the box office was the patron of art.

Meyerbeer's 'Robert the Devil' made a fortune for the Paris Opera. A picturesque, heroic, allegorical story about a demon's influence over a medieval duke was enhanced by brilliant scenic effects and accompanied by music scored in dramatic style. There was something for everybody's taste. The 'Huguenots' went one better. The Jewish composer, in an officially Catholic country, presented to his free-thinking audience the fight for freedom of the sixteenth-century Protestants—all on a scale never before attempted in Paris.

Meyerbeer was not the only composer to follow the path suggested by 'William Tell.' Before the July revolution, the now almost forgotten Auber astonished his audiences, accustomed to a graceful and melodious style, by producing 'Masaniello.' This work, which seemed very inflammatory at the time, being about a Neapolitan revolution to the accompaniment of an eruption of Vesuvius, made a sensation in Paris (though musically it is not very important) and reached Brussels just when the Belgians were prepared to follow the French lead. The Belgian war of liberation against the Dutch was initiated, it is said, at a performance of 'Masaniello.' (Auber did not mean his text to be taken so literally. Louis Philippe appointed him director of the Conservatoire and, later, Napoleon III made him Imperial *Maître-de-chapelle*. Ironically, Auber's death was hastened by the terrors of the Paris Commune of 1870.)

In Dresden, during the riots inspired by the Paris revolution, seventeen-year-old Wagner wrote what he describes in his autobiography as 'a political overture, the prelude of which depicted dark oppression, in the midst of which a strain was . . . intended to develop gradually and majestically into the fullest triumph.'

CHAPTER XXI

The Unpolitical Romantics—and Their Background

Mendelssohn, Schumann, Chopin

IN Berlin, in the large dining-room of a well-to-do banker's house, a small orchestra and a party of amateurs assembled on alternate Sunday mornings to enjoy music-making with the gifted children of their host. Notable musicians passing through the city (for example, Weber in 1821) observed the precocious talent of young Felix Mendelssohn-Bartholdy.

The banker was the son of Moses Mendelssohn, the Jewish philosopher, but he had the children baptised, had himself turned Christian, and had had added the name Bartholdy to his own. He knew that all his father's philosophy could not mitigate the disadvantages of being a Jew (and, in any case, that same philosophy supported great broad-mindedness in religion). Felix grew up not particularly race-conscious and sincerely devout in his Christian religion.

The family retained, however, the Jewish clannishness that usually remains for a generation or two after release from the Ghetto; and Felix with his talented brothers and sisters enjoyed the affectionate support of the patriarchs and matriarchs among their relations.

In due course they moved into a home that was less than a mansion-and-park but more than an ordinary house-and-garden—a ten-acre property including something larger than a music-room if smaller than a concert-hall. This is worth noting because, with the waning influence of the aristocrats in their baroque palaces, the importance of the well-to-do middle-class people increased. Such people as these would sit on the committees of concert-giving societies, guarantee the expenses of festival performances, and donate scholarships to music schools.

The removal took place when Felix was sixteen, but already he was a little celebrity, so that his father was moved to declare 'Formerly I was the son of my father: now I am the father of my son.' It was in this year (1825) that Felix, after appearing in Paris as pianist and composer, revealed the trace of priggishness often to be found in his letters, complaining that French musicians lacked seriousness and reverence for their art. His determination to write oratorios is said to have been due to his distaste for the prevailing low moral standards of opera.

At the age of seventeen he wrote the 'Midsummer Night's Dream' overture. Mozart and Schubert were not more mature at so early an age. But Mendelssohn did not devote himself to music exclusively. He found time to study a wide variety of subjects, and to cultivate such accomplishments as dancing, swimming, and other recreations.

Before he set out to earn a living, which was not until he was twenty, he showed the genuine public spirit that later endeared him to Queen Victoria's Prince Consort—a man who understood this kind of virtue. He rescued Bach's choral works from neglect. It is hardly credible, yet true, that the performance of the 'Matthew Passion,' which Mendelssohn organized and conducted with the help of an actor friend, was the first since Bach's death. And it was carried through against scepticism and opposition. In the end it led to the founding of the German Bach Society (Bach Gesellschaft), which has devoted itself to spreading the knowledge of Bach and to publishing worthy and reliable editions of the music.

Mendelssohn for once referred to his racial origin. 'It was an actor and a Jew who restored this great Christian work to the people,' he said.

Now he went on a grand tour to see where his abilities might be most welcome, and in the course of it came to England on a paddle-steamer (the engines of which broke down on the way). Success was immediate. He played for the Philharmonic Society, which elected him a member, and he visited Scotland, which gave him material for the 'Fingal's Cave' overture, and perhaps also for the Scotch Symphony which he would write later.

Further travels took him to Vienna and Rome. His letters tell of the degeneracy of taste in Vienna (it was two years after Beethoven's death), and they are somewhat unkind about Berlioz, then studying in Rome. He met Liszt and Chopin in Paris.

By 1833 he was able to announce that he had found a regular job, as director of all musical enterprises in Düsseldorf at £90 per annum.

Two years later he accepted the conductorship of the famous Gewandhaus concerts in Leipzig, having found the Düsseldorfers unwilling to succumb to all the reforms he proposed. Mendelssohn had great reformist zeal but not of the political kind. He concerned himself with musical education and propaganda, improvements in professional conditions, the elevation of public taste, and so forth.

Schumann was also concerned to educate the public and to persuade it to acquire a taste for romantic music. So much was this true that for a number of years he appeared to his contemporaries as more journalist than musician. As a boy he seems to have been as much immersed in poetry as in music, and as an unwilling law student (his mother was antagonistic to music) he attended to music only in the fashion of an enthusiastic amateur. He was taught the piano by Wieck, whose nine-year-old daughter, Clara, was destined to be Schumann's wife and interpreter-in-chief of his piano works. He attended the Gewandhaus concerts at Leipzig. Whether there or at Heidelberg, whether at university or on holiday, he listened to the greatest performers. But not until he was out of his 'teens did he really settle down to music. Fortunately he had a little money of his own.

Now, he was in a hurry to improve as a pianist; and to help his weakest fingers he devised a little mechanical exerciser. Unfortunately it dislocated a finger so thoroughly as to ruin all prospects of a career as a virtuoso.

This was in 1833, and he was now twenty-three. Schumann proceeded to devote himself more thoroughly to composition. At the same time he felt that the musical public, often indifferent to the masterpieces of the great men who had lately died, were not likely to understand either his own music or the music of the other young men of his day.

And thus he was stimulated to launch his *New Musical Journal*. Vastly superior to the magazine that Breitkopf and Härtel published in Leipzig, it began a new era in musical criticism, a new stage in the development of the power of the Press in musical affairs. He modestly refrained from referring overmuch to himself, and hid his journalistic identity under peculiar pen-names, some of which appear as titles to the pieces in his 'Carnaval.' Other names were devised for the members of a kind of mythical musical society consisting of the several selves that made up his own personality, his friends, and his heroes. The finale of 'Carnaval' depicts the march of this society of 'Davidites' against the 'Philistines,' who opposed progress. For ten years Schumann carried on his disinterested propaganda, showing remarkable critical discernment. On the strength of early and untypical works he sensed the genius in men as diverse as Chopin and Brahms. His writings were inclined to gush, but there is genuine penetration in his estimates of the music of the past, of the music of his present, and, within limits, of Wagner's 'Music of the Future.'

Perhaps Chopin ought not to be included among the non-political romantics. He always regarded himself as a Polish nationalist, and certainly he was tied by many associations to a circle of writers, artists, and politicians, who were mostly liberals or socialists, or, at any rate, reformers of some kind. (In those days there was not the conflict between nationalism and socialism that has since appeared.) Yet, somehow, despite his Polish songs and his Polish mazurkas, despite the young-man impulse he had to die fighting for his fatherland, it is impossible to place him in the company of Wagner-of-the-barricades or Senator Verdi. Though his music is at times full of energy and fire, it never seems to be a kind of manifesto, as Beethoven's or Wagner's often is. Though it is pianistically designed for concert-virtuosi, it appeals intimately, as Schubert's does. (Like Schubert's, it has inspired many unworthy drawing-room effusions, unfortunate by-products of romanticism.)

Chopin's sense of exile in Paris is extraordinary in that his father was a Frenchman. But the sense of attachment to his birthplace persisted, though in many respects he became a thorough Parisian. Perhaps it is hardly fair to assert French ancestry, for the Chopins were more strictly Lorrainers, whose country has German affiliations as well as French and a history of many invasions from both sides.

Chopin's childhood was happy. His father had become a professor of French at several distinguished schools in Warsaw, and maintained aristocratic connections that were advantageous to his talented son. Young Frédéric grew up in the midst of nationalist and romantic art, and he had every encouragement to absorb folk songs and peasant dances—native possessions that could not be influenced by the hated Russian Government.

His adolescence brought travel abroad to several German towns and to Vienna, where he gave two concerts. It brought a love-affair as well as a passionate attachment to a young man-friend. He suffered all the pangs and indecisions of a temperamental youth before he finally left home to seek a career abroad. He carried away with him a silver goblet full of Polish earth—the parting gift of his most intimate friends.

Hardly was he in Vienna than Poland, fired by the 1830 conflagration in Paris, rose in revolt against Russia. This was fortunate for Paris, for it prevented the Tsar from interfering in France, but it did Poland no good.

Chopin had thought of returning home to fight, as his friend Titus had done, but his family urged him to remember that he was not strong enough for a soldier's life. He continued therefore with his travels, and was in Stuttgart on his way to Paris when he heard that Warsaw had fallen to the Russians. The tumult in his mind found expression in his Étude in C minor (No. 12 of the first book)—still customarily called 'The Revolutionary Study.' 'Was God a Muscovite?' Chopin enquired bitterly.

Paris, where many a Polish savant was fleeing for refuge, was now to be his permanent headquarters. Fortunately Chopin had excellent letters of introduction. Cherubini, the head of the Conservatoire (how Berlioz hated Cherubini!) was kind to Chopin, and at the old man's *salons* there were all the musical celebrities of Paris to be met— Rossini and Meyerbeer, Liszt and Mendelssohn, and many other celebrated composers and virtuosi. A concert at Pleyel's was a failure financially, but Liszt and Mendelssohn agreed with a leading critic that Chopin's music and playing were admirable.

After only the shortest period of financial uncertainty Chopin began to enjoy great success as a teacher of aristocratic ladies. Their names and titles appear in many of his dedications. Some of these people were of the new aristocrats, replacing those liquidated during the Terror—Madame the Baroness de Rothschild, for example. Of the genuine-antique titles some were German or Austrian or Polish. There were a few English misses, an American of New Orleans, Berlioz's faithless Madame Camille Pleyel. This is how Chopin described his circumstances in 1833 (he was twenty-three).

'I move in the highest circles among ambassadors, princes, and ministers. . . . You will imagine that I must have made a fortune by this time; but the cabriolet and the white gloves eat the earnings almost entirely, and without these things people would deny my good form. I love the Carlists, hate the Phillippists, and am myself a revolutionary. . . .'

We are told, however, that he avoided earnest political discussion, and he made little attempt to move outside his own artistic and aristocratic circle. More than any other composer he seemed to think with his fingers. This is not to say that he composed, amateur fashion, groping at the keyboard, but that his music is so purely pianistic as to lose almost all its savour when transcribed for other instruments. All kinds of poetic fancies, it seems, went into his romantic ballades and dramatic scherzos, his somewhat rhapsodic sonatas and his not-always-slumberous nocturnes, his swiftly-contrasted preludes and the studies that transmute every known technical problem into patterns of beauty. Yet the poetic fancies often defy literary description, as the music defies formal analysis. Deeper than the elegance and the sentiment, deeper than the tricks of Polish idiom in the mazurkas (and occasionally in the waltzes), there lies, as in Mozart's music, a mystery. Chopin's music is quintessentially romantic, but he refrained from giving descriptive titles to his pieces, and the public, which is so ready to coin its own titles, has managed to provide only two or three—the Butterfly Study, the Raindrop Prelude. . . .

At the Gewandhaus concerts Mendelssohn had an efficient orchestra, a committee that looked after all business arrangements, and almost unanimous public appreciation. He was now a European figure of importance, and he played his part zealously. Successful and authoritative, he insisted on better pay for his orchestra, and took every opportunity to agitate for the establishment of a great music school.

A fifth visit to England saw a production of his oratorio 'St. Paul' at the Birmingham festival. Birmingham makes its first appearance in the standard musical histories on this occasion.

New towns were appearing on the musical map. (There was soon to be a Philharmonic Society as far away as New York.) The new towns could not pretend to vie in glamour with Venice and Vienna and Paris. Mr and Mrs Hammond in their *The Town Labourer*, describe the growth of the industrial districts as occurring 'in a frantic monotony of disorder.' Only very gradually did the disorder resolve itself sufficiently to allow poor people to have access to Mendelssohn's music.

At first, little culture penetrated into the cholera-ridden hovels of the slum dwellers. Little leisure was allowed for it by the factory whistle

that aroused workers too poor to own clocks. Little impulse to sing
animated the children who, working on a shift system in the mills
of the Black Country, slept in the factories, tumbling to sleep in the
unmade beds of those who had just awakened. Though English goods
overflowed the warehouses in every far-distant port, there were as
yet few pianos in poor men's homes. It is true that Parliament spent a
million pounds building new churches, and churches mean organ-
music; but at that time one Englishman in every seven was a pauper,
and the best pews were reserved for the gentry.

But the Methodist revival was a sign of improvement. A missionary
religion, appealing to the poor, taught miners and textile operatives
and potters to organize their affairs, to read, to sing, and to study
the disturbing opinions of the prophets. Trade unionism, growing
up against the bitterest opposition, led towards improved conditions
that provided opportunities for recreation. In time there would exist
in every town some place—the town hall, the chapel hall, the gas-lit
meeting-room of the artisan's friendly society maybe—to which would
come, travelling over the fast-growing network of railways, Herr X
and Signorina Y to perform at the annual concert of Factorytown
Choral Society. Herr X and Signorina Y may never have heard of the
Parliamentary Reform Acts, the Chartist Riots, the Tolpuddle Martyrs,
the Co-operative Societies, the projects for abolishing slavery and for
providing free, conpulsory education; they may have had only a
rough (and generally false) idea, gained from box office statistics,
as to the proportion of mill-owners to mill operatives in their audiences;
but the swift growth of the profession of music depended on such
factors.

Mendelssohn was too well-informed to be quite unaware of these
happenings. During his visits to England he was careful to see the
sights, from the House of Commons to new Atlantic liners. But his
deeper sympathies were not actively engaged. He reserved them for
his more intimate relationships and for his musical life. In this respect
he was no worse than most people; but his biographers are nearly all
tempted to be a little scornful because his letters are so smug; he was
so conscious of being a more worthy citizen than the absentminded
Schumann or the fantastic Berlioz. Whereas Berlioz would almost
certainly have accepted a commission to write a festal hymn on the
emancipation of the natives in Ceylon, Mendelssohn, to whom it was
offered, thought the idea amusing, and declined the task. Playing to
Queen Victoria and the Prince Consort at Buckingham Palace in the
company of their gallant, elderly Prime Minister, Mendelssohn was
not the sort of man to remember (as Wagner almost certainly would
have done) that Lord Melbourne's female and juvenile employees

were slaving away in mines under conditions that many people now do not care to hear described. But it is only fair to say that he would certainly have been glad if some prophet had been able to tell him of the benefit millions of people would derive from the influence that spread out from the great Leipzig Conservatoire which he founded.

He was thirty-one years old, married, and with an increasing family, when the negotiations for the project began. A legacy had been left to the town of Leipzig, and Mendelssohn set himself to persuade the King and Government of Saxony that they ought to have a music school.

Before he finally achieved his aim he had to waste a good deal of time and energy over a project for an Academy of Arts in Berlin. He did not want to be its Musical Director, but Wilhelm IV of Prussia insisted. The new post, he guessed in advance, would be uncongenial, since Berlin was lukewarm; but more than a year elapsed before he was allowed to relinquish part of his duties.

The Leipzig 'Conservatorium' was opened in 1843. Schumann was one of its first professors. But the King of Prussia was still anxious to have Mendelssohn's services. Everywhere Mendelssohn appealed to people in authority as the very man to add lustre to a city without being a disturbing influence (like that dreadful Wagner). Queen Victoria, for example, was always glad to observe that music, unlike certain pictures or novels, was a moral art, and could safely by placed before anyone, however delicate her susceptibilities.

It is obvious that a man cannot write symphonies and overtures, albums of piano pieces and songs, a violin concerto, piano concertos, and oratorios in the midst of royal and municipal duties without overworking.

'Elijah' proved to be his last great effort. Though it received an ovation at the Town Hall, Birmingham, in 1846, he insisted on extensive revisions before publication. He would not abandon his plans for conducting and playing in London, Manchester, Birmingham, though it was not long since he had been heard at Aix, Düsseldorf, Liége, and Cologne. He must needs set to work on another oratorio intended to be called 'Christus.' The death of his favourite sister added depression to weakness. He died after a short illness at the age of thirty-eight.

In 1838, Schumann attempted to establish his journal in Vienna, seeking to propagate his ideas in the waltz-mad city of Strauss where 'serious' music largely consisted of demonstrations of power and speed by pianists of the Thalberg kind. But the consent of the police and the censor's office were too long withheld. For a moment he thought of living in England; and his 'Carnival-Prank from Vienna' (*Faschingsschwank aus Wien*) contains a well-hidden reference to the forbidden Marseillaise. But Leipzig called. Mendelssohn was at the Gewandhaus. Clara Wieck, now grown up, attracted him.

There were difficulties. Clara's father thought Schumann too careless about money and too fond of drink. Herr Wieck was afraid that his daughter's brilliant career might suffer. His anger did not stop short of a malicious campaign of slander, and the young couple had to take legal measures to force his consent.

Until now, Schumann had concentrated on writing piano pieces. Most of them were sets of small pieces strung together under a general title—'Papillons,' 'Scenes of Childhood,' 'Carnaval,' and others. There were the more closely knit 'Études Symphoniques,' in which most of the pieces are variations on a theme. There were a few more architectural works, including the Fantasie.

Marriage released a flood of songs. Schumann found inspiration in Heine's lyrical poems, and produced, besides a few separate songs, the great song-cycles—'Dichterliebe' and 'Frauenliebe und Leben' revealing all the aspects of love as experienced by a poet and by a woman. Full of romance and tragedy—too full for some modern tastes —they are masterpieces of lyrical art.

Marriage meant money worries; but there was the journal, then the professorship (for a while) at the new Conservatorium, and Clara's concert tours which took her as far afield as Russia.

From this time onwards there arrived the bigger works. The symphonic pieces suffered from Schumann's inability to write really effectively for anything but the piano or the voice, and perhaps the happiest results were to be found later on in the piano concerto where the orchestra merely shares the interest. Even the chamber music betrays the 'prentice hand, except one work which also includes a piano—the E flat major quintet.

Now there began (at the age of thirty-four) the nervous weakness that was destined to end in mental collapse. But ten more years of creative activity preceded the final two years in an asylum. A move to Dresden (where he knew and did not much like Wagner) improved his health. And he was able to move to a village out of harm's way during the 1848 revolution that drove Wagner into exile. Surrounded by five children and devotedly served by Clara, he continued to work, producing, amid some now forgotten operatic and sacred pieces, the piano concerto (expanded from an earlier work) and 'Manfred.'

In 1850, Düsseldorf offered him the conductorship of its orchestra and choir. Mendelssohn's earlier work in this town was bearing fruit in a general development of municipal music in Germany. But now

Schumann's growing inability to adapt himself to his surroundings was becoming plain. His critical faculties were clear enough, for it was at this time that he recognized, on little evidence, the genius of the young Brahms. But the music committee at Düsseldorf were compelled to suggest that he should hand over the conducting of all works but his own to a deputy.

The impending disaster held off for a while. But in 1853 Schumann attempted to drown himself. There were two melancholy years in an asylum during which Brahms was Clara's deeply sympathetic friend. Schumann was forty-six when he died in 1856.

If Chopin's 'revolutionary' enthusiasms did not go very deep, he was little likely to forget politics in the company of Madame Dudevant —that pioneer campaigner for women's freedom who called herself George Sand. Though she had aristocratic blood and had inherited a considerable estate, she liked to emphasise the humbler elements in her heredity. In the 1830's she dared to smoke and wear trousers. Long before Chopin came to her house she had separated from her husband and, since then, had loved (among others) Prosper Mérimée and Alfred de Musset. She had enjoyed the friendship of Liszt and the mother of Liszt's children—the Countess d'Agoult who wrote under the name of Daniel Stern.

Now she set out to look after the invalid Chopin. (She was 34, with two children; he, 28.) She conceived the idea that the climate of Majorca would improve his health. Unfortunately they went there at the worst time of the year, and the return nearly killed him. Nevertheless their association continued for ten of Chopin's most creative years before the final quarrel.

The fact that she portrayed him, not very flatteringly, in a novel[1] does not endear her to us, but music owes her a debt. She gave Chopin comfort and security, nursed him through many bouts of illness, and loved him in a half maternal fashion.

After they had parted, Chopin, fighting consumption, carried on with his career for two more years. He visited London (and played to Queen Victoria), he toured the English provinces, he endured the infinitely boring conversation he found in Scottish country houses. His illness found an ally in London fogs. He died at the age of thirty-nine in 1849.

---

[1] Heine, writing of *Lucrezia Floriani*, said, 'She has hideously mistreated my friend Chopin in a repellent book divinely written.' Chopin affected not to recognise the portrait, but the parting came soon after. George Sand's earlier affaires appear in other novels. It is only fair to add that there was abundant generosity and much nobility in her strange character.

Mendelssohn was born in 1809. Schumann and Chopin both in 1810. Mendelssohn and Chopin were dead before they were forty: Schumann before he was fifty.

The gentler spirits were dead: the fiercer ones remained in conflict with circumstance and one another.

CHAPTER XXII

Composers at Work

THE processes of artistic creation are always obscure. But those of composition are particularly mystifying. With other arts the on-looker can at least see how materials are assembled. He can accompany the painter to buy some canvas, he can take a seat in the studio and see the colours being mixed and the brushes prepared, he can handle the engraver's tools or lend a hand at the press. He can see how the sculptor's clay is built up into a design that reveals qualities in a living model. Anybody who has attempted amateur carpentry or has erected a shed for gardening tools can persuade himself (it may be falsely) that he can 'get the hang' of how an architect goes to work.

We can all draw and sketch a bit, we all wrote poems and stories when we were children, we have all played with bricks or made sandcastles.

But only a few of us have ever invented tunes, and still fewer have written them down. Children nowadays learn more of the practice of simple composition than they used; but their little tunes and the lectures that they endure on appreciation do not go far to illuminate the processes of making a symphony.

Of all kinds of composition, songs and dances are the easiest for the amateur to attempt. The metre of a poem suggests a musical rhythm. Its structure helps to determine the appropriate musical form. Like a painter with his easel set up on a hill-top, or a sculptor searching for a Venus in the features of the young woman who is looking out of a north window across the chimney pots of Mont-parnasse, a song-writer has a subject, a model to work from. His task is simplified when he is working within a small, conventional form such as the average musical-comedy refrain. Here an untrained composer who has enough inspiration to influence his memories of other men's tunes, can write 'song numbers' that are so like thousands of others as to be catchy—yet sufficiently unlike to be novel.

A dance, in a similar way, solves many of the composer's problems in advance. A waltz *must* be in three time. A polka must go one-two-*Hop*, one-two-*Hop*. The cadences of a czardas, the castanet rhythms of a bolero, the anticipated half-bar beat of a charleston are fixed by tradition. And, as we discovered in the chapter on form, there is a natural tendency for these pieces to work out in 8, 16, or 32-bar rhythm.

It is when your imitation composer desires to write an extended, developed piece—the untitled, 'abstract' sort of piece that is called *sinfonia concertante*, opus umpteen—that he cannot imagine how anyone sets about the task.

The general plan of a big work may be obvious enough. For example, put a libretto—an operatic 'book'—before an amateur composer and he may quite well be able to discern which parts of it are lyrical and which are narrative. He may know which sections call for the more or less set pieces destined to become excerpts suitable for concert performance, and which others are purely narrative or explanatory. He is sure to know the usual method of giving out the parts—the hero's to a tenor, the heroine's to a soprano, the villain's to a bass, the maternal part to a contralto—and he is unlikely to question traditional usage in this matter since lofty sentiments seem to call for a high voice[1] and deep intrigues for a low one.

Other decisions may bother him more. Ought there to be a full-blown overture, or only a short prelude? And of what type should it be? On all grounds of artistic propriety there is everything to be said for a composition which is based on the leading themes of the opera. But the eighteenth-century type of overture which makes no musical references to the work that it is introducing can be very effective, in defiance of all argument about propriety. And for a light opera there is nothing very reprehensible in making a *pot-pourri*—almost as sketchily constructed as a 'musical switch'—of the 'song-hits' of the show.

The layout of the libretto, then, may be a matter of comparatively simple organization in its earlier stages. How far the composer will interfere with the librettist's work depends on personal temperament. Handel complied with convention and worked in a hurry for audiences who, in any case, were inattentive. He would compose a first act before the dialogue of the last had been written. Gluck, on the other hand, found that a libretto 'commonly cost him a year and, oftener than not, a serious illness' before he was satisfied with it. Few composers are as fortunate as Richard Strauss, who for many years worked in the closest collaboration with Hugo von Hoffmansthal—a partner worthy

[1] The medieval tradition in Passion Music, however, was to assign the part of Jesus to a bass.

of his genius. Few Sullivans find a Gilbert. Few composers can write their own books, as Wagner did.

In laying out a big work, a composer may be attempting something in the nature of a manifesto; but if he regards himself as the leader of an artistic revolution he must consider his strategy. Nobody has prowess enough to inaugurate reforms in every department. Wagner, it is true, laid a spell upon harmony and orchestration, dramatic development, and vocal technique. Yet even he had nothing to contribute to rhythm, and his stage-craft was more grandiose than skilful.

The value of experience to a composer is difficult to estimate. Even a great genius, so long as he is without experience, may make the impression of a bungling amateur. But experience of itself produces mere hack composers—facile people who could write a correspondence course.

Experience cannot produce an original idea: ideas are not substitutes for experience. Among the students at our music schools there are some destined to be critics who know everything about writing an opera except producing the material: others who can sketch out a cor-anglais tune for 'childhood memories,' a fanfare for 'the mysterious knight,' a violin melody for 'the eternal feminine,' and as many vengeance, resignation, redemption, or recognition themes as any romantic could desire, yet who produce only a few songs.

It is doubtful whether a natural born composer consciously weighs up all the problems before him. He is not a musical building contractor working out an estimate for forty gross of semiquavers, a crateful of sharps and flats, 500 gallons of sentiment, and a varnishing of orchestration. On the other hand he is not a creature of pure instinct, a songbird full of rapturous impulse. No analogy is exact. As good a comparison as any can be made between a composition and a plant. A plant grows and has a wilful life of its own that defies the gardener. But it cannot defy its own nature, producing a rose from a bulb. A composition grows: it has a way of defying the composer; and if it is conceived as a fugue it should not end as a mazurka. Nevertheless the comparison is not a safe one. The gardener knows that if a seed germinates it will almost certainly produce such and such a plant. The composer is not absolutely sure. The natural history of composition is full of freaks. For centuries, writers of music have sought for comparisons. The words associated with childbirth are borrowed. A work is said to be conceived; it gestates; it is brought to birth; it is the offspring of the composer's genius.

A composition is and is not a building; it is designed, yet it grows. It is and is not a cry from the unconscious; it is intuitive yet it is logical.

It is and is not a child; it is born, yet only *before* birth does it develop.

Thus there is no precise way of describing how a composer arrives at a course of action. To say he decides on it is to use a rather misleading term, yet what other word is there ? He *feels* that there should be so many movements in his symphony. He has a hunch that the themes should be of such and such a style or length. Perhaps he likes music to be ingenious. Perhaps, on the other hand, he fears academic cleverness—he is a rhapsodist. Nobody knows why a composer will write a funeral-march slow-movement in one sonata and not in others, or why he will finish his pieces abruptly this year and write elaborate epilogues next year.

But here are some recurring problems that we can all understand: (1) the number of movements; (2) whether to use a general title, or a title for a section, or no title; (3) the rival claims of the story in a programme piece and the inner life of the musical development; (4) the resources to be used, and so on. These are not quite purely creative problems. Composers' friends dare to give advice about them. Friends do not advise about the course of a modulation. Indeed a looker-on does not often advise about purely technical matters, though there have, of course, been splendid examples of composers learning technical dodges from fine players.

Composition is mostly a lonely affair.

Some composers nevertheless have the gift of making it almost sociable. Romantic writers are too apt to make artists conform to a few stock types, of which the two most popular are the gay young Lothario and the old hermit—young Liszt and old Beethoven, both in a state of frenzy. A tidy and methodical Haydn, a sober paterfamilias like Bach, a professor of chemistry like Borodin, for whom pathology remained a career to the end, are not people from a theatrical costumier's stockroom.

Mozart preserved a remarkable calm when at work, and Schubert could retire into the world of music while around him were the sights and sounds of a beer-garden. They could achieve a kind of creative tranquillity under adverse conditions. Beethoven, on the other hand, would seek solitude by going for a long walk in the fields, and there stir himself into a kind of creative tempest, singing and waving his arms about when he was not scribbling and scratching in his notebook.

Some composers erupted the fires of genius in an intermittent fashion, like a Vesuvius that lies dormant between earthquakes. Wagner and Verdi both had long periods of deceptive inactivity in creation. Rossini, after scattering showers of sparks with great violence for his youthful years, became practically an extinct crater in early middle age. Bach was of the Stromboli type—a continual fire sending up a punctual flame at frequent intervals—away from the mainland, hurting nobody, apparently inexhaustible. The comparison with a mountain returns to the imagination when we read Wagner's dictum about composers—a heart of fire, a head of ice.

A composer's feelings have no dependable relationship with the mood of his work. Some artists refer darkly to the pain and distress of creation as though they were victims of a visitation. Some are like industrious farmers who take a pride in tilling their genius under a changeable sky. There is the question of external stimulation. With Wagner it is a case of *cherchez la femme*. With Haydn one seeks in vain.

Although these considerations make us wary of fake-scientific classifications for composers, there is no excuse for regarding the practice of composition as completely unaccountable. A chilly August or a muggy Christmas would not justify us in saying that there is no way of distinguishing between summer and winter. We can, in fact, make a number of valid observations. For example, eighteenth-century composers were more prolific than nineteenth-century ones. This is not to say that they were cleverer or more hardworking. Speedy writing was easier in those days. Composers and public alike accepted conventions—contrapuntal, harmonic, formal—that explain why musicians in those days seemed so skilful in the art of improvisation. A good fugue, like a classic game of chess, is rare; but one can always play chess; and with practice one can always write—even improvise— a fugue.

Then again, figured bass left much to the performer to fill in; in *de capo* arias you wrote two-thirds of a song and left the 3rd third as a mere repetition of the opening; in *secco* recitatives there was the merest skeleton of accompaniment for a patter of narrative; all these devices were conducive to high-speed writing. Orchestration was not complex. It could, of course, be subtle; but when we read of the odd assortment of instruments that were assembled as orchestras in those days and learn of the defects in wind mechanisms, we wonder all the more how Mozart was able to contrive his scores so economically yet effectively. But we do *not* wonder quite so much at the sheer speed of composition. Mozart wrote for comparatively few instruments; and, whether because of the bias of his mind or because of the limitations of the players, he left more empty spaces in his scores than almost any other composer. Silence is an important ingredient in Mozartian sound.

With the nineteenth century there occur two important changes.

Firstly there is, so to speak, a statistical change. The quantities of notes, the reams of music paper, the gallons of ink, the foot-pounds of energy, the decibels of sound per *opus*—all manifest remarkable increases. And since three-score-years-and-ten are a more or less constant factor, the opus numbers diminish by inverse ratio to the number of notes per piece. There is also a psychological change. There is greater insistence on originality. Themes have to be more striking, development more surprising. The very purpose of a piece may be half-philosophic or sociological. Formerly, in the eighteenth century, people listened to new music a great deal: their new music, unlike ours, did not contain a series of shocks. From Beethoven's time onwards, however, new music becomes less and less acceptable at a first hearing until we, in our twentieth century, make a first favourite of Bach, who was regarded as a conservative a couple of hundred years ago, and write to the *Radio Times* to protest about too many contemporary music concerts.

There were, of course, exceptionally prolific composers even in the nineteenth century. There was Schubert; but then a song is more likely to be written in a burst of inspiration than any other type of piece, and Schubert was apt to construct even his big works out of a series of song-like melodies. There were the minor composers who held to convention in their salon pieces, their little ballets and operettas, their conservatoire specimens, their ballroom confections. But the broad rule holds, and we observe how the pace of Verdi's writing slowed as he brought himself more into line with the ideas prevailing in his later years.

Although the germination of a musical idea is a highly mysterious process it is not entirely obscure. Composers have told us of some of the sources of their thoughts, and we can trace some of the others.

It is quite possible to breed one musical thought from another. Quite apart from the old habit, prevalent among Handel and his contemporaries, of borrowing without acknowledgement from one another's works, there is the Beethoven method of detail transformation. It reminds one of the schoolboyish habit of adding to illustrations in a book, so that a portrait of a girl becomes, by the addition of whiskers and a clay pipe, a likeness of a tramp. Such a practice in the ordinary man's hands nearly always leads to a debasement of the original idea, as in reminiscent jazz. In Beethoven's, it transformed the most unpromising subjects into pregnant utterances capable of enormous enlargement.

Somewhere between casual borrowing and magic transformation is the habit of weaving folk melodies into the texture of a work. Three methods offer themselves: one is to bring in the melody as a quotation, almost as one writer might quote from another; the second is to inject folk-style into a work, much as a writer might make one of his characters speak in Zummerzet or Cockney; the third is the method of subtle reference—the use of allusions and unusual terms such as, in another field, might reveal that the writer of a book on economics was born in a gypsy caravan.

All the musical sources of composition are aided by visual stimulation. If dancers can find suggestions for movement in the sound of a piece, we may be sure that the reverse process is possible, and that many a musical shape has been indicated by a gesture of the hands, a toss of the head, a leap into the air, the swish of skirts, and the tapping of feet. Many an accompaniment for a sea-song owes more to the *appearance* of breakers on the shore than to their clamour, and an audience is more likely to day-dream about the *picture* of white wings swooping above a wave-defying cliff than about the sound of the undertow or the cry of a seagull.

Yet sounds of a non-musical or only half-musical kind have a contribution to make. Galloping horses, church bells, ticking clocks, the splash of fountains, bird-song—even the postman's knock—have had their place in music. The rhythms of train travel and the clatter of factories have been heard in the concert hall.

Less powerful nowadays is the influence of ideal and moral conceptions. In the days when capital letters indicated that a writer was in a reverent mood, composers were apt to suggest aspiration by an upward soaring melody . . . that fell . . . only to rise higher. Liszt called a piece 'The Blessing of God in Solitude'; it consisted of a saccharine tune over a harplike accompaniment—a musical counterpart to Victorian paintings of Heaven. Sighing was often suggested by an appoggiatura—by a note that clashed a little with its underlying harmony and then melted into it by a small fall in pitch.

The trick of imitating gasps and sobs and laughter evolved into a settled technique. For agitation, turn to the page of the orchestration treatise that deals with tremolo effects. For determination, recall the colours of military music. Brass instruments have always been associated with hunting and war; and besides this factor of historical association there is the effect of brass timbres on our nervous systems. They serve for rousing occasions. Nobody knows quite why some harmonies seem 'sweet' and some 'harsh,' and there is perhaps no logical basis for the popular idea that major keys are cheerful and minor keys sad. Nevertheless, only one great funeral march, the Dead March in Handel's 'Saul,' is in a major key.

Undoubtedly many effects in music are the result of conditioning during our childhood years, yet there is an astonishing degree of agreement about the characteristics of certain combinations of sound. According to all logic, our equal-temperament tuning should make one key exactly like another in character, the only difference being that of pitch. Nevertheless, many composers feel that the tonalities which include many black notes on the keyboard are more vividly coloured than the white tonalities. They turn to B flat minor for tragedy and to F sharp major for glittering gaiety. C major spells simplicity and innocent joy. Perhaps the structure of orchestral instruments accounts for this state of affairs. Violins, which are comparatively sweet instruments, play most easily in sharp keys. Brass instruments, which have a quality of pageantry about them, usually play best in flat ones. As for C Major, it is the key of childhood—the one we all began with in infancy.

How does the composer work in his study? He does not need to grope for ideas on a piano, as amateurs do. The stage picture of a composer seated at a keyboard is misleading. But we cannot be sure that he will keep away from the keyboard. Beethoven thought out many of his ideas in the open air, but Wagner had a desk built over a piano keyboard so that he would not have to walk over to the instrument if he needed to test an idea. Berlioz condemned working at the piano: Rimsky Korsakoff is known to have recommended the practice to some of his pupils. Both men were great masters of the orchestra. Obviously we must keep an open mind. Some composers shun the piano even when they are writing for it: others like to have it nearby. Only this much is certain: a real composer does not sit at the piano in the hope that a lucky stumble will produce a theme like that 'great Amen' in 'The Lost Chord.' It is worth noting in passing that a large majority of the great composers were pianists. It is easier to pick up a vocabulary of chords on the keyboard than on most other instruments.

The actual writing of ideas in their first form is nearly always in a kind of crude shorthand. A few methodical composers keep a notebook for jotting down ideas for a rainy day. But many find that their minds work better when they sit down to do a definite job. The common belief that works commissioned for an occasion are usually poor because they do not spring from the composer's own impulse is not well founded. Some such works, of course, are admittedly like the sort of ode a poet laureate produces for a state reception to the Emperor of Ruritania, but a truly professional composer is not for ever mooning about awaiting a visitation from the muses. He sits down at his desk and begins to think.

His first thoughts may run above a rhythmic scheme—one that

belongs to a certain type of piece by tradition or one that is produced as an act of clever arrangement. Many music-lovers think that they ought to despise cleverness (which they learn to call 'mere' cleverness), but cleverness is not only an ingredient in the making of fugal patterns, variations on a theme, and so forth, but is often a means of stoking up the fire of inspiration. Almost every set of *études* begins with the impulse to manufacture something out of standard technical devices. The composer says to himself 'I'll do an arpeggio study, then something for left-hand octaves, then a four-against-three rhythm, then a slow melody surrounded by arabesques, then something to exploit pedalling, and finish up with a cascade of double-thirds.'

A harmonic basis is equally possible. A series of chord-clusters can be broken up, and then all the notes reassembled in an unusual time-order, making a melody that traverses the chords in a series of to and fro leaps.

A colour scheme is another starting-point—the desire to do something, for example, for an unusual ensemble of instruments.

To the amateur composer who thinks primarily in terms of bits of melody, these methods are indeed mysterious.

To the professional composer who understands them all, they remain mysterious. Each composer has his own individual way of thinking on these lines—thinking along all of them at once maybe—and bringing to the task the quality which no analysis can determine. The difference between talent and genius is like that between inorganic chemistry and organic chemistry—the difference of being alive. It cannot be produced in the laboratory.

Some writers on music have said that composers will be able to rise to greater achievements when they can record their fleeting thoughts more rapidly than is possible with pen and paper.

Few professional composers think so. The ordinary concert-goer persuades himself that he, too, could compose if only he could commit his lovely ideas to paper before they fade. The professional composer, however, smiles at this romantic notion. He doubts whether the amateur's vague dreams of celestial harmony would amount to much if they could be performed under concert conditions.

Nevertheless, here, too, we must keep an open mind. Recording pianos so far have had no discernible influence. Film recording is still new. Few composers can understand that Dutch system of notation—'Klavarskribo'—which enables music to be printed as it is played—but not in conventional notation. They would have to learn to use this highly ingenious but easy system which gives, not a diagram of pitch, but a picture of note positions on the piano keyboard. A born composer can succeed very well under the handicaps of our existing system, and he suspects that those who fear such handicaps are probably not composers at all.

But we must not be prejudiced. The art of composition is intimately bound up with developments—social, industrial, scientific—which at first sight seem to be irrelevant.

CHAPTER XXIII

The Controversialists (1)

Berlioz, Liszt, Wagner, Verdi

WHEN Berlioz did experience good luck it was always sensational. There was, for example, a commission from the Ministry of the Interior to compose a Requiem Mass to commemorate some people who had been killed during a vain attempt to assassinate King Louis Philippe. It is true that the original scheme fell through; but warfare in Algeria provided some more dead heroes to be commemorated, and the 'Messe des Morts' was performed in 1837. It brought Berlioz 4000 francs.

Then there was Paganini's desire to have a great work for viola—something for a 'Strad' he had just bought. This, after alterations to suit Paganini, had been performed in 1834; but now at last, after a lapse of four years, Paganini himself heard it and sent Berlioz a letter of praise enclosing a cheque drawn on Rothschild's—for 20,000 francs. There is a story that Paganini was really acting only as intermediary for the owner of the *Journal des Débats*, and that this M. Bertin wanted to help a brilliant contributor without hurting his feelings. Whatever, the truth of the matter, there is no doubt that Paganini could afford so princely a gift. His fortune grew to £80,000: one English tour produced £16,000. And so strange—not to say demoniac—a character as Paganini, for all his charlatanism, was quite likely to desire to rescue the viola from neglect as a solo instrument and to pay handsomely for 'Harold in Italy,' even though it is no virtuoso-concerto. Another 10,000 francs came from the Ministry of the Interior in 1840 for the 'Symphonie Funèbre et Triomphale' to celebrate the tenth anniversary of the July revolution and to accompany the unveiling of a column erected in the Place de la Bastille.

Meanwhile Berlioz had known disasters too. He had desperately wanted to see a work of his performed at the Opera, but 'Benvenuto Cellini' was a complete failure there, except for the overture.

But with a number of considerable works to his credit, including the 'Romeo and Juliet' symphony, he set forth on foreign tours. A reputation preceded him as a master of orchestral effect. Even Wagner, who was reluctant to praise anyone, had been impressed by the Funeral Symphony as performed by a military band of 120 combined with a symphony orchestra of 130. Nobody knew more than Berlioz the possibilities of all the instruments which were being so swiftly developed and improved at that time. Nobody else was capable of writing the great treatise on Instrumentation that was to appear a few years later. (In the chapter on Orchestration we shall discuss the inventions that enriched the orchestra, the technical devises of which Berlioz was swift to avail himself.)

Berlioz, now separated from Harriet Smithson, travelled with Marie Recio, the second-rate singer who was destined to be his second wife. With her, too, he was unhappy—not least because it was hard to dissuade her from singing. He reached Germany with the disappointing knowledge that the Conservatoire had rejected his application for the directorship and had preferred a more conventional practitioner named Onslow.

For the next six years he toured Europe, with occasional visits to Paris and holidays in the south of France. A great many German and Austrian towns saw him, and some of the German rulers, particularly Prince Hohenzollern-Hechingen, were helpful. As always, he was rewriting or adding to earlier works (the 'Carnaval Romain' overture is an afterthought for 'Benvenuto Cellini'), and as always he put his immediate experiences into his works. The most extraordinary example of this was his writing an Hungarian March for his 'Damnation de Faust.' The original Faust had no connections with Hungary, and the libretto had to be modified to suggest that he had. But Berlioz in Hungary had been struck by its national tunes, and incorporated some of them in the 'Rakóczy March.'

Amidst the first mutterings of the revolutionary storm that was about to sweep across Europe, the March had a sensational effect on the patriots of Budapest, and Berlioz altered 'Faust' accordingly.

His post-chaise took him onwards to Russia, where he enjoyed great success. But not before he had celebrated the downfall of post-chaises in a 'Song of Railways,' to mark the opening of the *Chemin de Fer du Nord*. The Russian tour, like the German, opened with a disappointment—the failure of 'Faust' in Paris. A year later the opera failed again in London, largely because of the director's extravagance. Berlioz gave two concerts in London.

In 1848, the year of revolutions, his father died; and, on a visit to his old home, Berlioz learned that his first love, Estelle, was a widow with a son practising at the Bar.

The railways were spreading. It seems appropriate that Liszt, one of the first and perhaps the greatest of the travelling virtuosi, should have arrived in England in the year when Stephenson was completing the first passenger railway—the Stockton and Darlington. It seems apposite too, that the doughty warrior in the cause of new music should have received his early training at the expense of the Esterhazy family. (His father had been steward on one of their estates.)

In this year (1824) when he was thirteen, he dazzled London Society by his extraordinary performances on the 'New Grand Piano Forte invented by Sebastian Erard.' His natural gifts had grown under the guidance of Beethoven's pupil, Czerny, whose books of studies continue to this day to appear in new editions. The world had shown its readiness to appreciate a phenomenon like Liszt by buying Czerny's music in such quantities (symphonies and sacred works as well as the studies) and by paying for his services as a teacher so handsomely (services which Liszt obtained for nothing) that Czerny was rich. His *études* had announced the age of the new pianism with such titles as 'School of Velocity.' And now his pupil, Liszt, would show just how much velocity was possible on Monsieur Erard's improved piano.

Like the wandering minstrels, he would also contribute to his age something more than mere entertainment.

For six years he practised and studied in Paris. He lived frenziedly, falling from rapture to despair over an adolescent love-affair and wondering whether to embrace religion. Love and religion were to be *motifs* throughout his life—many love-affairs, and then religion in his later years when he became Abbé Liszt. As a youth he yearned to be a great lover, saint, and social reformer all at once. Also to be as great a master of the piano as Paganini was of the violin. In the year 1830, when he met Paganini, he met Berlioz and Chopin, too. In such people he found qualities that inspired him to work and study untiringly.

His recitals became orgies of excitement. He was not above pretending to faint with anguish at the beauty of the music. To us there is something comic in the story of his having to be carried out by the man who was turning over the pages of a 'Song without Words,' something comic in his playing one of Mendelssohn's unsensational pieces from the score. But his audiences were enraptured by the play of expression on his striking countenance, and the ladies pursued him as they now pursue film stars.

With one aristocratic lady he eloped. The Countess d'Agoult—married and with three children—became his wife in all but name, and bore him a son and two daughters. Scandal failed to ruin his career.

For six years the Countess observed Liszt's extremist dual personality. She saw his true nobility marred by vulgarity, his desire for a life of dedicated service submerged by his fondness for applause, his broad social sympathies hidden by a snobbish seeking for the applause of people of rank. It was typical of him to rush to Vienna and give concerts in aid of Hungarian victims of a flood disaster: it was equally typical of him on his return to talk to the Countess only of his successes among the Austrian ladies. They parted in 1839. She later made him the scarcely disguised chief character of a novel. He never forgave her, as Chopin never forgave George Sand.

He was not yet thirty. His triumphs, pianistic and amorous, continued in a series of glittering concert tours all over Europe. Particularly in his native Hungary, he was received with music and jewelled gifts and torchlight processions. Even in the stately homes of England, where there was a little chill at the memory of that dreadful affair between a real lady and a professional musician, there was the countervailing thought that Queen Victoria had heard him with pleasure at Buckingham Palace.

In Russia, at Kiev, he met the Princess Carolyne von Sayn-Wittgenstein. With her, too, he eloped. Like the Countess she was already wife and mother. Wife she was destined to remain, for her husband never consented to divorce her, even though at one time the Pope himself was prepared to arrange an annulment.

With this twenty-eight-year-old lady—not beautiful but intellectual and wealthy—the thirty-seven-year-old Liszt went to Weimar as Court Musical Director to inaugurate a reign of musical enlightenment and to become involved in every one of the prevalent musical controversies. Particularly those that raged around Richard Wagner.

Warfare attended Wagner's infancy, the enmity of governments pursued him in manhood, threats of murder enlivened his love affairs. He was the son of . . . he was not quite sure. His first wife *had* an illegitimate daughter. His second wife *was* an illegitimate daughter. His personality made many enemies. His music made so many friends that he lived to see a festival theatre dedicated to his works alone.

His official father died during Wagner's babyhood and was succeeded by a family friend who became stepfather, an actor named Geyer. Some people said that Richard, who went to school as Richard Geyer, ought properly to have held that name permanently. Nobody knows. Nobody knows for certain if Geyer had any Jewish ancestry. But if he had, as some authorities (on little evidence) assert, he was an odd parent for so violent an anti-Semite as Richard became.

Both fathers were interested in the theatre—the first as an amateur, the second as a professional. One of Richard's brothers and three sisters followed theatrical or operatic careers.

There is nothing surprising then in Wagner's early enthusiasms for Greek mythology. Shakespeare, the stories of E. T. A. Hoffmann. What *is* extraordinary was his ability to learn the crafts of playwriting (in verse) and composing (for full orchestra) with very little settled tuition, and without being able to play any instrument respectably. He was extremely resistant to tuition. He had to learn in his own way from Weber and Beethoven scores. He remained a kind of inflated amateur bungler for years. But he was never a dilettante, and he had an enormous capacity for work. All his projects were on the scale of the colossal.

He was seventeen when an overture of his was first performed—to the audience's justified amusement. But he derived useful lessons from the disaster, as he derived lasting impressions from the riots in Leipzig. Like the ill-fated insurrection that barred Chopin from Poland, the Leipzig riots were an echo of the 1830 revolution in Paris. Wagner's fellow students at first fought the police, but when law and order seemed seriously threatened, they mounted guard over the printing works of Wagner's brother-in-law. Ironically the students were indifferent to the fate of the exiled Poles who soon came drifting through Leipzig, and it was the master printer who entertained the leading exiles to dinner and sang the songs of their fatherland. Wagner's life was to be full of such contrasts.

He was no more than twenty-one when he became conductor at the Magdeburg Theatre, and gained his first experience of the easygoing, impecunious, inefficient troupes of performers that passed as operatic companies in many towns in Germany. The Magdeburg Theatre enjoyed a small subsidy from the Saxon Court, but the director often had to be diplomatically absent on pay-days.

Wagner organized several special performances, including one of Beethoven's 'Battle of Vittoria.' His own account, in *My Life*, says that the firing of cannon and musketry was so realistically contrived by special apparatus that the audience, deafened, took to flight. 'Wellington's victory was finally celebrated in a confidential outburst between myself and the orchestra alone.'

A 'benefit' for the conductor at the end of the season was disastrous —'few people in the audience, and a free fight behind the scenes.'

Thence to Leipzig again, in search of a job. 'Owing to my evasion of military duty in Saxony, I never again succeeded in obtaining a regular passport until I was appointed musical director in Dresden.'

Penniless—worse, he was in debt—he went to Königsberg, chasing after attractive Minna Pläner who had played in the Magdeburg

company. She had a job in Königsberg; and Wagner, hopeful of
getting one, married her there, against her better judgment.

Their temperaments clashed from the first. She was older than he
and more prudent. Opera to her was not an exalted, artistic vocation:
it was merely a means of livelihood. She desired respectability and
little else, for in her childhood she had been poor, and in her adolescence she had been seduced. She found it enough to try to bring up
a six-year-old daughter and to persuade the world that the child was
a little sister, without having to cope with Wagner's endless debts.

At first she showed a disposition to run away from her difficult
husband. Later it was he who could not be held.

The year in Königsberg was unsatisfactory, but Wagner's optimism
sustained him. If Meyerbeer could make a fortune in Paris, why not
he? If the influential dramatist, Scribe, could write librettos for other
composers, why not for him, too? Wagner sketched a story and sent
it to Scribe.

Paris took no notice. Furthermore the Director of the Königsberg
Opera went bankrupt.

And so to Riga where a new opera house was being started. Wagner
and Minna sailed—they had not yet seen a steamer or a railway—
and were ushered into Russia by officials of a government that Wagner
as a student had hated and would have cause again to hate. Russia
was a country where nationalist music was still almost unheard of,
and where Glinka's works, full of folk-tunes, were being described
by some of the old aristocracy as 'coachman's music.'

In Riga the tide of accumulating debt mounted. But 'Rienzi,' a
grandiose work based on a story by Bulwer Lytton, was beginning
to grow. In this work Wagner, though far from mature, ceased to
be an apprentice in his craft.

Creditors were not to be put off any longer; Paris, despite Scribe's
silence, seemed to call; if only Paris took 'Rienzi,' there surely it would
appeal to Meyerbeer's 'fans.'

The young couple and their pet dog, deciding that a chance of
success in Paris was better than the certainty of trouble in Riga, fled.
They were smuggled across the Russian-German frontier during the
changing of the guard. A little more alertness on the part of the Cos-
sacks while this strange trio were struggling across ditches and through
hedges, and another mute Milton would have died inglorious.

Lacking a passport, the Wagners bribed and cajoled their way
aboard a sailing-ship and travelled to London, after a long-drawn
agony of storms and shelterings in unforeseen ports that made Richard
think of the legend of the Flying Dutchman. England gave them the
experience of railway travel; an attempt to see 'Rienzi's' author

introduced Wagner to a House of Commons debating anti-slavery measures.

A steamer took the Wagners to Boulogne. And there, as though Fate had arranged it, Meyerbeer happened to be staying—Meyerbeer whose success Wagner envied, whose friendship he solicited . . . and whose hatred he eventually earned in full measure.

Meyerbeer, who worshipped success, always made friends wherever possible. He listened to Wagner's recitations of 'Rienzi': he gave him letters of introduction to take to Paris. Whether his kindness was genuine or calculated, it was not enough for Wagner, who in later years violently attacked Meyerbeer in a pamphlet *Jewry and Music*. Nothing less than unquestioning admiration and endless generosity was ever enough for Wagner.

In Paris, where Berlioz had to fight for existence, the two newly arrived Germans, despite their introductions, very nearly starved. Literally at times they lacked enough to eat: their shoes leaked and they could not pay a cobbler. Wagner's only compensation for living there lay in the excellence of the orchestral performances that at last enabled him to hear Beethoven's Ninth Symphony much as he had imagined it. Though Wagner was poor, there was money in Paris, and occasionally some of it was spent worthily.

But not at the Opera. Opera had become the entertainment of men-of-the-world in search of women-of-the-half-world. Every kind of vice was for sale. The admission of clients to back-stage provided a subsidy that helped to relieve the French Government of loss on this cultural enterprise, and made a fortune for the lessee. This lessee was one Véron, a patent-medicine monger, whom Ernest Newman describes as an 'amateur assassin.' Heine wrote of him: 'The name of Véron will live for ever in the annals of music. He has adorned the temple of the goddess, but shown the goddess herself the door. Nothing could surpass the luxury that rules at the Opéra, which is now the paradise of the hard-of-hearing.'

Véron profited by the fact that the new, bourgeois dandies paid: the old aristocrats had had free seats. He charged special prices for the box nearest the stage, and the Opéra became, according to Newman, 'one-third temple of the Muses, two-thirds ante-chamber to a seraglio. It was this institution, hoary with iniquities, cynical with long experience of human cupidity and folly, towards which the green young German provincial named Richard Wagner had bent his hopeful steps from the other end of Europe.'

Wagner was green enough to set Heine's 'Two Grenadiers' to music. As in Schumann's setting, Wagner's introduced a fragment of the 'Marseillaise,' a song then only to be sung to the accompaniment of civil disorder. He was green enough to hope for quick success with his early opera 'Liebesverbot,' but the theatre that promised performance went bankrupt. The stack of unpaid bills that always accumulated wherever Wagner might stay was augmented by publication of some music at his own expense.

Wagner agreed to pay for this by writing articles for the publisher's *Gazette Musicale*, though most of the fees would have to go to translators.

An introduction to the manager of the Opera brought only the truly superb suggestion that Wagner should write a ballet—*in collaboration with another composer*. Wagner, as though he had not heard, offered a brief sketch of his projected 'Flying Dutchman' and continued with 'Rienzi.' He must have appeared crazy to the business men. They, after all, were not to know that he would one day write 'Mastersingers' and 'Tristan.'

And so Wagner had to accept hack-work from Schlesinger, the publisher—commissions to write a cornet tutor and to arrange Donizetti operas for various small orchestral combinations.

Wagner, living in one room to save fuel, and borrowing not to go hungry, derived what little comfort he could from the praise which Heine and Berlioz offered for . . . his journalism. When he at last got his early Columbus overture performed—badly—Berlioz glumly observed that it was very difficult to get on in Paris.

So difficult was it that Wagner was very glad when a 'surprise party' of guests who brought their own food and drink turned up on the New Year's Eve of 1841. (It stimulated him to make an hilarious speech on Freedom in America.)

The wolf was still at the door. The 'Flying Dutchman' libretto he had to sell for some other composer to set to music. (A ghostly *Vaisseau Fantôme*, not by Wagner, is still to be found mentioned in the encyclopædias.)

Gradually Wagner reconciled himself to the thought of failure to conquer Paris. His mind turned more and more to 'The German Ideal.' Under its influence he thought more and more of the folk-tales—of Tannhäuser, of Lohengrin, of the Minstrels' Contest on the Wartburg.

In 1842, hearing that the Dresden Opera would perform 'Rienzi,' he returned to Germany. He had been helped by a Christmas gift—a five-hundred-franc note tactfully sent in the beak of a goose by a friend of his sister's. A brother—a professor of Oriental languages at Leipzig—paid the fare.

Dresden's resources seemed poor after those at Paris. But Dresden did perform 'Rienzi.' Wagner (now nearly thirty) had his first taste of real success. The opera was terribly long, but the audience stayed and was emphatically favourable. Bigger audiences, paying enhanced prices, appeared at repetitions of the work.

By contrast, the 'Flying Dutchman,' produced a little later, seemed gloomy, but it achieved at least a partial success.

All in all, the Dresdeners were impressed; and when deaths left two important posts vacant, Wagner became conductor of the German Opera, and occupied a place formerly held by Weber. (One of his first official tasks was to help Berlioz give a concert.)

The new Royal conductor enjoyed a salary of £225 per annum, and was asked to supervise operas on three or four evenings a week and a certain amount of music for plays on other nights. There was also music at Court and at the Royal Church. There were leagues of Royal Red Tape to unravel. All this work devolved on Wagner and one subordinate director.

Nevertheless, Wagner, deep in Grimm's *German Mythology*, projected new works. He observed that people from outside Dresden were coming specially to hear his opera. They had heard Liszt play a piano transcription of 'Rienzi.' And Liszt, who in Paris had seemed to be only a display pianist ('beleaguered by the cream of Parisian female society'), on further acquaintance revealed himself as an ardent champion of the new music.

In Paris the Opéra continued to present its glittering entertainments. Its patrons, the people who had followed the Government's advice to get rich, the bankers, the ironfounders, and the mill-owners, the old aristocracy, the parvenus, and the climbers, amid the clamour of grandiose entertainments could not hear the songs that were being sung in their factories. Heine could have told them. 'People in our gentle walk of life,' he wrote, 'can have no idea of the demoniac note which runs through these songs. One must hear them . . . in those enormous workshops . . . where the half-naked, defiant figures keep time to their songs with the mighty blows which their great iron hammers strike upon the ringing anvil.'

The political parables of yesterday have a way of dwindling into the fairy-tales of to-day, and a rebel Robin Hood becomes a kind of mythical boy scout. Already the operas which sang of national liberators seemed to have changed their emphasis and to be more about the glory of the nation than the liberty of the subject.

In any case, M. Véron's clients manifested an increasing interest in ballet. And if they carried this to the point of pursuing the ballerinas, it was not in order to conduct an inquiry into the dancers' rates of pay, their hours of labour, or their conditions of employment.

But the songs in the factories, and the pamphlets that the police

could not always suppress, were precisely about such things. So were
the discussions in George Sand's circle. The poor found champions
in the artists; and the artists discussed a variety of 'burning questions'
from the emancipation of women to freedom of the Press, from
Cobden's theories on free trade to Marx's on the class war, from
Kossuth's insurrectionary campaign in Hungary to Saint-Simon's
plea for international peace organizations.

Like Heine's 'Two Grenadiers,' many artists forgot Napoleon's
destructiveness and remembered only that he was a man of the people.
Like Beethoven, many of Napoleon's enemies wondered if his defeat
had not after all been a misfortune. So far had repression reached.
The authorities in country after country were fantastically nervous
of any kind of art that was not frivolous or juvenile or erotic . . . or,
in the Victorian sense, 'sacred.' If there had been any feasible method
of censoring a Czerny exercise, Metternich's spies would have combed
it for subversive semiquavers.

It is only fair to Wagner, if he is blamed for being (as he often was)
'impossible,' to remember the conditions in his world, to remember
that Schumann dared not be a music critic in Austria; that Mendelssohn's relatives hardly dared be Jews in Germany; that Chopin's
compatriots in Paris dared not return to Poland; that . . .

If another example is needed of the operations of censorship, there
is Verdi in Italy.

Verdi's father, a man of peasant origin, was a village innkeeper
and general storekeeper. Verdi's first patron was no Esterhazy or
Cardinal-Archbishop: he was merely a well-to-do grocer—the innkeeper's wholesaler. Here there was no violent contrast between exalted
aristocrat and humble peasant; indeed there was practically social
equality, for in those days the middle classes and the peasant classes
of Italy were both more interested in throwing off the last fetters of
feudalistic government than in fighting one another. There were as
yet few people who foresaw that the more successful tradesmen would
themselves presently become aristocrats.

Signor Barezzi, the grocer, was an enthusiastic amateur musician,
and in his house there met the Philharmonic Society of the small town
of Busseto in the Duchy of Palma. He was soon interested in the innkeeper's boy who trudged from the village into the town to learn music
and from the town back to the village to play the organ on Sundays.
It was with Signor Barezzi's help, supplemented by a charitable trust,
that Verdi at eighteen was able to go to Milan to study. He was too
old for the Conservatoire, and not yet brilliant enough to persuade
the directors to make an exception in their rules. Nevertheless

he obtained good tuition and some experience with a choral society.

Then the conductor of the Busseto Philharmonic died. His several jobs fell vacant, and Verdi felt in honour bound to return and take over. One of the posts was that of organist at the Cathedral; but the clergy, who frowned on Verdi as one chiefly versed in profane music, gratified their moral indignation by giving the place to another. This decision led to so much fighting between the Philharmonic Society and the Church authorities—even to riotings and imprisonments—that the Society was prohibited to meet at all.

In 1836 Verdi married the grocer's daughter. Now his works were beginning to be in some demand. In 1839 an early opera was done at La Scala, Milan. Ricordi, the publisher, paid £64 for the score, a sum which Verdi shared with the impresario who had had faith enough in him to risk the new and unknown.

This impresario, Marelli, powerful both in Milan and in Vienna, was Verdi's great benefactor in his early years; gave him many commissions; encouraged him to bear up after the tragic illnesses that wiped out Verdi's wife and both children in three months; introduced him to librettists; suggested subjects; and forbore to take umbrage at one or two outbursts of temperament.

The Italian audiences, accustomed to the sentimental melodies of Donizetti and Bellini, were struck by the vigour of Verdi's style. These opera-goers were not always people of the most refined taste; they applauded a singer's top notes as an English football crowd applauds the scoring of a goal; but at any rate they were keen—they were 'fans.' Further they were patriots, and in Verdi they recognized the bard of freedom. We can easily be too impressed by the fact that Verdi was always having to fight the Austrian authorities, for there was hardly a subject that did not arouse dark suspicions in the Censor's office. We can remind ourselves that Verdi, peasant-like, was really more interested in country affairs than in national politics. But it is impossible to ignore the fact that a number of his operas provoked patriotic demonstrations, or that he set the fiery works of Victor Hugo to music. Indeed, it was not until after 1848, in which year he wrote a patriotic opera for the revolutionaries, that he partially abandoned the heroic emotions of most of his early works and began to portray the more intimate feelings of his characters.

The Austrian censor continued to be obstructive even then. (The Austrian censor, at one time, forbade the printing of all the works Heine had written *or might yet write*.)

CHAPTER XXIV

The Controversialists (2)

IN Italy, the middle classes, the town workers, and the peasants were united in acclaiming Verdi's music. In the presence of Austrian rule in some parts of Italy and Bourbon despotism in others, everyone who was a patriot, everyone who desired a united, free Italy, was a revolutionary.

In France, however, patriotism and revolution were not alternative battle-cries for one party. The middle classes were divided on the subject of the 'Marseillaise.' The bigger business men agreed with the King, the Church, the remnants of the old aristocracy, and the advance-guard of the new, in hating the sound of the tune. It seemed to them more revolutionary than patriotic. (Time had not yet transformed it into a formula-utterance for State occasions.)

The lesser tradespeople, however, and the professional men, the smaller officials and many artists, were agreed with the factory and railway workers in asking for improved representation in the Government, and greater freedom in argument and education. They sang again of Liberty, Fraternity and Equality.

After the crash of 1848—the violent cymbal crash that momentarily stopped all singing—a new contrapuntal arrangement was heard. There was a re-orchestration of political themes. Louis Philippe abdicated, and the monarchist melody sank to a whisper.

On the other hand the fierce songs in the factories were also suppressed, as 'National Workshops' for the unemployed—hastily improvised by the more extreme revolutionaries—were dismantled. The stately measures of the old aristocracy were heard only occasionally; but the gay, glittering waltzes and galops and can-cans of Offenbach's impudent operettas proclaimed the continuing vigour of the big business men.

The upshot of the 1848 revolution was a not very republican republic—in France. Its influence elsewhere, as in 1830, was to provoke a series of risings across all Europe.

Wagner's music-director, Röckel, was elated when Louis Philippe fled. The prospects of a successful progressive change seemed excellent. In Saxony, the King took warning and permitted the formation of a new liberal ministry. From Vienna the news of revolt particularly satisfied Wagner because the youth of the educated classes were supporting the poorer classes. Röckel, from being only a moderately distinguished musician, suddenly revealed himself as an inventive tactician. But his comrades were shallow thinkers, and Wagner's mood changed to impatience. He, however, was far from clear. He asked for a new-type king, not a despot, not a constitutional king directed by ministers either; but 'a leader among the free'—'the first among equals.' This exercise in mental gymnastics did not save him from being labelled as a dangerous revolutionary.

This dangerous revolutionary went on a short visit to Weimar, to witness the installation of Liszt at the Court of the Grand Duke there. Liszt, to his eternal credit, was turning his back on the dazzling career of greatest of virtuosi, and accepting a post that would enable him to conduct new music, to compose new works, and to stage new operas.

In Dresden, Röckel was arrested. On being bailed, the erstwhile musical director abandoned his job, grew a challenging beard, and with unsuspected efficiency founded a new paper, the *Volksblatt*. The more militant townspeople, welcoming the fugitives beginning to arrive after the Vienna revolt, now began to applaud Wagner more and more heartily as they thought they recognized in the Royal conductor a man sympathetic to them. The orchestral players formed a debating union.

Early in 1849, Bakunin appeared at a rehearsal of the Ninth Symphony. Bakunin, son of an influential Russian family, had renounced inherited wealth to become one of the most conspicuous revolutionaries in Europe. Wanted by the police in Prague, he found asylum in Röckel's house.

This strange figure, in private life a gentle and considerate person, did not shrink from whatever penalties his political logic might lay on him or his associates. Democracy and republicanism he regarded as makeshifts. He did not believe that any human being was good enough to govern anybody else without becoming corrupted. He desired to destroy all government.

Wagner tells us that in his intercourse with Bakunin he 'fluctuated between involuntary horror and irresistible attraction.'

When Röckel had to escape, Wagner undertook to manage the *Volksblatt* in his absence. Meanwhile the poorer townsfolk of Dresden grew impatient of discussion.

A clang of bells from the Church of St. Ann sounded the tocsin of revolt. 'To the barricades' was heard. Barricades . . . mostly market stalls.

So that the local troops might not act in ignorance, Wagner exhibited placards on the barricades, 'Are you on our side against foreign troops?'

This action was a fair sample of the amateurish tactics on the revolutionary side. Bakunin philosophically set himself to enjoy his few days of freedom while the Prussian troops and the inevitable end drew near.

Wagner, crossing a square that was under fire, climbed a tower to see the skirmish. At the top he found a schoolmaster in possession, and the two of them, protected from shot by straw mattresses, passed a night in philosophical discussion.

A thousand miners from the Erzgebirge arrived singing the Marseillaise. The opera house had gone up in flames before Wagner reached his own home again.

Disciplined soldiers, however, are apt to win their battles. Bakunin advised the provisional government to retreat. Wagner, returning from a wagon-requisition in the country, met them in full flight towards Chemnitz. Chemnitz proved to be a trap. In Dresden the Prussian soldiers were soon 'cleaning up.'

Wagner knew he would be wanted by the police. With all possible speed he went to Liszt in Weimar. Thence, under an *alias* to Magdala. Thence, on another friend's false, out-of-date passport to Zürich in Switzerland. His wife, now quite unsympathetic, bewailed his having lost a respectable job for a silly ideal.

For a while he was in Paris again. He had escaped from a revolution and found a cholera epidemic. He observed: 'The old capitalist régime, after its triumphant struggle against the once dreaded socialist propaganda, was exerting itself vigorously to regain the public confidence by its almost insulting pomp.' But the régime neglected sanitation, and the cholera was unimpressed by pomp.

Helped by the ever-generous Liszt, Wagner returned to Zürich and wrote an essay on 'Art and Revolution.' Zürich was a place of refuge for many political exiles, but it was no place for a career. Wagner, unexpectedly assisted by a gift of a thousand marks from an unknown admirer, went off to France yet again, there to become involved in a love-affair in Bordeaux with a married woman (who had fallen in love with 'Tannhäuser').

It came to the point where Jessie Laussot's husband threatened to shoot Wagner. In actual fact he seems to have contented himself with inciting the police to investigate the refugee's passport, which meant the expulsion of Wagner from Bordeaux. The affair fizzled out in a long-distance correspondence between Madame Laussot's mother, and Wagner, and poor, jealous, would-be-respectable Minna.

Liszt, living with a princess (and scandalizing Weimar) and enjoying the patronage of a Grand Duke, did not recoil from the 'dangerous revolutionary' who demanded his help after the Dresden rising. Liszt was in no position to be shocked by other people's unconventional behaviour. Nevertheless he might have been so, for sinners are often censorious. Fortunately for Wagner and for many another composer then anxious to be recognized, Liszt was a man of extraordinarily wide sympathies.

He produced 'Lohengrin,' though its composer was forbidden to return to Germany. He produced the masterpieces of the dead and the more promising works of the living. In addition to acquainting his audience with the merits of Berlioz, Schumann, Mendelssohn, the Russian Nationalists, and some lesser composers, he found time to write his popular Hungarian Rhapsodies, a series of stupendously difficult 'Transcendental Studies,' two programmatic symphonies on 'Faust' and 'Dante,' and a round dozen of symphonic poems.

For some ten years Liszt conducted his crusade. During the latter part of the time his personal life fell more and more under the domination of Princess Sayn-Wittgenstein, who, once she was banished from Russia, became more and more possessive, cutting off all correspondence between Liszt's children and their mother, and disparaging rival composers (particularly the begging and borrowing and commanding Wagner).

Scandal and Court intrigue culminated in the open hostility of the Grand Duchess of Weimar, who, as a sister of the Tsar, was outraged by the Princess's behaviour. A production of 'The Barber of Baghdad' (an opera by Cornelius) was hissed. Really it was Liszt who was hissed.

The Weimar era was at an end. For a while it seemed that Liszt and the Princess might be able to avoid further antagonisms by getting married, for the Pope was willing to grant the lady a divorce from her Russian husband. But even this plan fell through. The opposition persuaded the Pope to reconsider his decision.

(Liszt was now fifty.)

What were the leading ideas in Liszt's crusade? In an age of theorizing, even those who were 'artless' could rely on being supplied with theories. Most of the composers were occupied with nationalism. Some, led by Brahms, sought to preserve formal traditions amidst changes in harmonic style. But without doubt Wagner's theories were the storm-centre of controversy; and Liszt's methods in his bigger works were in some respects a contribution to Wagnerism and in some a derivation from it.

The 'Music of the Future' demanded much more endurance from its devotees than the music of the past. From the state of affairs we have already observed in eighteenth-century opera, when audiences strolled about during a performance, there was a change to an almost church-like atmosphere. Wagner's acts were long. (At Bayreuth, with intervals for unhurried meals, a performance extends over most of a day.) The system of characterizing ideas and people by recurring 'motives' demanded concentrated attention. And everything was *durch-komponiert*—composed on and on in an endlessly narrative way without formal endings that might invite applause. For opera had become Music-Drama, and, as such, had to satisfy the canons of epic-dramatic art. For the third time in musical history, a composer sought to recall the condition of Greek art. But, unlike the Renaissance pioneers, and unlike Gluck, Wagner remembered that the Greeks regarded music-drama as part of their religious worship; and Wagner's attitude to the old gods of his people was something more than a connoisseur's attitude to a picturesque legend.

A great many critics found the legends tiresome, the music long-winded. But there was a sustained power in Wagner's music that converted thousands to admiration. The unfamiliar idiom was soon revealed as being full of melody. The thick score contained elaborate detail that captured the attention on rehearings of the music. It attained heroic stature. It was not only great music; it was greatness-music.

Whereas Wagner had fled from the police to find himself in the midst of an epidemic, Verdi fled from that same Parisian cholera to begin a conflict with the police.

After the failure of the 1848 attempt to achieve Italian independence, Verdi produced three of his most popular operas: 'Rigoletto,' 'Il Trovatore,' and 'La Traviata.' The first was based on Victor Hugo's story, *Le Roi s'amuse*. To treat of kings otherwise than reverently was enough to cause trouble.

Verdi escaped from prosecution as Beethoven had done—because the authorities were too fond of good music to be robbed of it by unpalatable opinions. It was the local chief of the *Austrian police* who suggested, among many alterations, that the King should be transformed into the duke of an unimportant town and that the title should be changed to 'Rigoletto.' His adjustments were so skilful that even Victor Hugo came to accept them with a good grace.

'Trovatore,' as a drama of chivalry and a portrayal of aspects of mother love (Verdi's mother had recently died), was immediately successful. But 'La Traviata' (based on Dumas's *La Dame aux Camélias*) was at first regarded as being as immoral as 'Rigoletto' was seditious.

For six more years Verdi had to face these fights with censorship before Italy became free. And on one occasion—writing an opera for the Paris Exhibition of 1855—he quarrelled with Scribe because Scribe's libretto, 'I Vespri Siciliani,' was not to a patriotic Italian's taste.

It was in the year before the Austro-Italian war that the battle against censorship reached a climax. 'Un Ballo in Maschera' (to a Scribe libretto about Gustavus III of *Sweden*) had to have its background moved to—*Boston*, this time to satisfy the Papal censorship. The Neapolitans, for whom the opera had been written, chalked up on their walls, 'Viva Verdi.' The composer's name concealed the name and title of their future King, and thus the inscription was doubly seditious:

Vittorio Emmanuele, Re d'Italia (Victor Emmanuel, King of Italy).

The Austrian War interfered for a while with Verdi's life in the country. There he was the complete farmer, attending to crops and livestock and indulging in a little shooting. He was forty-six when he married the lady who had been living for some few years on his estate. He was a year older when, rather against his inclinations, he allowed himself to be elected deputy in Cavour's first Italian parliament.

Once Italian independence was achieved, Verdi left the conduct of the affairs of the new nation to others. He was never an active parliamentarian, and his political station was midway between the right and the left parties. He remained a deputy for five years.

The Paris Exhibition of 1855 at which Verdi had quarrelled with Scribe had been held in rivalry to an earlier exhibition in London. In 1851 the Crystal Palace was erected in Hyde Park to house samples of the Empire's goods together with exotic treasures from foreign lands, and to be a seat of judgment on artistic wares.

Both exhibitions were milestones in Berlioz's career, for at the London Exhibition he was a member of the jury, and on the eve of the later Paris Exhibition he heard his 'Te Deum' (through the generosity of an organ-builder). The 'Te Deum' had originally been planned when Prince Louis Napoleon became President of the French Republic. It was offered for the coronation when this same prince, forgetting his oaths and upsetting the constitution, made himself Emperor Napoleon III. It was now brought forward again at the opening of the exhibition. For the closing ceremony Berlioz wrote a cantata 'L'Impériale.' He was now a half-successful celebrity, an often-attacked musician-laureate, a campaigner who consoled himself for many bitter disappointments with a few great public triumphs.

One of his greatest triumphs had been the Berlioz Festival Week at Weimar in 1852, when Liszt had produced 'Benvenuto Cellini.'

One of his greatest disappointments had been the failure of the same work in London. It had been hissed—in the presence, too, of the Queen—and what was to have been a complimentary after-theatre banquet dwindled away into a little supper for Berlioz and *The Times* critic. But the rival Philharmonic Societies in London competed for his services, he possessed the order of the Legion of Honour, and a great exhibition offered occasion for performances.

So while Napoleon III, crying 'Empire is Peace,' proceeded to make war, Berlioz composed State works in his rather war-like style to celebrate the triumphs of peaceful industry.

While Berlioz had been conducting for the New Philharmonic Society in London, Wagner had been conducting for the old (and still existent) Philharmonic Society.

Wagner, on this visit, gives us a glimpse of Victorian musical England—a performance of 'The Messiah' at Exeter Hall, London. 'An evening spent in listening to an oratorio . . . is almost as good as going to church. Everyone in the audience holds a Handel piano-score in the same way as one holds a Prayer Book in church. . . . At the beginning of the Hallelujah Chorus it is considered proper for everyone to rise from his seat. This movement, which probably originated in an expression of enthusiasm, is now carried out at each performance of The Messiah with painful precision.'

(Mendelssohn, in similar circumstances, had said, 'I thought on the immense improvement which such a number of *real amateurs* must necessarily produce in the country which may boast of it.')

Between 1848 ('Lohengrin') and 1853 (the beginning of the first opera of 'The Ring') Wagner had sorted out his ideas in a series of arguments and pamphlets. He ceased temporarily to be an active composer. (He found time for the Bordeaux affair.) Such prose works as *Art and Revolution, Jewry and Music,* and *Opera and Drama* reveal the spirit that animated him. Like Beethoven's excursions into political music, they help us to understand the sociology in 'The Ring,' his attitude to love and sex in 'Tristan,' his mystical journey to Christianity in 'Parsifal.'

Gradually he abandoned the political enthusiasms of his youth. He fell under the spell of Schopenhauer's *The World as Will and Idea*. Commenting on it, Wagner wrote: 'For those who hoped to find some philosophical justification for political and social agitation on behalf of so-called "individual freedom" there was certainly no support to be found here, where all that was demanded was absolute renunciation of all such methods of satisfying the claims of personality. . . . It is from this perception of the nullity of the visible world

. . . that all tragedy is derived. . . . On looking afresh into my Nibelun-
gen poem I recognized with surprise that the very things that now
embarrassed me theoretically had long been familiar to me in my own
poetical conception.'

The 'Ring of the Nibelungs' was complete as a poem, though the
music for its four constituent music-dramas would not be completed
for many years to come. The original 'Siegfried's Death' project
grew into 'The Ring' very slowly. 'Das Rheingold' was finished in 1854;
'Die Walküre' in 1856; 'Siegfried' after a promising beginning was
set aside for *twelve years* ('Tristan and Isolde' and 'The Mastersingers'
being composed meanwhile). Wagner was in his sixties by the time
'Götterdämmerung' completed the whole scheme.[1] By then, the one-
time friend of Röckel and Bakunin had become an idol in a new,
imperialist Germany.

Bernard Shaw, in his *Perfect Wagnerite*, suggests that 'The Ring'
is an allegorical poem about capitalism written by a Socialist. Wagner's
'Socialism,' however, is rather like the 'National Socialism' of Fascist
Germany. It is mixed up with cloudy assertions about the Nordic
Race, folk-lore, leadership, and so forth. Siegfried is a Führer's ideal.
Sword in hand, he makes it his job to vanquish the unidealistic, money-
grubbing dwarfs, to assert his masculine superiority over Woman,
and to sweep aside the doubts of the intelligentsia gods.

Wagner, endlessly frustrated by commercial society, fighting his
way through a tangle of debts multiplied by usury, and suffering an
exile's homesickness, came to glorify a mythical, uncorrupted true-
German. Compared with this ideal specimen, all the tradesmen who
had trusted Wagner with goods, all the friends whose friendship had
foundered on the rock of unpaid loans, every publisher or theatrical
director who had not foreseen the greatness of his achievements-to-
come, began to crystallize out into one clear-cut form. The capitalists,
the men who give up everything for Gold after they have been rightly
spurned by Beauty, appeared in dramatic form as the dwarfs of 'The
Ring.'

The dwarfs were not unlike Wagner's picture of the Jews.

Wagner's pamphlet on the Jews anticipates the arguments of the
Nazis. According to him, the Jew is always a foreigner; the Jew's
voice betrays his foreign origin even if his German accent is good;
the Jew has forgotten all but a little Hebrew and is therefore without

---

[1] 'If an architect were to spend half his life designing a huge and elaborate
building which was not only unauthorized and unwanted, but for which
the very materials did not at the time exist anywhere in the world, that
would be a fair parallel to Wagner's chosen task.' (Dyson in *The Progress
of Music*.)

a native language or a native culture or a folk-lore; the Jews are money-manipulators; a Jewish-German marriage produces only Jews. . . .

In order to bolster up his case in the realm of art, Wagner attacks Mendelssohn, Meyerbeer, and the poet Heine. Mendelssohn, he says, writes music as Jews write German—with a foreigner's regard for style, but without inner comprehension. Meyerbeer is merely 'a Jew banker to whom it occurred to compose operas.' Heine, as an alien, is a mere spectator—an observant wit, but not a poet. Wagner's argument implies that however much a Jew's verse may seem to be like poetry, it cannot really be so. The closer the resemblance, the greater the deceit. (Among those deceived by Heine were all the most notable song composers in Europe.)

History's sequel to this attack is tragi-comic. Jewish musicians, like Mahler and Bruno Walter, were leading Wagnerians during times of bitter anti-Semitism. And later, in Palestinian communities where German refugee musicians sought to restore a treasury of folk-song in a revived Hebrew, the home-sickness of the exiles still turned their thoughts to a Germany that used to be. The ancient Israelites by the waters of Babylon thought of the good old days in Jerusalem. The new Israelites by the waters of Jordan thought of the good old days in Bayreuth.

Though Wagner the poet and musician was withdrawing into philosophy and religion, Wagner the man, pursued by political influences, was pursuing—Frau Mathilde Wesendonck.

She was the young wife of a German engaged in the silk trade with America. The Wesendoncks lived near Zürich. They were rich and generous. Otto Wesendonck had paid for an Italian holiday for Wagner.

It was after Wagner's return from his London visit that events began to move. The Wesendoncks were building a new house. In friendship for the Wagners, Otto Wesendonck bought a little house nearby which the Wagners could occupy at a nominal rent.

For us, the product of this dangerous proximity is 'Tristan and Isolde.' Wagner was beginning to doubt whether 'The Ring' would ever be performed; he was inspired by his Schopenhauerian mood; Mathilde gave reality to Isolde, or maybe his thinking of Isolde stimulated a passion for Mathilde.

'Tristan and Isolde' was not finished in Zürich. The Wesendonck affair lost its savour as soon as Minna Wagner was able to intercept a letter from Richard to Mathilde.

Wagner went to Venice, and his relationship with the Wesendoncks became distant. (Otto Wesendonck was large-spirited enough again to help Wagner financially on a later occasion.) Minna went to Dresden.

She was not a political exile; and she still hoped to gain a pardon for her husband in Saxony.

It was at the time when Wagner was putting aside the uncompleted 'The Ring' that Berlioz set to work on his great twin Virgilian operas— 'Les Troyens.' The Trojan Wars had long haunted him as subject-matter for opera, and after two years of hard work he completed 'The Capture of Troy' and 'The Trojans at Carthage.' Wagner had neglected 'The Ring,' fearing it would never be performed: Berlioz could well hope for better fortune. But fortune was niggardly; she allowed Berlioz to hear only the second opera before he died. And although she granted him hearings of his next, and final, opera ('Beatrice and Bénédict' based on 'Much Ado about Nothing') they were not Parisian performances.

Years earlier he had told Wagner that it was hard to succeed in Paris. His last triumph was not there but in St. Petersburg. Instead of a little supper with a music critic, there was a banquet with five hundred aristocratic guests.

But Berlioz, now sixty-five, was ill. His only son, on foreign naval service in the West Indies, had died of yellow fever. His second wife was dead. Even Estelle, his first love whose memory he had cherished since childhood, would permit him nothing more than an exchange of letters, though he had called on the astonished grandmother and offered marriage.

Paris, which had provided him with few of his triumphs, accorded him a triumphal funeral (1869).

If Paris was often unkind to Berlioz it was insulting to Wagner.

We left Wagner in Venice—where the Saxon Ambassador made an attempt to get him expelled. Wagner, however, remained until he observed that the music-loving Venetians were not applauding the best Austrian military bands, and that war was imminent. When the war of Italian liberation was over, Wagner visited Paris once more. (Paris was in triumphant mood. Napoleon III had helped Cavour and Garibaldi establish Victor Emmanuel and had received in exchange Victor Emmanuel's family possessions in the Savoy, and the town of Nice which was Garibaldi's birthplace.)

Paris was hostile to Wagner. It stayed away from his concerts. It attacked him through the Press. It shared Meyerbeer's not surprising dislike for the exile.

A few Frenchmen did, it is true, become Wagnerians—the poet Baudelaire, and the young musician Saint-Saëns who was so uncannily skilful at improvising piano-versions from Wagner's full scores.

(Wagner said in later years that he heard that Saint-Saëns had 'set himself up as a composer.') But most of Wagner's adherents were foreigners. The erstwhile revolutionary could count on the Prussian Ambassador and Princess Metternich; and the Princess was persuading the Emperor to permit 'Tannhäuser' to be given at the Opéra. Indeed Wagner's revolutionary past was being forgotten. He could now return to all Germany except Saxony.

Despite ambassadors and princesses, Paris remained obstructive. It wanted ballet. If only Wagner would write a ballet for the second act of 'Tannhäuser,' all would be well, since fashionable late-diners never arrived for the first act of an opera.

The fashionable late-diners resolved to teach Wagner to respect Parisian customs. The gay young men-about-town, members of the Jockey Club, arrived in force for the second act of the second performance of 'Tannhäuser' and made an uproar.

The third performance was postponed to a Sunday, when box-holders could usually be relied upon to stay away. But *Les Jockeys* forwent *le week-end* for once. They whistled; they played flagcolets; they yelled. Princess Metternich observed with patrician scorn: 'Away with your free France! In Vienna, where at least there is a genuine aristocracy, it would be unthinkable for a Prince Liechtenstein or Schwarzenburg to scream from his box for a ballet in "Fidelio." '

Wagner withdrew the piece. But it inspired interest in him. There was even a short-lived project for a *Théâtre Wagner*.

In the next year Schott, the publisher, gave Wagner 3,000 marks as instalment on the as yet uncompleted 'Mastersingers.' (Wagner suggested that Schott should support him for two years to a limit of 20,000 francs.) The earlier operas were gaining favour throughout Germany.

The Saxon Government, too, was relenting at last. It gave Wagner permission to join Minna in Dresden.

It released Röckel after thirteen years.

Support came from far and wide. St. Petersburg arranged a concert of Wagner's music, and the composer conducted a picked orchestra before the Society of Nobles. The Grand Duchess Helena, who had helped Berlioz, helped him too.

Another patron of Berlioz's helped Wagner in Germany. Prince Hohenzollern-Hechingen arranged a concert at his castle and sent Wagner away with 4,000 marks (roughly £200) with regret that it was impossible to be more liberal.

Nevertheless Wagner was still heavily in debt.

Travelling from town to town, arousing interest in his music dramas, he found time to work on 'The Mastersingers'; to pay attention to one mistress and then a second; and to begin to upset another marriage.

Liszt's one surviving child, Cosima, had married a celebrated young pianist-conductor, Hans von Bülow. The young couple, like Liszt, were Wagner mad. Before long, Cosima and Wagner were in love. The situation, ordinary enough in superficial appearance, was unusual in that all concerned were people of exceptional quality; and when, in the course of years, there developed a crisis, they remembered Liszt's motto—'more than *Noblesse oblige, Génie oblige*.' (By that time Minna was dead.)

But meanwhile there occurred an incident so melodramatic in character as to read like fiction. Wagner had been chased by creditors and had gone to Switzerland. Then he had gone quietly to Stuttgart, hoping that his debts would not find him out.

One evening he was annoyed to receive a visiting card. The fact that it was inscribed 'Secretary to the King of Bavaria' suggested that the caller was not a bailiff. Nevertheless Wagner said Not at Home. The landlord of the hotel insisted that the gentleman from Munich had urgent business. Reluctantly, Wagner made an appointment, anticipating disaster. Next morning, the Royal secretary arrived with a letter. Says Wagner, 'In words which, though few, penetrated to the very core of my being, the youthful monarch' (Ludwig II of Bavaria, then eighteen years old) 'confessed his great partiality for my work, and announced his firm resolve to keep me near him as his friend, so that I might escape any malignant stroke of fate.'

Before long not only was Wagner established at the Court of his Royal protector, but von Bülow, too—as Court Pianist. For a while von Bülow did not suspect that he had a rival in Cosima's affections; nor did the jealous young King know that *he* had a rival in Wagner's. The King, who was abnormal and already advanced on the road to madness, may be forgiven for not understanding the situation. But that Hans von Bülow should have accepted Cosima-and-Wagner's first child as his own is extraordinary.

Whatever the state of domestic affairs may have been, the state of public affairs was unhappy. The Bavarians were hostile to the Royal favourite. They resented so much attention and support being given to him, to the neglect, so they felt, of the common weal. After two years he had to go away from Munich.

For a while he was able to return, because the defeat of Bavaria (by Prussia) in the Seven Weeks' War had led to the downfall of the minister who was Wagner's chief opponent. 'The Mastersingers' was produced. It was conducted by von Bülow, who by now had accepted, or appeared to accept, a second daughter as his own.

But emotional storms in private and a campaign of calumny in public drove Wagner to confess to King Ludwig. Wagner had found in Cosima a woman with whom, he felt, he could live permanently in a state of sympathy. There was no alternative but departure. Once again Wagner went to Switzerland; and there, domestically quiet at Triebschen (the villa near Lucerne where he had lived the first time he left Munich), he settled down with Cosima. There Cosima bore him a third child—a son. The two daughters had been named after Wagnerian heroines, Isolde and Eva. The son was called Siegfried, for Wagner had resumed working on 'The Ring,' and 'Siegfried' was being composed after the twelve-years break. When at last divorce made marriage possible, Wagner's tribute to Cosima was 'The Siegfried Idyll,' first performed outside her bedroom on her birthday (Christmas Day, 1870).

The other people concerned in the affair behaved well. Cosima's husband and her father both remained devoted to Wagner's music. Neither let his private feelings affect his artistic judgment. Only the mad young King never recovered from the blow. The world at large scarcely noticed, for the Prussians were defeating the French in the 1870 war that made France again a republic and welded the German States into a united empire.

Wagner was now the most discussed musician in Europe. (To this day, book after book is written about him.)

But while he was climbing to eminence there were newcomers on the musical scene. Before we bid farewell to him, to Liszt, and to Verdi, we must observe some of their contemporaries, and travel to new countries. There were the Russians. There was Brahms. We must extend the musical map to Scandinavia in the north and Spain in the south. We must remind ourselves that Bohemia had a voice of its own long before Czecho-Slovakia became a political entity. We must observe the folk-tales, which the earlier Romantics presented quite seriously, transform themselves into 'romances' with plenty of 'local colour' splashed on the scenery. We must see how the hero-stories about peoples' liberators became either mystical allegories or parade-ground displays. We must listen to the symphonists borrowing from the old folk-musicians, and hear the popular song-writers borrowing from yesterday's symphonists.

But before we do that we ought to see by what chemistry the age of science was mixing the newly imported outlandish pigments on the orchestral palette. We must see what the inventors of an age of engineering were able to contribute to the assemblies of tubing and wiring and carpentering that we call musical instruments.

CHAPTER XXV

Science and Orchestration

WE have already observed how the violin and its family companions supplanted the old viols. Since the days of the great craftsmen of Cremona there has been no advance in quality. Violins, violas, violoncellos (cellos), and double basses, which were brought to their finest pitch during the 'classic' period, were ready to give an almost human, song-like quality to the orchestral music of the 'romantic' era. The romantic composers always regarded the strings as the foundation of the orchestra. It is only recently that an anti-romantic age has shown less and less respect for the violin family.

As compared with the string family, the wood-wind and brass-wind instruments have been modified again and again. Craftsmen have experimented endlessly with the length and thickness of tubes, the positions of valves and vents, the shape of brass mouthpieces, the arrangement of the 'saltspoons' on the wood-wind instruments, the selecting of reeds. And while they have been exhibiting their wares in shop windows and trade exhibitions, teachers have argued about systems of fingering and methods of lip-control.

Of the great inventors in this field, special mention must be made of Adolphe Sax, whose name is recalled by the saxophone—an instrument that attempts to combine brass and wood-wind characteristics. Sax, following the example of his father, pursued the calling of instrument maker with enormous success. He produced new families of instruments—saxhorns and saxophones—and improved various existing instruments in detail. Many composers of his day sang his praises—particularly Berlioz, whose sense of orchestral effect and whose courage in assembling enormous orchestral forces was unique. Sax gained many gold medals at those industrial exhibitions that Paris and London delighted in, and continued to be an important influence until, in old age, he fell on hard times.

We are reminded of other inventors when we look at the makers' names on our best pianos. It is interesting to note that the history of the pianoforte shows how the nations of the world gradually joined in the race for industrial supremacy against England. Though the pre-pianos were made in the great musical centres—Italy and Germany—the kind of piano that ousted the harpsichord came to be made in the first industrial country. A piano is a species of machine, and England was the machine-shop of the world. Beethoven obtained his best piano from John Broadwood of London.[1]

Then, as France became more and more an industrial power, we begin to hear of Pleyel and Erard. (Erard, by the way, made the harp what it is to-day.)

Supremacy shifts to Germany, a late-comer in the industrial field. The German makers were, some of them, pianists—Bechstein, for example—dissatisfied with existing instruments.

Lastly to America. Steinway's were originally a German family; but a branch went to America after the troubles of 1848 and Americanized the spelling of their name. By 1876 they were a firm of a million and a half dollars. . . .

Piano-making is now a giant industry. To understand piano music we must not merely discuss Chopin's private life, we must give a moment's thought to the workaday lives of lumbermen and ironfounders, metallurgists and cabinetmakers. It is true that there is only one Chopin, but the workman must not be forgotten. He it is who decides whether Chopin can fling a web of cadenza-notes wider than Beethoven could, and ensures that Debussy's bass octaves will vibrate over a period that would have been impossible in Weber's day.

There are two kinds of orchestration. Musicians are generally most reverent about the kind that is so intimately part of a composition that we simply cannot imagine any rearrangement of the existing score. As against this there is the kind that is an afterthought. Academic musicians are inclined to cite jazz as a dreadful example of this, for a dance-tune originally composed for piano reappears in a bewildering variety of orchestrations.

A great deal of orchestral music is, however, composed in a spirit of compromise. The composer does not write every detail straightaway in its final form; neither does he dig his ideas out of the keyboard and then transplant them. He sketches his work on a 'short score'—drafting out his string passages and brass chords and wood-wind arabesques in the rough, and leaving until later the decision whether the violas shall stand on their own or be supported by bassoons.

As in the chapter on harmony, let us follow a student through a course of orchestration.

[1] Muzio Clementi (1752–1832) a composer, virtuoso, and teacher still remembered for études and sonatinas, established the pianistic style on instruments manufactured by his firm in London. His assistant and pupil, John Field (Dublin 1782–Moscow 1837), was the first composer of pieces called 'Nocturnes.'

Firstly he learns to recognize instruments by their sound, and then to imagine their sounds in his head. From this, by dint of careful listening, he has to become acquainted with combinations of sounds —flute with clarinet, or trumpet and oboe.

He will discover that string tones blend easily; that trumpet and trombone have affinities, but that the horn tone, being less 'brassy,' is often more easily blended with wood-wind than with the other brass tones; that wood-wind tones are often easier to blend with horns or strings than with one another. He will observe which percussion notes merge into the general tone and which 'stick out.' That is to say he will contrast the tuned drums (tympani or kettle drums) with the 'fire irons' (cymbals, triangles, and so forth).

Then, having understood each instrument's main characteristics, he has to learn its exceptional ones. He has to know at which point a voice gets lost in the general conversation and at which it becomes shrill and insistent. He has to know what tonal modifications can be made by 'mutes.' If he is to be a dance-music orchestrator he must understand the mysteries of playing into bowler hats or using a 'wa-wa' mute. If he is to understand radio work, he must know the difference between blowing hard a long way from the microphone and blowing soft nearby—the difference, that is, between a faint shout from a distance and an equally faint whisper in the ear. This complicates matters. In a concert hall, a *fortissimo* is loud. In a radio studio, however, a *fortissimo* may be soft if the instrument is distant, but the soft sound will have the forced *quality* of a loud note. Conversely, near the microphone, we can hear a *pianissimo* note quite loudly, but with the unforced gentleness of a soft note.

There are a few technical stumbling-blocks. The worst is provided by the transposing instruments.

A trumpet will serve as an example. A trumpet does not have a separate piece of machinery for each note, as a piano has. It is based on the principle of a bugle, which has no machinery at all. Yet a bugle can produce an arpeggio—the notes of a chord one after another— by simple manipulation of the bugler's lips. (In the chapter on sound we observed that one string, or one tube, can produce several sounds.) Let us assume that the bugle produces the chord of B flat and is therefore a B-flat bugle.

By modifying the bugle, and adding pistons to it, we enable it to add in extra lengths of tube. We now have a trumpet. Each piston shifts the trumpet into a new key. The original tube-length and the three pistons altogether provide four positions; and, with three notes available in each position, we have the twelve notes that music demands.

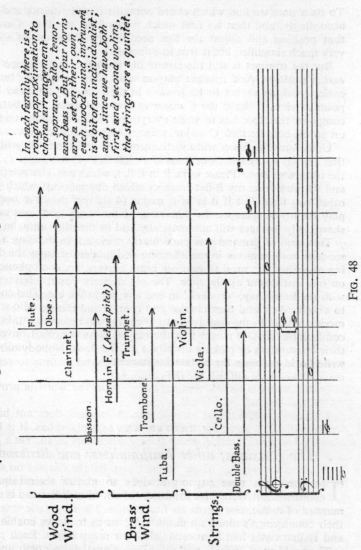

Approximate Range.
(Upward range can be extended by good players.)

In each family there is a rough approximation to choral arrangement — soprano, alto, tenor, and bass. — But four horns are a set on their own; each wood-wind instrument is a bit of an individualist; and, since we have both first and second violins, the strings are a quintet.

Flute.
Oboe.
Clarinet.
Bassoon.
Horn in F. (Actual pitch)
Trumpet.
Trombone.
Violin.
Viola.
'Cello.
Tuba.
Double Bass.

Wood Wind.
Brass Wind.
Strings.

FIG. 48

To fix a note we find which chord contains it and adjust the pistons accordingly, and then we find which part of the chord to aim at in that position and adjust the lips accordingly. (This explanation is very much simplified but is true in principle.)

But the trumpet is still fundamentally in B flat. B-flat chord is its *easiest* position. And trumpet players when they are playing in their easiest position expect to be *reading* in their easiest key. From their point of view, B flat is the *C major of their instrument*. The unhappy composer therefore has to write everything for them a tone too high on paper, because *their* C major is consistently a tone too low.

Unfortunately, many wind instruments are difficult to play in keys that employ many sharps or flats. If a piece is in D flat major (5 flats) the trumpeter says, 'Please write it in E flat, which has only three flats, and I'll play it on my B-flat trumpet which automatically adds in the other two flats. But if it is in E major (4 sharps) then I'd prefer to play on my A trumpet. In that case, please write in G major (one sharp). My trumpet will automatically add in the other three sharps.'

This kind of demand was particularly prevalent in the days before modern improvements in manufacture and modern standards of playing abolished the need to pamper brass players, some of whom play on one instrument all the time. The old masters would begin a piece with the horns, say, 'crooked' in one key, and then change the crook to another key, and then change and change and change as the piece modulated, all in the endeavour to keep the wind players within their comfortable keys. It meant that the players were constantly adjusting their instruments or picking up others off the floor. Nobody dared to write florid passages for certain instruments. And reading scores was made exceedingly difficult for the conductor.

CHAPTER XXVI

The Russians; other Nationalists; and Brahms

THE romantics were patriots anxious to glorify their respective countries. But Weber, for instance, did not have to invent a German manner of music, nor Verdi an Italian one. Their operatic texts and their countrymen's mood no doubt inflected their music, but German and Italian styles had been established for many generations.

The problem of devising a specifically national manner did, however, present itself to the Russians. Russia emerged into musical history during the romantic era. Her musicians, too, were patriots. Even in

Russia the echo of new ideas had been heard, and artists were discussing the Russian people as something more than mere possessions of the Tsar and the Grand Dukes.

But there was no point in bringing out old Russian stories, the myths, the histories, and the legends, and then dressing them up in German or Italian music.

The problem was solved by Glinka. Glinka is one of those composers, like Gluck, whose influence is felt mainly through the works of other composers.

His first contribution came from childhood memories. 'My father would send for my uncle's musicians, a small orchestra drawn from the serfs on his estate, which lay eight versts away from ours . . . During supper Russian national songs were played . . . and perhaps the songs which I heard in my childhood first suggested the idea of making use of our national music.'

Glinka's second contribution was borrowed from Berlioz. He was an enthusiastic supporter of Berlioz's Russian tours and avidly learned what there was to know of the new-style orchestration.

The old tunes and the new orchestration were both heard in his opera, 'A Life for the Tsar.' But these were not the only elements that made it a pioneer work. Whereas many of the earlier romantic operas in Germany and France had been attacks on despotic monarchy, Glinka's was a loyalist work. It is true that some of the older nobility, accustomed to French and Italian music, sneered at the 'music of coachmen,' but nobody said it was seditious. In fact its first performance (1836) took place before the Imperial family. Its composer, hailed as the Patriarch of genuinely Russian music, was afterwards made choirmaster of the Imperial Chapel.

Glinka had yet another contribution to make to the craft of music. He went abroad to study other people's folk-tunes, and the result of his travels was that he wrote some Spanish music.

Musicians were quick to learn his new ideas. Patriotism of Weber's and Verdi's kind, full of peoples-versus-tyranny, was rivalled by patriotism of a loyalist kind. The two kinds existed side by side. Some composers cried king-and-country with genuine feeling because they lived contentedly and proudly under monarchies which, in their view, were not tyrannies. Some cried the same slogan because they knew on which side their bread was buttered. And some devoted their chief attention to scenery—the forests and mountains of their native lands—and to the quaint old customs of the peasants.

'Local colour' became a commodity. Most musicians, it is true, were faithful to the folk-music of their own country, and used it as an important ingredient in their nationalist recipes. But others imported it. If the nations of Europe could import South Sea pineapples to add to their menus and Chinese jade to set off their clothes, the musicians could import Arabian tunes to weave into the fabric of Oriental fantasies and Negro tunes to impart the right touch to new-world symphonies.

Glinka pointed the way.

Balakirev followed him. Balakirev's enthusiasm attracted disciples, some of whom turned out to be greater than their master. These composers, a group that included Borodin and Rimsky-Korsakoff, transformed Russia into an exporter of some of the most picturesque music the world has ever known. Some of it, like Rimsky-Korsakoff's 'Scheherezade,' is pure fairy-tale, come from a Baghdad that is peopled by Tartars rather than Arabs and set among steppes rather than in the desert. Some of it is full of vodka spirit and peasant carousals. But most of it is infused with the melancholy that romantic observers used to see in every Muscovite. Even when the gaieties of St. Petersburg are expressed in an elegant waltz there is a suggestion that outside the ballroom the snow is falling.

Of the thoroughgoing nationalists the most striking figure, perhaps, was Moussorgsky.

Outside the Balakirev group, but friendly to it, stood Tchaikovsky. (Moussorgsky, born in 1839, was the older of the two, by one year.)

Moussorgsky has only recently been rescued from the effects of too much editing. That the present-day Russian State publishing department should have gone to great pains to do this becomes understandable when one reads Rosa Newmarch's description of the composer.

'He was a true child of the sixties, of that period of moral and intellectual ferment which followed the accession of Alexander II and the emancipation of the serfs. Of the little group of composers then striving to give expression to their newly awakened nationality, none was so entirely carried away by the literary and political movements of the time as Moussorgsky. Every man was asking himself and his comrades the question posed by the most popular novel of the day, *What shall we do?* The answer was: "Throw aside the social and artistic conventions. Make art the handmaiden of humanity. Hold out the hand of fellowship to the liberated masses and learn from them the true purpose of life." To this democratic and utilitarian spirit . . . Moussorgsky strove to give expression in music . . . as Dostoievsky and Tolstoy expressed it in fiction. . . . His songs are a series of human documents. . . . The whole army of the "humiliated and offended" supplied him with subjects. He had also a vein of sardonic humour, and his musical satires upon the critics, priests, and minor officials of his day are unique in their clever mimicry and mordant sarcasm.'

It seems almost incredible, but we have Borodin's word for it, that, as a foppish young officer in a crack regiment, Moussorgsky would play the piano at parties 'and with coquettish gestures play bits from "Trovatore" or "Traviata" while around him all sat entranced, murmuring "Charmant! Delicieux!"'

A later picture of him is very different—a picture of poverty and drunkenness and also of a fierce idealism that rejected the quest for beauty for its own sake. 'The goal of the artist,' said Moussorgsky, 'should be to study the most subtle features of human beings and of humanity in the mass.' Much of his work remained unfinished, and his one enduring masterpiece, 'Boris Godounov,' was misunderstood even by his friends. We have only to compare Borodin's 'Prince Igor' (which has been described as having as much historical significance as the Arthurian legends) with 'Boris,' a work in which the people, customarily in the background, are active participants in the drama (and the love scenes only incidental), to understand the critics' perplexity. The committee of the Imperial Opera rejected the work even after Moussorgsky had made considerable alterations to please them. Rimsky-Korsakoff persuaded himself that Moussorgsky's unconventionalities in harmony and orchestration were merely signs of incompetence, and drastically revised and edited the works after Moussorgsky's death. The Russian composers who regarded their country as a decorative subject for glowing pictures, and who felt quite able to present the customs of Persians and Spaniards and Chinese in their fantasies, could not appreciate a colleague who mistrusted his ability to understand even such near neighbours as the Ukrainians. But, to do them justice, they did stand by Moussorgsky in his personal misfortunes, and tried to make life comfortable for him after he lost his humble Government job and before epilepsy and paralysis killed him.

Tchaikovsky was among those who never understood Moussorgsky. They were children of the same era and they were both typical Russians. But Tchaikovsky was a European as well as a Russian; and perhaps he felt the same about Moussorgsky as he did about Wagner, who, he said, 'killed his colossal creative genius with theories.'

Whereas Moussorgsky was concerned with the Russian masses, Tchaikovsky spoke as one melancholy person to all other melancholy persons, pouring out his many troubles and his few joys to a world that listened because he never alienated its sympathies by sarcasm or aloofness. His wretchedness never becomes squalid; his resignation is never cowardly; he does not philosophize. He is the poetic sufferer, all the more attractive because he can assume an expression of gaiety and brilliance. Eloquent melody, rich harmonies, and a ballet-composer's sense of rhythm hold the listener's attention and add to his memories.

Moussorgsky once complained that 'whereas he often heard painters or writers express live ideas, musicians, to his knowledge, never did anything of the kind.' He declared that writers and scientists had done more to mould his style than ever a classical composer had done.

But in an age of advancing science and developing industry most musicians were at a loss to deal with 'live ideas.' Artists, looking at steam engines and factories and slums, felt only aversion. Neither their own ancient alchemy nor the modern scientist's formulæ could show how to transmute such things into music. Mountains and torrents and oceans—yes. But not bricks and steel and coal.

More and more, music became an art of escape. It escaped into the twilit world of Delibes's ballets, the romantic mountains of Grieg's Norway or Smetana's Bohemia, the ballrooms and theatres of Offenbach's Paris or Strauss's Vienna. Even the theatrical 'realism' of Bizet's 'Carmen' meant flight into a land of sunshine and bullfights. And the profound philosophy of Goethe's 'Faust' could be withdrawn from the libretto of Gounod's opera until only a melodramatic legend was left.

Many people found in music a perfect exit from a world full of problems. Wagner, it is true, remained full of problems and theories. But he was a symbolist. And, ignoring the symbolism, you could accept 'The Ring' as a story about gnomes and giants and enchanted goddesses; you could regard Tristan as someone like Tennyson's Sir Lancelot or any other schoolgirl hero-knight. Even when they were producing religious music the composers took you away into a legendary world where Parsifal went in search of the Holy Grail. Verdi's 'Requiem' and Brahms's, for all their nobility and sincerity, seemed like some music on the subject of Christianity; not, as with Bach or Palestrina, like Christianity transformed into music.

But the problems remained. The manufacturer in the orchestra-stalls came back from music-land to the problem of exporting pianos to countries where piano factories were many and efficient; the student in the gallery came back to the problem of paying for lessons that would enable him to give lessons in towns where teachers' brass plates shone on countless front-doors and pupils were too poor to pay fees; the second flautist in the orchestra changing into Hungarian military uniform in an after-concert cab, on his way to appear in Herr Donau's orchestra at the Duchess of Mayfair's all-night dance, came back to the problem of finding time to practise, so as to continue to be good enough for a symphony orchestra that could not afford to pay for sufficient rehearsals. . . .

In this world there was always a warm welcome for the artist who could tell a 'human story' in an epic manner, contrasting public triumphs with personal frustrations, exulting in the bustle of affairs yet remembering each man's lonely end.

Tchaikovsky in his Russian way and Brahms in his German were masters of this kind of storytelling.

Tchaikovsky's music is more nervous, more swiftly exciting than Brahms's. It has a lighter texture, a more brilliant surface, and more varied colouring. Also, for all its excesses of temperament, it is not sentimental in a spinsterish fashion as Brahms's occasionally is.

But Brahms's music is, somehow, healthier, less sick and morbid. Sometimes, it is true, his music overflows with conventional sentiment, but for the most part the emotional impulse is restrained. Sometimes the form of his pieces is pedantic—slavishly following patterns set forth by Beethoven—but it is always well knit. Sometimes his rhythms seem a little heavy-footed after Tchaikovsky's, but they are more interesting on second and third hearings.

And because of his respect for classical tradition and his complete lack of theatrical flair, the narrative and personal quality in his music is more disguised than in Tchaikovsky's. To many critics a Brahms symphony seems more purely musical than a Tchaikovsky one. They prefer to ignore its romantic elements and to listen to it as 'abstract' music.

To people who think very readily in musical terms, instead of daydreaming their way through a performance, this kind of music often seems superior to the obviously narrative kind. But it is easy for trained musicians to be over-pedantic on this point.

Brahms, born in 1833, was exactly seven years older than Tchaikovsky (they were both born on the 7th May) and lived some four years longer. The same world events, then, bore on them both. And a certain number of comparisons ask to be made in their private lives.

Both owed a great deal to a woman friend older than themselves. In Brahms's case the woman was Clara Schumann. After her husband's death she maintained a deeply affectionate, maternal interest in Brahms, who had been a sympathetic friend during Schumann's madness.

In Tchaikovsky's case it was a Madame von Meck, an elderly, wealthy widow with eleven children. He was thirty-seven and already well known when she first offered to give him a yearly income (some

£600), sufficient to enable him to devote himself entirely to composing. Until then, although such works as the third symphony, the piano concerto in B flat, and two or three dramatic works had been performed, he still had to endure a great deal of uncongenial teaching in order to gain a living. Like Berlioz he had also to supplement his income by writing musical criticism—on one occasion of Wagner's Bayreuth festival.

Neither Brahms nor Tchaikovsky provide the biographer with any romantic love affairs. Brahms was too distantly adoring in the presence of cultured women, and too easily satisfied by casual affairs with others for whom he had little regard, ever to get married or even entangled. Tchaikovsky was psychologically incapable of loving a woman. Unfortunately he did marry. He married a romantic girl— she had fallen in love with his music—in the hope of ridding himself of his abnormal inclinations. The result was tragic. They separated after a short, disastrous life together. He suffered a breakdown—even attempted suicide—and she went away, ultimately to die in an asylum.

No such possibilities could arise in his friendship with Madame von Meck, for the good reason that he never spoke to her. They corresponded copiously, he dedicated the fourth symphony to her, and the association remained satisfactory until late in his life—when she suddenly withdrew her support, announcing that she was ruined. Tchaikovsky found out afterwards that she was not; he did not know that her odd behaviour had been occasioned by a nervous breakdown. He broke off the friendship. Fortunately by that time he was not in need of help.

Both Brahms and Tchaikovsky introduced folk-tunes into their music. Brahms got his from Hungary. (The German, Italian, and French composers hardly ever used the folk-music of their own countries.) Or rather he learned Hungarian music from a Hungarian-Jewish fiddler named Reményi, for whom Brahms as a young man acted as accompanist on concert tours. (Reményi had come to Brahms's birthplace, Hamburg, as a refugee from the 1848 revolutions.) From this association there came the popular Hungarian dances.

Tchaikovsky's folk tunes are Russian. They occur here and there in his music, but are not as important as in the other Russian composers' works.

Both Tchaikovsky and Brahms became widely known and reasonably prosperous in their own lifetimes. Brahms's reputation grew swiftly, and for most of his life he had the steady support of Simrock, the publisher. Tchaikovsky's music provoked hostility in Vienna and Paris at first. But in England and America it strode into popular favour. In the piano and violin concertos, the travelling virtuosi found trump cards, and these brilliant pieces drew attention to the solider achievements.

Tchaikovsky wrote little chamber music and several ballets and operas (the 'Swan Lake' ballet and the opera 'Eugene Onegin' are the most popular examples). Brahms wrote much fine chamber music and nothing for the theatre.

In character the two men were very different. Brahms had a knack of annoying people. (At Weimar, as a young man he went to sleep while Liszt was playing to him!) He had an unworthy prejudice against England—a country which he had not visited. He made himself look rather foolish by his antagonism to the Weimar modernists and to Wagner.

Tchaikovsky, though shy and difficult, was never boorish or prejudiced against foreigners.

Brahms and Tchaikovsky hated one another's music.

CHAPTER XXVII

An Era Draws to a Close

BETWEEN 1881 and 1901 there died Moussorgsky, Wagner, Liszt, Tchaikovsky, Brahms, and Verdi. Twenty years. . . .

If we extend the period to thirty years we must include Hugo Wolf, Dvořák, and Grieg.

The ranks of the romantics were sadly thinned. There were still determined warriors in the field, led by Elgar and Strauss, fighting a magnificent rearguard action. But only a few veterans survived the first Great War.

The earlier romantics had been crusaders. Some, like Weber, were well-informed men who could expound the causes they fought for, and who knew what forces were arrayed against them. Others, like Schubert, fought rather blindly and were perplexed by opposition.

Until their day, musicians had relied on aristocratic patronage. The time came when some of the aristocrats were unwilling to be patrons: some, reduced in wealth by the wars, were unable. And those who continued to pay the piper were not prepared to call a romantic tune.

An alternative system of patronage was being developed, a commercial system that rested on publishing and concert-giving as a trade. Opera was becoming more and more a state-and-municipality affair. Royalty and the new aristocracy paid for and decorated the best seats, and they still had a way of making their influence felt (as Wagner found in Paris), but musicians were more and more bound to consider the people in the gallery and the pit.

The new patronage developed slowly. Some of the romantics went hungry—Schubert in Vienna, the young Wagner in Paris. Some might have gone hungry had they not been able to subsidize their composing out of what they made from public performance or teaching—Liszt and Chopin.

Those who lived long enough, and those who were born late, enjoyed the greater prosperity which spread over the world of music in the latter part of the century. By that time the new patronage was established; and musicians, less concerned to be crusaders, were writing for a market. Getting one's wares taken notice of was sometimes a long job; but there were now millions of customers, and among them one could find at least a few, even if one's goods were not the fashionable stuff that is quickly observed and as quickly discarded. Writing for a market did not necessarily mean 'writing down' to the market.

Let us look at the departments of the market.

There was the operatic section. Although there was as yet only the beginning of a properly regulated international system of copyrights and performing-rights, there was money in Opera. Verdi became very rich; Wagner's Bayreuth Opera House received support from all over the world; the later Italians—Mascagni ('Cavalleria Rusticana') and Leoncavallo ('Pagliacci')—were destined to receive enormous incomes from the sale of music and to be helped by the propaganda of barrel-organs; Puccini, still later, would receive a performing right from every orchestra that in silent-film days played a selection from 'Madam Butterfly' or 'La Bohème.' (It meant thousands upon thousands of pounds.)

In the realm of light opera and operetta, Sullivan was making the kind of income that even a jazz-and-musical comedy composer of to-day might envy—and that without the aid of gramophone sales.

There was America—a growing market. In 1883 the Metropolitan Opera House was opened. Before that time Opera in America had been a second-rate and risky business. Mozart's librettist, Lorenzo da Ponte, who had emigrated to New York, had tried it. But the author of 'Figaro' and 'Don Giovanni' had seen his operatic ventures fail and had been reduced to selling tobacco and liquor, to teaching Italian, and to book-selling. The Metropolitan was a sign that New York considered itself well able to sustain a fashionable opera house. America was buying vast quantities of European music, and publishing some herself. She was manufacturing instruments. Two years after establishing the opera house New York founded a conservatory, and in

1892, and for two more years, it paid Dvořák fifteen thousand dollars a year to act as director.

On his arrival in New York he was given a silver wreath and a welcome by a giant chorus and orchestra. This must have embarrassed the unassuming, peasant-like composer of whom we are told that he 'did not show much interest in anything outside his own *métier* . . . a child of nature, who did not stop to think, and said on paper anything that came into his head.' Continuing in the folk-song vein that had attracted the attention of musical Europe to his native Bohemia—to his own music and to Smetana's—he wrote works that showed sympathy with the Negro and Indian music of America. The symphony 'From the New World' and the 'Nigger' quartet contain melodies that are recognizably like Negro 'spirituals.' They are interspersed among the tunes of a Czech type that are the more usual material of the other symphonies and chamber works, the operas and songs which were, and still are, ambassadors of a culture that has survived all attempts at suppression. Not only in his quasi-American pieces, but by the very nature of his career did Dvořák appeal to New Yorkers, for he progressed from behind the counter of his father's village inn to a place among the holders of the Austrian Iron Crown of the third class.

The 'star' singers and performers were going to America. Jenny Lind toured there, invited in the first place by Barnum, the circus proprietor. It was said that she made £20,000 in a couple of years. In so vast a country one could sing the same programme in town after town without fearing that anyone would hear it twice. Tchaikovsky conducted in New York, Baltimore, and Philadelphia. Grieg was constantly invited to America but was too delicate to venture the journey. New York had a Wagner society, one of the many that collected money for his festival theatre.

An enormous publishing market grew up in Europe. As the middle classes grew in numbers and wealth, they bought instruments and took lessons; they played at musical evenings; their teachers sent them to the music shop to buy four-handed arrangements of symphonies for sight-reading, the Slavonic dances of Dvořák, the Norwegian dances of Grieg, the Hungarian dances of Brahms, and, later on, the dances from every country by Moszkowsky. Chamber music enthusiasts were on the look-out for Brahms's latest quartet. The lesser pianists who could not tackle Liszt or Chopin found refuge in Grieg's 'Lyric Pieces.' The Wagnerians plodded their way through piano arrangements of the music-dramas. The choral enthusiasts supported the festivals. If a town like Birmingham lacked the resources to stage Dvořák's glowing nationalist operas, it could commission a cantata: Worcester could give his 'Stabat Mater' in the Cathedral. An enthusiastic amateur, making a hobby of singing at a whole winter's rehearsals, would spend a deal of money at the music shop. Later on, the publishing trade was further helped by the growth of an examinations system and by the competition festivals.

In a market where great composers could make money there was plenty of room for lesser ones, too. An enormous amount of the worst, most trumpery pieces was sold. Outrivalling even the popular piano pieces of the 'Maiden's Prayer' variety, there were the 'ballads'— sugary concoctions about love and gardens and dickey-birds and sweet children who had become angels and silver-haired mothers who remembered their erring sons. The amateurs who bought these things insisted on hearing them sung at concerts. But the celebrated singers who gave way to this popular demand could sometimes manage to insert something more serious into their programmes, and they thus helped to popularize the songs of the greater composers.

The market continued to be prosperous until after the First Great War. Then people began to listen to radio. Musical parties were not to the taste of flat dwellers, and there was not time enough in life to play bridge *and* the piano. Musicians felt themselves harmed, and could not foresee the good that radio might accomplish.

The romantic era began at a time when the system of aristocratic patronage seemed still quite healthy. The romantics were prophets of the downfall of aristocratic rule. 'Modern' anti-romantic music made its appearance at a time when the system of commercial patronage seemed still quite healthy.

In the year of Prussia's victory over Napoleon III, Wagner saw the laying of the foundation stone of his new festival theatre at Bayreuth. (Liszt was present.) All over Germany and wherever there were people of German sympathies there had been formed Wagner societies, to forward the very kind of project calculated to appeal to the victors. Following the war, the separate states of Germany became a united nation under one German Emperor, and the Germans were full of the feeling that not only German armaments had been triumphant, but German *Kultur* also. As if to corroborate this, Wagner wrote a Kaiser March and Brahms a Song of Triumph. To give Wagner a theatre of his own, there to present 'The Ring' in its entirety, seemed a musical way of announcing the status of a new Great Power. The one-time associate of Bakunin became the hero of imperialists, and to him was erected a temple of music-drama, where 'The Ring' was first performed in 1876.

Bayreuth completed found Wagner with a £7,500 debt. A grandiose concert-festival in London produced only £700 towards its reduction. It was no longer financially feasible to restrict performances of 'The Ring' to Bayreuth, and thereafter it was released to the world.

Soon Wagner was at work on his 'Parsifal,' in which the self-denying aspect of Christianity is presented to the accompaniment of voluptuous music. But his health was failing. He went to Venice to seek relief from erysipelas and to rest an unsound heart. Liszt stayed for a while, and the two men were friendly. But Wagner could not be idle. He had to contend with 'Parsifal's' production difficulties. Early in 1883 he died.

He thought that his music would be the Music of the Future, and that his trick of providing each character and idea with a theme ('leitmotiv'), to be quoted at moments of crisis, would be widely adopted by composers. But only for a short time did Wagnerism continue to be a general mode of writing. Strauss, Elgar, Mahler, Delius, and a number of lesser men show Wagner's strong influence. But in the post-Wagnerian decades there developed an anti-romantic spirit— aloof and derisive. In conquered France there grew up the anti-German spirit of Debussy, who hated anything *kolossal* and grandiloquent, who loved brevity and subtlety, who was suspicious of emotion, and who worshipped the kind of beauty that appeals to the senses without disturbing the heart.

Wagner's way of writing long stretches of narration and explanation, and his avoidance of set arias, are an encouragement to the long-winded. He himself was incapable of brevity, and his disciples have nearly all been inclined to spread themselves.

But despite the interminable length of his works, Wagner's music has held itself in favour through the years when confident critics (now forgotten) were prophesying its decline. For even if his music, for long stretches, sinks to a slow smoulder, it is redeemed by the occasions when it maintains a white-hot flame. Such a flame annihilates criticism.[1]

After the failure of the divorce plan for the Princess Sayn-Wittgenstein, Liszt turned to religion. He did not suggest marriage when, at last, the Princess's husband died. Instead he took minor orders in the Church and became an Abbé. The Princess shut herself away in darkness in an unventilated room, there to smoke black cigars and write a treatise on religion.

For his remaining years, Liszt divided his time between Rome, Weimar, and Budapest (where he was director of the new conservatoire). His playing continued to send women crazy, and they pursued him indefatigably though he was in his seventies. To the end, he was

[1] But amidst the German bombs of the Second World War many Europeans found Wagnerism somehow less palatable than of yore.

true to his half-dozen characters—he was a true saint, a true Mephisto-phelian, a true gentleman, a true mountebank. He would seek out a new talent (Grieg's, for example), forgive Brahms's rudeness, and give lessons without payment to any pupil who was talented enough. Yet he could remain quite unmoved when the mother of his children died.

In 1886 he went on a grand tour. Two of his great religious works were given in Paris and London. He was heard by Queen Victoria at Windsor. It was a triumphal progress, but inwardly Liszt was lonely. Wagner was dead: Liszt felt that loss keenly. Cosima was too busy managing Bayreuth to pay attention to her father; and she had asked him not to come to Wagner's funeral. The Princess was writing her treatise. It is impossible to tell how much consolation Liszt derived from religion, and how much his role of the Abbé who composed choral works in a cloister at Rome was a pose.

At the Bayreuth festival of 1886 he insisted on hearing 'Tristan und Isolde,' though he was unwell. Pneumonia set in. Liszt's last word was 'Tristan.' His Princess died seven months later. She had just finished the twenty-fourth volume of her treatise on the *Inner Causes of the Outer Weakness of the Church*.

It was after his enormously successful American tour that Tchaikov-sky devoted himself to a great 'programme' work. This, the 'Pathetic Symphony,' he described as 'penetrated with subjective sentiment.' Perhaps he loved this work above others because it seemed most completely to express his sufferings from 'torments which cannot be put into words,' his 'indefinable terror.'

It was his last work. He died swiftly of cholera in 1893, shortly after declaring that he felt that he would live a long time.

Brahms's end, like his life, seems out of scale for the composer of such noble music as his. He faced death with terror, finding no con-solation in the sentiments he had expressed in the 'German Requiem' or the 'Four Serious Songs.' And death came slowly and lingeringly in the form of cancer. His pitiful end closed a career that had been a tale of success. But the success-story is undramatic. The biography of Brahms must be sought in his music, for the events of his life—his residing in Vienna, taking holidays in Italy, receiving honours at universities, and so forth—make a rather uninteresting tale. Only occasionally are the anecdotes told of him other than commonplace. He had his moments of nobility; he produced flashes of somewhat rough wit. But to many people he seemed a rather boorish person living a rather ordinary, bourgeois life, and showing little understanding of the quality of rival composers—except Dvořák.

Yet he wrote symphonies and concertos which are spoken of in the same breath as Beethoven's, songs which rival Schubert's, pianoforte pieces which seem to rebuke Liszt's sensationalism while fully exploiting pianistic technique, and lighter pieces which compare with those of the Russians and Bohemians. He must have had a rich inner nature. Perhaps one reason why it revealed itself so little was because there was hardly any conflict between it and the world. Like Haydn, Brahms was in sympathy with his patrons. His music found a ready welcome. He had no impulse to go a-crusading; in fact he was inclined to dislike the disturbers of the peace. The post-Brahmsian music lasted no longer than the post-Wagnerian.

Verdi's life was as dramatic as his operas: his death an effective curtain. A cantata for the 1862 international exhibition in London provoked trouble because of its political flavour. (This is yet another of those works in which a quotation of the Marseillaise appears.) The opera 'La Forza del Destino' was found too gloomy in St. Petersburg, and 'Don Carlos' (written during a second war with Austria) made Paris wonder if Verdi was becoming a Wagnerian.

In 1869 Verdi was asked by the Khedive of Egypt to write an opera to celebrate the opening of the Suez Canal. The result was 'Aïda'— an Italian opera with an Egyptian story to celebrate a French engineering triumph. It was produced under difficulty, because Paris, where the costumes and scenery were being manufactured, was undergoing a siege. Some critics found it Wagnerian—Wagner bees buzzed loudly in many critical bonnets. Verdi cannot have been pleased, for though he admired Wagner's music he regarded Wagner's influence as the musical counterpart of Germanism. And successful Germanism, he prophesied, would lead to more wars.

After the Requiem, produced in 1874, Verdi seemed to retire. He was in his sixties and pessimistically inclined to leave the European stage to Wagner and to Wagner's young followers.

It was not until Wagner was dead that Verdi returned to the musical world. The old man, apparently discouraged, content to rest on his past successes, and devoting himself to his cattle and his vines, now astounded the world by presenting to it a work full of youthful vigour mated to mellow wisdom. 'Otello' was a staggering achievement for a man of seventy-four—a thoroughgoing masterpiece. Verdi, however, continued depressed. His librettist Boito (himself the successful composer of an opera—'Mefistofele') contrived at last to interest him in the idea of making an opera of a Shakespearian comedy, to contrast with the tragedy.

For some three years they laboured at the new work. 'Falstaff' showed that, at eighty, Verdi was, if anything, still improving. It was his last operatic effort. In his final eight years he produced four sacred works which include the 'Te Deum' and the 'Stabat Mater.'

He survived the shock of the death of his wife for two years, and died at the outset of 1901.

He was buried in the oratory of the Musicians' Home in Milan. He had founded the Home, and provided for its endowment in a will that indicated the lavish financial rewards of a successful operatic career.

Enormous crowds attended his funeral. They had lost in him a national hero.

The romantic impulse continued by a momentum not yet dissipated.

César Franck, living a comparatively retired life as cathedral organist and teacher in Paris, synthesized romantic emotion with the theology of his Flemish forefathers, and Wagner's harmonies with the contrapuntal devices of the Church composers, producing a modern-gothic music for those who no longer believed in hell but clung to heaven.

Mahler and Bruckner synthesized elements from Brahms, Wagner, and Tchaikovsky, and upheld the grand manner in large-scale symphonies and song-cycles.[1]

Hugo Wolf, abnormally sensitive to poetry, produced masterpieces of song almost too finely wrought for concert performances to mass audiences.

Scriabin abandoned himself to mystic ecstasies.

Nationalist music continued most vividly in Spain. Every province of Spain has its typical dances, and in its music there is a dash of Oriental colour—relic of the Moors. The incisiveness of this cabaret music, its supple rhythmic quality, and its gay thoughtlessness captivated those audiences, particularly the Parisian ones, to whom Wagnerian seriousness was antipathetic. Albeniz, Granados, and, later, de Falla became associated in many minds with those French and Russian composers who, far from taking sides in the Wagner-Brahms warfare, lumped both composers together as ponderous blusterers.

All this picturesque music placed great burdens on performers. Whereas earlier music had made its chief demands on the voice, romantic music encouraged the intensive training of fingers. Liszt and Paganini had been specimens of things to come, and more virtuosi *had* come, moulded on their pattern.

[1] The music of Mahler and Bruckner particularly appeals to the German peoples, as Elgar's appeals to the British. None of these composers has become a world-favourite, like Beethoven. Mahler, a Jew, was temporarily under a cloud in Nazi Germany.

CHAPTER XXVIII

Pre-War

(before 1914)

IT was during the Paris exhibition of 1889 that Rimsky-Korsakoff first conducted the new Russian music in Paris. The half-barbaric artistic wares of Muscovy and Tartary were therefore displayed at the same time as the imports from the French Empire—from Indo-China, Senegal, and North Africa. In barbaric art there is no romance; in Eastern art there are the refinements of sensation, but, often, no 'heart' as Europeans understand the term.

Paris was ready to welcome anti-romantic art. The grandiloquences of Napoleon III's empire had been revealed as shams. German art was associated in Frenchmen's minds with the brutality of the conquerors who had tactlessly crowned their emperor, not in Berlin, but in Versailles. French art, when it was not frivolous, cultivated satire, criticism, and realism. Whether it was Zola's or Maupassant's documented realism or the painters' impressionism, there was a general agreement not to magnify, not to pontificate, not to indulge in glorifications of chivalry and heroism and poetic love.

Debussy's music was opportune. It was objective and subtle; it was pictorial. Quite early he had shown an inclination to abandon formal harmony and to use chords, not with text-book logic, but as a series of sensations. Like Berlioz he had scandalized the Conservatoire by his music, and, again like Berlioz, he had made little use of the *Prix de Rome*. Even the then dominant Wagnerian influence affected him only for a short while.

When Rimsky-Korsakoff and the exhibition coincided, he became enthusiastic about Moussorgsky's music. Like Moussorgsky he had learned more from writers and painters than from musicians, and, as Moussorgsky would have done, he observed the exhibition and found musical raw material in its merchandise. But he did not follow Moussorgsky in addressing the mass of people: he addressed his art to artists.

In 1889 he was twenty-seven—a Bohemian person whose parentage was a mystery and whose private life was bound up with a green-eyed mistress. He soon began to make a reputation with small piano pieces and songs, but his real fame arrived with 'Pelléas et Mélisande' and 'L'Après-midi d'un Faune.' 'Pelléas' is a pale, misty work, as un-Wagnerian an opera as possible. 'L'Après-midi' is an orchestral illustration, glowing, sensuous, voluptuous, completely unsentimental. 'Pelléas' never became popular, but 'L'Après-midi' swiftly made its way.

Nevertheless Debussy remained poor. The world-market was great and prosperous, but it dealt chiefly in romance, religion, nationalism, and frivolity.

Marriage (not with the mistress) had not augmented Debussy's slender means, and a post as critic on the *Revue Blanche* brought only a little money. 'Pelléas,' so long as it remained the centre of a storm of controversy, did improve matters, but not for long.

What ultimately set him up was a second marriage to a well-to-do woman. This could not occur until two divorces—hers and his—had been completed. The new union (which drove Debussy's first wife to attempted suicide) resulted in a daughter, before the divorces were pronounced.

Thereafter Debussy could devote himself to composition. His titles reveal his preference for imaginative over-emotional music—'Images,' 'Prints,' 'Sketches.' In his piano preludes he puts the titles at the end of each piece—in parenthesis—in order that no emotional associations shall bring disturbing preoccupations into the listener's receptive mind. Everything is exquisite, consummately subtle, witty, charming, but not sweet, and never aggressive. His *fortissimos* are bright streaks of colour, not palpitating excitements.

His most distinguished contemporary, Ravel, in a paradoxical phrase, demolished those people who complained that since his and Debussy's music was 'artificial' it could not be sincere. 'One can be artificial by nature,' he said.

The delicate pieces continued to arrive until the first Great War. Debussy, always anti-German, always pro-Russian and pro-English, hoped to see France revenged for the loss of Alsace and Lorraine. But he died during that German offensive that preceded the final German defeat. Cancer carried him off nine months too soon.

He lived long enough to see the collapse of France's ally, Russia.

The Russian musicians had been following a similar path to Debussy's, abandoning 'poetic feeling' for impressionism. It is not surprising that they failed to follow Moussorgsky's lead. That might have been dangerous. For example, during the unsuccessful 1905 revolution, Rimsky-Korsakoff wrote a letter to the Press complaining of the stringent police supervision over the students of the St. Petersburg Conservatoire. His fame did not save him from being dismissed from his professorship. Glazounoff and Liadoff had to resign before Rimsky-Korsakoff was reinstated.

Perhaps it is unfair to suggest that musicians were afraid to follow Moussorgsky. They were not inclined to. Many musicians, both in and out of Russia, were not interested in Moussorgsky's ideas. For musicians, like most other professional men, were tending to become 'cultured' without being well informed.

To realize this, we have only to imagine the reactions of Rimsky-Korsakoff and Debussy to the Paris exhibition, and compare them with what Beethoven's or Wagner's might have been. Or we have only to imagine Elgar at, say, the (early twentieth century) 'White City' exhibitions in London strolling about with the ghost of Verdi.

The older musicians would have been full of enquiries about the condition of the peoples, the nature of their Governments, the emotions of the peasants and workers who produced the merchandise, the songs of the sailors who transported it.

Rimsky-Korsakoff and Debussy, however, would have been more directly concerned with æsthetic problems—the quality of Chinese paintings, the orchestration of Senegalese music, the attitudes of Javanese dancers, and the colour combinations in Indian shawls. If Debussy thought about the crowds at the exhibition it was quite probably with distaste, for he was an aloof person. If he thought about the countries represented by the various pavilions it was in terms of the Franco-Russian *entente* against Germany.

Elgar might have been expected to see the exhibition more from the older romantics' point of view, for he was no Debussyite, but a continuing upholder of the romantic tradition. But Elgar had little of the critical crusading spirit of the earlier men. He loved his country as they loved theirs, and nobody knew better than he how to transmute its beauty into noble melodies and rich harmonies. But he began where Wagner ended. Whereas Wagner had arrived at the German victory of Siegfried over the dragon by way of revolution, persecution, and exile, Elgar began immediately with the English victory of St. George over *his* dragon. Whereas Wagner found the Holy Grail only after tasting the earthly delights of Venusberg, Elgar, dreaming the Dream of Gerontius, seemed to know of sin only by hearsay. Whereas an early romantic like Schubert sang of Death and the Maiden, Elgar sang in memory of his King-Emperor.

This is not to say that Elgar's music is either better or worse than the other men's. A man may as poignantly express sorrow over the death of the squire in the mansion as of the peasant in the cottage. Indeed he had far better write of the people he knows than those who are so many statistics in a Government blue book. We observe these changes, not to estimate Elgar's merit, but to understand his manner. In this way we learn why the external nature and style of music was changing.

If the late romantics and the early moderns ceased to write about Beethoven's moral questions, or Schubert's homely emotions, or Verdi's political enthusiasms, or Wagner's sociological philosophies, it was partly because they were less and less in touch with these things.

Whereas a *kapellmeister* was almost as familiar with his patron as with his own peasant relations, a middle-class, twentieth-century composer was only well informed about conditions. It seemed that wars and revolutions of any serious character were banished from Europe. Nobody foresaw that in a few decades music might again become politically partisan.

Yet the twentieth-century musician was not less educated than his predecessors. He was as able as they to speak a couple of foreign languages. One could not say that Richard Strauss, whose operas and symphonic poems were based on Sophocles, Molière, Cervantes, Nietzsche, and Oscar Wilde, was restricted in his outlook—only that music was more and more addressed to those who were neither in the gallery nor in the royal box.

Nevertheless the moderns were waging a war of freedom—of æsthetic freedom. What kind of freedom this is, people could see at the Russian Ballet. A great many external forces were compelling artists to revise their beliefs. Photography made painters wonder whether they had not something better to do than make likenesses. Electricity shed a new light on stage *décor*. New textiles provided a wider range of costume, and since they were cheaper they were more widely studied. Public libraries and museums allowed choreographers to compare the attitudes of the ancient Greek and Etruscan and Egyptian dancers with those of the 'classical' school. Later on, motor cars and flying machines and the spread of organized sport fostered the movement for dress reform, and in that fashion brought tolerance for the exposed bodies of ballet dancers. A long list of such processes could be compiled.

Settled ideas were being challenged from many directions in an era that saw the formation of numerous societies for promoting all sorts of objects—vegetarianism, Esperanto, atheism, and so forth. Many conventional people persuaded themselves that 'cranks' were becoming a danger, but the cranks gave us many new freedoms and ideas.

There were cranks and greater-than-cranks in music too. As usual, music was late in following the lead of the other arts. While Montmartre was issuing a fresh manifesto about some new 'ism almost every other month, music was only just beginning to bring out anything analogous to, say, 'futurism.' The man who, more than any other, brought music into line with the new painting, and provided the patronage for such a composer as Stravinsky, was Diaghileff.

The Russian Ballet of Diaghileff represented a breakaway from the Imperial Russian Ballet. It took advantage of the rigorous technical training imparted by the Imperial School, but it persuaded many Imperial dancers to set out on a voyage of artistic exploration. Diaghileff assembled a caravan of glamorous merchandise and toured it round the capitals of Europe. Appealing to much the same people as thronged the opera houses to hear Melba and Caruso sing the superbly effective melodramas of Puccini, he gave them the Arabian Nights, ancient Greece, old Russia, provincial Spain, and all the scenes of Europe's carnivals. Diaghileff, a man as capricious and despotic as Haroun-al-Raschid, dispensed patronage to a great many very remarkable artists. Of the composers, Stravinsky was the one most intimately associated with the ballet. He took advantage of all the new freedoms —unresolved discords, unsymmetrical rhythms, orchestral colour combinations that 'clashed'—and applied these resources realistically to highly fantastic subjects. He was an alchemist performing black magic with the aid of Vickers-steel crucibles and Röntgen rays.

Was the pre-War Stravinsky an escapist into fairyland, or did the curiously poignant death of Petrouchka—a puppet with human feelings —represent a universal tragedy? One thing was certain. The new composers were determined not to be moralists.

Diaghileff's repertoire included 'classical' ballet. Much of the music was adapted from Schumann and Chopin. But the ballet's chief influence was exerted by way of Rimsky-Korsakoff, Stravinsky, De Falla, Debussy, and the Parisian group of modernists known as 'Les Six.'

Gradually the Russian Ballet became more and more nomadic, without roots in any soil. When the 1914 War came, and later the Russian Revolution, Diaghileff, always anxious to be in the vanguard, flirted with the idea of returning to his native land. But his artistic revolution and Lenin's social one had only a little in common; and the post-War period found him *déraciné*, as much an exile as any taxi-cab-driving Grand Duke in Monte Carlo.

Diaghileff's caravan made London one of its halting places. London, as in the days of Handel, of Weber and Rossini, of Mendelssohn, Liszt, and Wagner, was still buying foreign music in enormous quantities.

Some musical historians speak of this import trade as though it were a military invasion, suppressing all native activity. In actual fact it provoked a great deal of musical work in England. Bundles of music and crates-full of pianos arrive more swiftly than musicians can, and they do not come merely on a visit. For every concert grand played by a foreigner at Queen's Hall there were hundreds of uprights played by English amateurs in English homes. For every sheet of music held in the hands of Italian prima donnas at Albert Hall there were dozens issued to the choristers at the cathedral festivals. But it is true that

English music was operating under foreign direction. It is impossible to tell whether Nature was niggardly in not providing English mothers with composer-sons, or whether English musical conditions were stifling promising infants at birth. Elgar's career supports both theories. It seems to say that if Nature had 'done her stuff' we should have heard about it. It also suggests that England was unprepared to nourish a genius. For Elgar was forty before he 'arrived,' and might not have arrived then but for the appreciation of German musicians.

Elgar's life and music are of a piece. His early life was spent in or near Worcester, where his father was a music dealer; and a great deal of his music is the noblest kind of cathedral-city music. His religion was Catholic, and his greatest sacred work has a text by Cardinal Newman. His private life was based on a very happy marriage, and there are no erotic storms in his music. His friends were not like Schubert's beer-garden cronies or Liszt's free-lovers; they were the sort of people one might meet in a novel by Galsworthy—the people affectionately portrayed in the 'Enigma Variations.'

Patriotism—that of Kipling's 'Recessional' rather than of Shelley's 'Men of England'—was a recurrent theme in his music. In his early work 'Caractacus' we have the spectacle of the hero, captive in Rome, prophesying England's future greatness. A 'Coronation Ode' marked the accession of Edward VII, and the Second Symphony was dedicated to the same monarch's memory. (Elgar enjoyed the friendship of the King.) 'Cockaigne' was a tribute to the sort of London the sightseer knows. The two 'Pomp and Circumstance' marches and 'Land of Hope and Glory' are martial music that knows nothing of the casualty clearing station. It seems appropriate that Elgar in old age should so often have been described as looking like a retired colonel. (Lady Elgar was the daughter of a Major-General.)

By the time the Great War came, Sir Edward was the musician-laureate of Empire. He was never corrupted by the position. He did not turn out mere *pièces d'occasion*. 'For the Fallen' maintains his high standard. It is one of the few war memorials that are not just so much monumental masonry.

In old age, when he had almost ceased to compose, he produced a Nursery Suite for the Royal Princesses.

The post-War period discouraged him. Honours had been heaped on him, and fame in the age of gramophone-royalties meant comfort. But with the death of Lady Elgar in 1920, when he was sixty-three, he was left to face old age alone. He felt that the world was not disposed to listen to him.

It was only partly true. Certainly there were people who under post-War conditions were out of sympathy with Rule-Britannia

patriotism and who felt that an Elgar concert was at times too much
like an Abbey memorial service, for officers. But even those people
could be persuaded to listen to Elgar's *personal* music—the 'Enigma
Variations,' the 'Violin Concerto,' the 'Introduction and Allegro for
Strings,' and 'Falstaff.'

In such works as these Elgar found and expressed the beauties of
England and of at least one Englishman's life without needing to have
recourse to folk-songs or tricks of illustration.

Elgar's younger contemporaries were in the unhappy position of
suffering too many influences. If they sought for folk-songs, as Vaughan
Williams did, they were making use of melodies which had been nearly
forgotten. It meant they were virtually using period melody, for in
England most farm labourers had forgotten the songs their peasant
forefathers knew, and only by searching very diligently in the villages
could anybody rescue the surviving folk-songs. This was hardly using
folk-songs as the Russians or Bohemians used them. (Arnold Bax
was more fortunate, for in Ireland there was still a peasantry.)

If a composer sought to emulate the *Lieder* writers by making use
of the treasury of English verse—as, for example, John Ireland did—
he faced the task of mating modern music to, say, early Victorian
poetry. Fortunately there was fine contemporary poetry, too. For
example, A. E. Housman's 'Shropshire Lad' poems were as ripe for
music as Heine's had been in Schumann's day.

One kind of music that offered many possibilities was landscape
music. It could be poetic, or pictorial, or both, and it could express
more than conventional rapture about a sunset. Delius comes to mind.
But he cannot be simply labelled 'English Landscape School.' He was
born in England of German parents. He lived at various times in
Florida, Saxony, Norway, and, most often, France. Hating con-
ventional religion, hating commercialism, trying to steel himself against
pessimism by doses of Nietzsche and Walt Whitman, he gave expression
to the quieter moods of Nature without indulging in sentimentality.
He had an inordinate fondness for slow rhythms and misty colours.
The landscape influence is as obvious in his music as patriotism in
Elgar's, as a few specimen titles show: 'Summer Night on the River,'
'On hearing the first Cuckoo in Spring,' 'A Song before Sunrise,'
'A Song of the High Hills,' 'Sea Drift.' . . .

He waited long for recognition. By the time it came in full measure
he was blind and bedridden.

It was said by many people in the days before the first Great War
that England was getting behind the times. American commerce and

German science and French art all seemed to make English methods seem conservative. Quite certainly German cultural life was much more strenuous than ours. The German professor, whether scientist or historian, proclaimed himself front-line soldier in the cultural offensive. The scientist built up new industries out of optical instruments, chemicals and dyestuffs, heavy-oil engineering, and gasbag aircraft. The literary professor erected an imposing edifice of comment on poetry and research into art. He translated, he produced guide-books; and he argued that if a good thing were not German then at least it was first shown to be good by a German. Under the influence of Baedeker guide-books the American or English traveller was half persuaded that the Pyramids, the Parthenon, the Colosseum, and Versailles were all built by Krupp's, and that Christopher Columbus travelled on the Hamburg-Amerika Line. If genius belonged to the country that bestowed most attention on it, then Shakespeare and Shaw were certainly Germans.

Richard Strauss[1] has this trick of making the whole world German. Whereas Bizet, a Frenchman, contrived to write Spanish music for 'Carmen,' and Tchaikovsky and Dvořák tried not to be thoroughgoing Slavs in their 'Italian Caprice' and 'New World Symphony,' Strauss brought the old world and the modern world and the next world of death and transfiguration all to Berlin and Vienna. One listens to Don Quixote, Till Eulenspiegel, Salome, Don Juan, and Elektra and feels that, no matter what language each of them spoke, thus spake Zarathustra . . . in German.

Like Liszt, Strauss often disguises second-rate ideas under a cloak of brilliance, but his symphonic poems and operas sweep along with a conquering swagger. In the operas, in the midst of all the 'fine writing' and purple-patch eloquence of Strauss's music, one discerns the thoughtful, quieter spirit of Von Hoffmansthal's librettos. This spirit is very evident in 'Rosenkavalier,' making the work something more than a gay confection. Strauss lived to a great age and saw the ending of the second World War. Thereafter the world at large became more and more aware of his later works, some of which seemed to repeat earlier successes with less success.

Strauss's orchestration is a dazzling dress of sequins; Elgar's is a robe of rich brocade; Delius's a misty veil.

Sibelius's is not a costume. It is an animal's skin—a live skin, not a furrier's exhibit. The music of Sibelius is not exactly uncivilized. He understands conventional nationalism ('Finlandia'), conventional theatricalism ('Valse Triste'), conventional concert-music (the violin

[1] Richard Strauss must not be confused with Johann (Waltz-King) Strauss. See pp. 142, 186.

concerto). In Helsingfors, in Tsarist days, they knew the culture of St. Petersburg besides their own. In Lenin's day they heard all the arguments about the class war (for the revolution began in Finland) and accepted all the arguments for the nationalist war that made them independent. Finland must not be thought of vaguely as a kind of polar waste inhabited by Eskimos and Laplanders, grey wolves and reindeer, and completely 'off the map.' Nevertheless, it is true that Finland is a country where city streets are but a small clearing amidst endless forests. The struggle of all creatures to survive against a severe climate seems more important than the war of armies, and legend is more copious than history. Sibelius uses the late nineteenth-century orchestra, though he disdains to make it play tricks to imitate storms and waterfalls, and he agrees with his contemporaries in using a modified symphonic form. There is nothing Finnish in these practices. His use of unblended tone-colours is said to produce the stark effect for which his music is noted, but that again is not necessarily Finnish. Technically it is the music of modern civilization. It does not even introduce folk-song.

Yet one critic after another discerns in it something elemental, so that it hardly seems to belong to Europe or to this century. To some sensitive musicians it makes no appeal. It seems as tedious—as a forest. Oddly enough, it is enormously popular among the sophisticated moderns. They find strength and refreshment in the bleak symphonies. When one has been over-stimulated, and sedatives and pick-me-ups are alike useless, there are remedial qualities in keen air and cold water; and a log fire is better than an electric radiator.

Sibelius's music is primeval without being savage. Perhaps this is because his music, like his country, is sparsely peopled. Yet it is not inhuman.

CHAPTER XXIX

Post-War

(after 1918)

WHEN the War ended in 1918 it seemed that the musical profession in England might well resume where it left off. Musicians could fetch out the German songs again and sing them in German. They could put the national anthems[1] in the lumber-room.

---

[1] Paderewski, most famous of Chopin players, had championed the cause of Polish freedom before the Peace Conference, and for a while was Premier of his reborn country. See p. 139.

In pre-War days, music had become a considerable industry. For every symphony orchestra mentioned in the reference books, there were dozens of theatre orchestras, café bands, and bands for the parks and the seaside. After the War, the film industry began to create a further demand for orchestral players. All these executants were products of a large teaching profession which renewed itself by turning out more and more teachers. It looked for direction to Doctors of Music and cathedral organists, and it sent some of its most brilliant products to study abroad. Before the War, Leschetizky in Vienna and Leopold Auer in St. Petersburg attracted the best young pianists and violinists.

Concert-giving was a trade. Agents with affiliations all over Europe and America arranged tours, booked concert halls, ordered posters and advertisement leaflets, distributed publicity photographs, and raked in commissions from all sides. Concert-giving societies, often based on local amateur choruses or orchestras, operated in every town of any consequence and offered their patrons famous, celebrated, or merely well-known artists 'direct from the Royal Albert Hall, the Queen's Hall, Covent Garden, and principal provincial concerts.'

Similarly in other countries. In consequence there appeared a considerable quantity of display music—the diluted Chopinisms of Moszkowski, the fake period-pieces of Kreisler, and so on. Concert careers attracted many women, and composition a few.

A considerable output of music of a superficial kind for musical comedies, revues, and cabarets gave employment to scores of composers, some of them tracing a half-respectable kinship with Offenbach or Sullivan. Before the War, music-hall songs were the nearest modern equivalent to folk-music. They showed the change of style that accompanies the transformation of a peasant 'folk' into an industrial proletariat. Although they were commercial products, they were written for music-hall audiences by people who spoke the language of the 'gods.' Cockney and Lancashire dialects had not yet given way to those of East Side New York, and English popular music was still English. Orchestrators, conductors, and copyists applied themselves to this source of income.

A torrent of books and periodicals, pouring from the printing presses, dealt with personal history, æsthetics, methods of technique, voice production, theory, and 'appreciation.' Every big newspaper employed a critic.

There was big money in music; not perhaps as bankers understand big money, but at any rate some thousands of pounds. After the War the profession greatly improved its organization for collecting 'royalties' and performing fees. The Performing Right Society, acting in sympathy with affiliated bodies abroad, established the legal right to compel performers or the owners of concert-halls, theatres, restaurants, etc., to compile lists of all music performed and to pay sums of money accordingly. In the heyday of the silent films, when there was no minute of the day that did not witness the performance of 'Selection from "Tosca,"' a steady stream of performance-fees poured into Puccini's pocket.

And a great deal of imitation Puccini, watered Tchaikovsky, and debased Wagner was specially written under lucrative terms to supplement the operatic selections that were the mainstay of cinema music. Before sound films swept it all away, there was a regular output of pieces called, for instance, 'House on Fire,' 'Burglars at Night,' 'Cowboys chasing Indians,' 'Sea Music,' 'Suspense,' 'Anguish,' 'Reconciliation,' and so on. They were arranged with optional 'repeats' so as to be of any desired length. Orchestrations were so managed as to have one player's melodies 'cued in' on another's part. Thus, whenever practicable, the bassoon part was cued in on the cellist's copy, the flute on the clarinet's, the viola on the second violinist's, and everyone's on the 'Piano Conductor's' copy. If the band were big, the players ignored the cues. If it were small, they played their own parts and as many others as they could manage. A Mustel Organ added body to the tone.

Presently there began to be manufactured a sort of one-man-band called a cinema organ. Though it cost a great deal, the interest on the capital outlay was not so great as the wages of an orchestra. Organ alternating with orchestra was cheaper than two orchestras. Later on, a console that came out of the floor on a lift made the organist a player and a jack-in-the-box spectacle all at once.

The amateur performer was encouraged to improve his standards. A competition festival movement that had begun in the eighties with an attempt to bring culture to agricultural labourers in Cumberland grew enormously. In a given town at a given time, hundreds of players, singers (choral and solo), elocutionists, and dancers, adult and juvenile, would congregate to perform their test pieces before adjudicators, to endure public comment and advice, and, if successful, to receive certificates and medals. (The movement continues to flourish.) A parallel activity, the brass band festival movement dates back to 1853. It is essentially a poor man's enthusiasm, for brass instruments are on the whole cheaper than string ones, are more durable, and may be played in the open air.

A vast network of examinations spread out from the chief London schools as far afield in the Empire as Hong Kong, Cape Town, and

Vancouver. A considerable patronage was dispensed to educational publishers.

In spite of all these activities, the arrival of gramophones and radio caused concerts swiftly to dwindle away almost to nothing, outside London and a very few other towns. Maybe the competitors and examinees were at home listening to their radiograms.

For a while the post-War profession went on almost undisturbed. But the composers were behaving oddly. The older romantics seemed disinclined to write any more. We cannot tell if the third symphony which Elgar intended to write for the B.B.C. would have been such a 'come-back' as Verdi achieved with 'Otello,' and 'Falstaff.' But Elgar wrote little in his last years. Rachmaninoff was busier with transcriptions than with new works.

Those who had been anti-romantic before the War were equally at a loss. Ravel's output, always slender, became hardly visible. Some younger Parisian composers, diversifying a small output of serious works with many drolleries and eccentricities, formed themselves into a defence-group called *Les Six*, and faced some years of antagonism before Honegger, Milhaud, and Poulenc, at any rate, became celebrated. Stravinsky, turning this way and that, going back to the classics, making further cold-blooded demonstrations of the 'juxtaposition of timbres,' issuing manifestos about his erratic navigations in seas wherein the old charts were obsolete and no new ones were authoritative, produced a series of challenges which few accepted.

So many romantic illusions had been shattered on the fields of Flanders; and, as yet, there had been no time to develop new ones. But the public-at-large was unprepared for anything else. Serious composition, always a gamble, leading sometimes to fortune and sometimes to a pauper's grave, was soon transformed into a short cut to bankruptcy. All the organizations for collecting fees were still in existence, but modern music produced few fees for many reasons. Firstly there was so much music already in existence. A glut had produced a slump. Secondly, the new season's models were unpopular. Thirdly, the number of paying customers had vastly diminished. Perhaps this last cause was the most important.

The first effect of the rapid spread of gramophones, radio sets, and sound films laid waste whole territories of music. The gramophone enormously reduced the sale of sheet-music for home performance. The radio made concert-going a weariness to all except those who lived in places where absolutely first-rate concerts were readily available and who could afford a seat in an acoustically satisfactory part of the concert hall. While the B.B.C. were able to support a certain few performers and one first-rate symphony orchestra, they took from thousands any reason for continuing to follow the musical profession.

But perhaps the greatest amount of unemployment was caused by the sound-film. The silent film had brought into existence a great army of orchestral players who faithfully slogged their way through so many hours of playing per day and earned modestly satisfactory incomes ranging from about five pounds per week for the 'rank and file,' to a thousand a year for the conductors of West-end 'symphony' orchestras.

In less than two years, three-quarters of them were disengaged at a time when a financial slump was deepening and the dance-craze had ceased to call for more players.

Just as a few 'classical' musicians found work with the B.B.C., so a few of these players—some of them men of high accomplishment —anchored themselves in film studios, and provided background-music measured out by minutes and seconds in accordance with so many feet and inches of photography.

A few composers, invading the film cities, wrote rather better music than many of these occasions deserved.

Here, as elsewhere, music became something in the background, to be listened to inattentively. The career of 'serious' composer became desperate. The critics might attend first performances and write about them copiously: the musical public, none too large anyway, turned a deaf ear. A few composers grew to their full stature, even in this unfavourable climate, but many seemed to write in a more and more secret language.

Long before these external events imposed their influence on composers there had been a turning away from established procedures. A decade or more before 1914 Schönberg had laid the foundations of a kind of writing that abandoned tonality in favour of a patterned arrangement of notes that never gave the impression of being in a key. The note-row on which a composition was based was subject to laws of permutation and combination that recall the strictest counterpoint of earlier times. Many people found this music incomprehensible and inhuman, yet Schönberg was lavish in his use of expression marks.

For some musicians his system came to life most triumphantly in an opera composed by his follower Alban Berg. 'Wozzeck' tells a sordid story with uncompromising realism but touches the heart of anyone whose ear has been conditioned appropriately. 'Wozzeck' made its way slowly. Written in the 'twenties, and gradually becoming familiar by way of broadcasts and recorded excerpts, it was not given at Covent Garden until the 'fifties when, in the climate of post-World-War-II, it made a profound effect.

Meanwhile it had suffered denunciation by the Nazis as *Kultur-Bolschewismus*.

Strangely enough it was precisely the Russians who were least 'bolshie' in their music. Though, at the time of the revolution, they had shown a taste for anything irreverent and untraditional, they became more and more committed to the doctrine that music must be comprehensible to the masses. The works of such composers as Prokofieff (who in his early years outside Russia had been gaily modernistic), Shostakovitch (whose first symphony promised more than the later ones fulfilled), Katchaturian (hardly more modern than Borodin) and the amiable Kabalevsky seem modernistic only to those whose radio sets are firmly switched to the Light Programme.

In other countries there were signs that an era of experiment was passing. In England, Arthur Bliss and William Walton, for all their modernistic energy and avoidance of sentimentality, belonged to a known tradition. In America, Ernest Bloch showed how quarter-tones might be introduced into chamber music without abandoning all the customary processes of composition. Hindemith, exiled from Germany, showed no disposition in his 'music-for-use' to write for mere sensation's sake.

Folk song had not ceased to be an influence. Béla Bartók, who was a great collector of folk-tunes of many countries, was never free from their effect, though a listener new to his fiercer works may not realize it.

With Vaughan Williams, folk-song sings out more clearly. But the music is not merely 'folky.' It reveals medieval, Tudor, and Victorian elements. It belongs to the tradition of English choral music. In opera it steers clear of Italian or German influences; in ballet it is not Russian; in the concerto style it is little interested in bravura. Yet, though it is rather too English for some foreign tastes, too remote for popular taste, and too traditional for vanguard-modernistic taste, it is of to-day and a power in the contemporary world. The Fourth Symphony, composed shortly before the Nazi War, seemed prophetic in the light of later events.

A composer of an earlier generation might well have prophesied that America—particularly the United States—must surely make a great contribution to music. Certainly Dvořák believed so, and certainly there were American composers who tried to put their country on the musical map in his way—by following the literary and folk-song tendencies of the romantics. Edward MacDowell, his younger contemporary, was the most distinguished of them, and his music, with its Grieg-like feeling for natural scene, holds the affections of a great many music lovers in his native country. But whether because

American creativeness was at first too occupied with engineering and
building—the arts of the pioneer—or whether because certain arts
could be readily imported to balance America's growing exports,
there was a neglect of the creation of 'fine' art. Literature was an
exception, of course, because there the language question made the
mere import of reading material unsatisfactory. English was not
quite the same as American, and other languages were beyond the
language barrier.

Pictures and statues and music speak a universal language—or so
it seemed to people who approached art by way of the appreciation
course. And since Americans were of every kind of European stock,
they could feel in sympathy with every kind of European music. Like
the Europeans, they ignored far-Eastern or African or Polynesian
culture when they talked of the universal language of art. For these
reasons, and for others that are still obscure, America in the early days
of this century was the patron rather than the creator of concert
and opera music. Statistics show that, shortly before the 1914 War,
there were as many foreign-born musicians in the United States as
native ones.

Imports, though they may frustrate home production, stimulate
distribution and marketing. After 1918 no country in the world conducted a more active consumer campaign than America. The endowment of orchestras, opera houses, and music schools was lavish
enough to make the States seem a veritable Eldorado to European
musicians. Music in the educational field was well respected. High-
power concert-agent publicity attracted the support of numerous
audiences, swelled particularly by the women's clubs. There was no
lack of money for fellowships and scholarships. And then there appeared the rich, if restricted, market provided by commercial radio
and Hollywood. During the slump in the 1930's the State attempted
to keep alive declining activities and to promote new ones. Workers'
organizations made up in the enthusiasm of individual members what
they lacked in money support.

Yet in the midst of all this activity there emerged only a very little
serious music to find a place in European programmes. Everything
else American was familiar in the Old World. Every type of American
music of the light type received the help of all the devices of publicity.
In England we paid the most flattering attention to American jazz, to
musical-comedy music, and to the hybrid symphonic-jazz works of
George Gershwin. But, though London concert programmes were
extraordinarily catholic—more so than those of any capital city apart
from New York—Londoners knew scarcely anything of the works of
Deems Taylor or Leo Sowerby or Alden Carpenter, and could not be

persuaded to regard Ernest Bloch—a race-conscious Jew of Swiss birth —as American.

To European audiences, American music was jazz. (Latin American music was little considered.) While some critics held that real American music had yet to appear, others averred that only snobbery prevented academic musicians from recognizing that dance music—however far removed from academic tradition—was the most alive of contemporary music. If it lacked the range and profundity or the ideals of classical music, that proved (so the argument ran) that the modern world also lacked these things, for jazz really represented our age.

The argument was much too superficial. One could easily say that jazz was the attempt of the age *not* to represent itself. However, nothing was or is gained by regarding dance music as a kind of plague from which 'real' music must be protected.

CHAPTER XXX

Jazz

THE gallant sea-dogs who fought for England in the wars of the Spanish Main were free-enterprise mariners. In those days before armed forces were state organized, the sea-captains who defended Queen Elizabeth looked for a share of the booty from the defeated galleons. They were not over nice in their methods. Schoolboy stories of derring-do fasten all cruelty on the Spaniards. The Spaniards were cruel, as the history of the Inquisition bears witness. But they could be brave too, as the conquest of Mexico by Cortez and his few followers demonstrates. The stories represent the English seaman as brave. So he was; and the voyages and battles of Raleigh, Drake, and Grenville stand witness. But he could be cruel too, as the beginning of the slave trade testifies. The floating concentration camps took their grim cargoes westward, and not until a hundred years ago were many white people shocked.

But guilt often lies deeper than the consciousness of it. And so, to help white people in the moment of meeting the Recording Angel, the Negroes were converted, harangued, prayed over. Churches that would admit no whites were built by whites who could not bear to proclaim the brotherhood of Man alongside a black. And so the Negroes were admitted to Christendom.

From the meeting of the Negro mind with European religion and music there emerged the Negro 'spiritual.' Songs of work, grief, exile, and exaltation accompanied the religious songs and were conceived, as folk-songs always are, by goodness-knows-whom and then amended and reshaped by the community that adopted them. The Birth of the Blues was the birth of many a haunting song of tenderness or bitterness or irony. There were jollifications too. Holidays, barbecues, festivals. The banjo twanged merrily.

The American Civil War freed the slaves not many years after slavery had been abolished in the British West Indies.

The negro musician began to know wider contacts. In the towns of Louisiana, originally French and still bearing French names—St. Louis and New Orleans—he learned something of Latin carnival music, the music of the street procession and the band wagon. (The saxophone was a French invention intended for theatre orchestras and military bands.) The wind orchestras of John Philip Sousa gave him standards of virtuosity, though he did not directly imitate. Show Boats plied the Mississippi. White composers wrote Plantation Ditties, like Stephen Foster's evocative 'Swanee Ribber.'

An American style of popular music developed. It included the vaudeville songs of New York, the hill-billy songs of the cowboys, the Spanish songs of California, the French songs of the South, the Federal and Confederate songs of the Civil War, the folk-songs of the British Isles, some of them better preserved in the Appalachians than in the Cotswolds, and all the songs of all the Europeans who emigrated to the great new land of freedom and opportunity.

But the Negro music was never swamped by the others. The French carnival music was transformed by players who had never been taught to play, and so Jazz was born. The origin of the word has never been positively determined. In later years the word was destined to be applied loosely to almost any example of popular dance music; but this was the Jazz, the Hot Jazz, that is still, for the enthusiasts, the only Jazz.

As for dance music, that too was developing. The Cake Walk, the Barn Dance, the Lancers, and so forth, flourished. A style of music called Ragtime—a crudely syncopated way of singing a music-hall song over an oom-pah bass—was already known at the beginning of this century. But ragtime did not become a world success until about 1911. 'Alexander's Ragtime Band' by Irving Berlin was one of the early best-sellers.

It is relevant to recall that Irving Berlin is not a Negro. He is a Jew born in Russia whose parents took him to America when he was an infant. Many of his popular rivals are also Jews. This is not surprising. Amidst all the jolliness of ragtime there was also a vein of sadness and homesickness. The emancipated Negro, finding no Utopia, was ready to remember that Dixie, after all, was the land where the sun was always shining. 'I wanna go back to me coal-black Mammy.' The European emigrants who had gone to the States to escape tyranny and poverty found that even in a democracy a man could be unemployed; even in the land of the free there could be bigotry. And when they sang songs of the Mississippi (darkies playin' de ol' banjo) they could affectionately remember the Volga and forget the Tsar, the Shannon and forget the hungry forties, the Danube and forget the Hapsburgs. The Jews could remember all the rivers that were not Jordan.

The first Great War set into motion a fantastic dancing craze in which this music became everybody's music. It was strident and escapist with lapses into tearful sentiment. It could be idiotic (Yes, we have no bananas). Its wallowing sentimentalities were shot with a certain humour (I left my Sugar standing at the corner of the street, and my Sugar melted away).

In the earlier years of commercial dance music, the Hot Jazz of the deep South was not greatly in evidence. Indeed such Jazz has never become widely popular. But many of the changes in popular dance music are pale reflections of the hot style. First-class hot players, performing and recording in the richer cities of the north, provided the vitamin content in the variegated dish of dance music; and this dance music was given universal appeal by the effect of radio, films, and records. Gone were the days when aristocrats danced one kind of dance and 'the folk' another. King and scullion danced to the hit of the moment, and, if they were both tuned-in to the same wavelength, to a performance that was impartially dispensed to both of them.

Jazz faithfully mirrored the public feelings. When American musical comedies first began to oust the English, the Viennese, and the French, the style was strenuously gay—the War mood. During the post-War boom it continued strident and frivolous. The saxophone was found to be an easy instrument to play and it made a great deal of sound. The other instruments, by using a variety of mutes, bowler hats and so forth, were able to produce grotesque noises. The drummer was much in evidence.

Soon the gay, confident mood dissipated itself. The boom began to seem less likely to be eternal. A maudlin, self-pitying quality began to be in evidence—the 'blue' mood. The erotic element was coloured by an inferiority complex. The new lyrics discussed the woes of the unwanted, the spurned, the forgotten, the regretful lovers of the world. When the slump of the early 'thirties deepened into something like a catastrophe, there was a moment of social abasement expressed in the title : 'Buddy, can you spare a Dime?' Stylistically, this blue music was the result of a significant blend. The harmonies of the most sophisticated examples were borrowed from the anti-romantic Debussy. Melodies were now more in accordance with the requirements of saxophone and trumpet technique. Rhythms were made subtler by the microphone, for a microphone makes it unnecessary for a singer to produce a large voice. He can whisper and croon in the easygoing rhythms of the speaking voice. Orchestrations became more and more scientific—and less academic. There was 'sweet' tone, and 'hot' tone, and 'dirty' tone, none of them like symphonic tone or military tone.

Calculated orchestration was challenged by an improvised kind. Some of the best Negro players in America, devotees of their cult, had been accustomed (particularly in the late 1920's) to assemble 'after hours' to practise their art in 'jam sessions.' On these occasions, only the merest skeleton of an arrangement was agreed on before a tune was played.

In the Memphis style, the first chorus was played simply; then each man in turn, on the spur of the moment, performed a solo variation on it, the others improvising an accompaniment. It was a competition in inventiveness and brilliance. The New Orleans style was even more reckless. Everybody improvised at once. Even when one allows for the fact that the harmonic basis was more or less fixed, and that a certain number of formulæ were exploited over and over again, the astonishing fact remains that such performances were recorded and found worthy to be issued to the world. These are the records beloved of hot music enthusiasts.

A quotation from Hugues Panassié's work 'Hot Jazz' shows us Jazz as it appears to an enthusiast.

'Louis Armstrong would improvise on the same theme for a full half-hour, taking twenty choruses in a row. Often he would be quite motionless as he played or sang—his eyes closed, like a man carried out of the world; tears would roll down his cheeks. His imagination seemed inexhaustible; for each new chorus he had new ideas more beautiful than those he had produced for the preceding chorus. As he went on, his improvisations grew hotter, his style became more and more simple—until at the end there was nothing but the endless repetition of one fragment of melody—or even a single note insistently sounded and executed with cataclysmic intonations.'

CHAPTER XXXI

Finale—for the Present

PERHAPS this is the point at which to stop. Nobody can write contemporary history. A middle-aged author has lived long enough to experience a great many changes in the climate of opinion. He has seen Béla Bartók and Vaughan Williams go up, and Scriabin and Bax go down. He has seen Benjamin Britten bestride the world like a colossus, and Carl Nielsen step out on to a wider platform than that of his native Denmark. It is too soon to guess who will be remembered in a hundred years time, or even in twenty.

The author could emphasize the debt that his own country owes to the Glyndebourne Opera House established by Mr. John Christie, to the Arts Council, and to the Edinburgh Festival, but his own country is only one of many in the world of music. He could summarize his own experiences of music in war, and war in music, but this would be grossly out of scale with the book as a whole.

Furthermore, in an era even more doctrinaire than Beethoven's, there are serious difficulties in the way of using the simplest adjectives. The Communists began by explaining that people's music was good: bourgeois music, bad. The Nazis followed by explaining that Nordic music was good: Jewish music, bad. Intellectual pressure-groups elsewhere seemed to say that difficult music was significant (good): easy music, eclectic (bad).

Music was everybody's solace during World War II, and after the war the musical public seemed to be larger and more adventurous than it was. But an enormous number of concerts and operatic performances 'flourished' without paying their way, and in every country the music-schools kept up a supply of brilliant performers for an industry that could employ only a few.

Similar conduct has been observed in earlier times and will no doubt continue in later ones. Meanwhile television has arrived—with the accent on vision.

The author has had considerable experience of music on television, yet he hesitates to make pronouncements about the future influence of television on music. Television is a dangerous game (out of sight, out of mind), but prophecy is a reckless one.

INDEX

A

Academy (*see* Schools of Music, *also* Handel)
Agoult, Countess d', 144, 156
Albeniz, 196
Alexander II, 184
Amati, 74
Ambrose of Milan, 21
America, 52, 60, 62, 102, 140, 161, 179, 190–1, 210, 212
Anna Magdelena (*see* Bach)
Aria, 60, 61, 74, 97, 149
'Arianna', 60
Arkwright, 95
Armstrong, Louis, 215
Arthur, King, 22, 40
Arts Council, 216
Atonality, 81
Auber, 135
Auer, Leopold, 206
Austria, 69, 72, 95–, 103–, 114–, 120–, 128–, 164–, 169–, 191, 195

B

Bach, 18, 48, 54, 74, 80, 81–, 95, 99, 110, 136, 148, 149, 186
Bakunin, 166–, 172, 192
Balakirev, 184
Ballet (*see* Dancing), 83, 162, 175, 186
Barbaia (*see* Rossini)
Bardi, 59–
Barnum, 191
Barry, Madame du, 96, 99
Bartok 210, 216
Bax, Arnold, 203, 216
Bayreuth, 169, 173, 188, 190, 191, 194
Beaumarchais, 106, 130
Bechstein, 179
Beethoven, 102, 103, 111–, 113–, 121–, 122–, 125–, 128–, 130–, 137, 138, 148, 150, 152, 156, 158, 160, 163, 169, 171, 179, 187, 195, 196, 199, 216

'Beggar's Opera', 89
Bellini, 164
Berg, Alban, 209
Berlin, Irving, 213
Berlioz, 130, 132, 137, 139, 141, 152, 154–, 156, 160, 161, 168, 171, 174–, 178, 182, 188, 197
Bible, 8–
Bizet, 186, 204
Bliss, Arthur, 210
Bloch, Ernest, 210, 212
Boccaccio, 49–
Boito, 195
Bononcini, 88, 99
Borodin, 148, 184
Brahms, 138, 144, 168, 177, 182, 186, 187, 189, 191, 192, 194–, 196
Britten, Benjamin, 216
Britton, Thomas, 88
Broadwood, 179
Bruckner, 196
Buffons, war of, 99
Bülow, Hans von, 176
Bunyan, 70
Burney, 13, 14, 19–, 74
Buxtehude, 82, 84
Byrd, 53–, 55–, 81, 114
Byron, 131, 133
Byzantium, 20

C

Caccini, 60
Cadence (*see* Form)
Calvin and Calvinism, 54, 69, 83
Canon, 44, 47
Cantata, 63, 85
Capitalism, 83
Carpenter, Alden, 211
Caruso, 201
Castrati, 88
Catherine the Great, 98
Cavalieri, 60
Cavalli, 61
Cavoni, 170, 174
Cervantes, 200

217